Business Adaptation to Climate Change

This book seeks to advance the understanding of how businesses may adapt to climate change trends. Specifically, it focuses on two general research questions: First, how do businesses adapt to chronic slow-onset nature adversity conditions linked to climate change? Second, how do firms adapt to weather-related natural disasters exacerbated by climate change? In the first part of the book, the authors develop a conceptual framework in response to these questions. In the second part, they test this framework using multiple empirical studies involving large data analyses of: (a) the Western U.S. ski industry adaptation to warmer temperatures, and (b) the effect of natural disasters on foreign investment by multi-national corporations around the world. This book will interest management and public policy students and scholars researching successful business climate change adaptation strategies, as well as business and non-profit organization leaders and policy makers involved in developing and promoting such effective strategies.

JORGE E. RIVERA is a Professor of Strategic Management and Public Policy and Tucker Fellow at The George Washington University's School of Business. He has published over 50 manuscripts and two books, including *Business and Public Policy* (Cambridge University Press, 2010) which received the 2011 Outstanding Book Award from the Organizations and the Natural Environment Division of the Academy of Management. Professor Rivera is founding co-editor of Cambridge University Press's Book series on Organizations and the Natural Environment.

CHANG HOON OH is William and Judy Docking Professor of Strategy at the University of Kansas School of Business. His research centers on non-market strategy in challenging environments, business continuity and sustainability, and globalization versus regionalization. He has published more than 55 papers in peer-reviewed journals. Currently, he is co-editor-in-chief of *Multinational Business Review*, a consulting editor of the *Journal of World Business*, and serves on the *Journal of International*

ORGANIZATIONS AND THE NATURAL ENVIRONMENT

The increasing attention given to environmental protection issues has resulted in a growing demand for high-quality, actionable research on sustainability and business environmental management. This new series, published in conjunction with the Group for Research on Organizations and the Natural Environment (GRONEN), presents students, academics, managers, and policy-makers with the latest thinking on key topics influencing business practice today.

Published Titles
Rivera, Oh, Oetzel, and Clement, *Business Adaptation to Climate Change*
Albright and Crow, *Community Disaster Recovery*
Grabs, *Selling Sustainability Short?*
Sharma and Sharma, *Patient Capital*
Marcus, *Strategies for Managing Uncertainty*
Marcus, *Innovations in Sustainability*
Bowen, *After Greenwashing*

Forthcoming Titles
Matisoff and Noonan, *Learning to LEED*
Potoski, *Corporate Environmental Strategy*
De Castro and Salvado, *Upcycling Strategy*

Business Adaptation to Climate Change

JORGE E. RIVERA
Geoge Washington University

CHANG HOON OH
University of Kansas

JENNIFER OETZEL
American University

VIVIANE CLEMENT

CAMBRIDGE
UNIVERSITY PRESS

CAMBRIDGE
UNIVERSITY PRESS

University Printing House, Cambridge CB2 8BS, United Kingdom

One Liberty Plaza, 20th Floor, New York, NY 10006, USA

477 Williamstown Road, Port Melbourne, VIC 3207, Australia

314–321, 3rd Floor, Plot 3, Splendor Forum, Jasola District Centre,
New Delhi – 110025, India

103 Penang Road, #05-06/07, Visioncrest Commercial, Singapore 238467

Cambridge University Press is part of the University of Cambridge.

It furthers the University's mission by disseminating knowledge in the pursuit of
education, learning, and research at the highest international levels of excellence.

www.cambridge.org
Information on this title: www.cambridge.org/9781108835725
DOI: 10.1017/9781108888691

© Jorge E. Rivera, Chang Hoon Oh, Jennifer Oetzel, and Viviane Clement 2022

First published 2022

A catalogue record for this publication is available from the British Library.

Library of Congress Cataloging-in-Publication Data
Names: Rivera, Jorge E., author. | Oh, Chang Hoon, author. | Oetzel, Jennifer Mary, author. |
    Clement, Viviane Wei Chen, author.
Title: Business adaptation to climate change / Jorge E. Rivera, Chang Hoon Oh,
    Jennifer Oetzel, Viviane Wei Chen Clement.
Description: Cambridge, United Kingdom ; New York, NY : Cambridge University
    Press, 2022. | Series: Organizations and the natural environment | Includes
    bibliographical references and index.
Identifiers: LCCN 2021063027 (print) | LCCN 2021063028 (ebook) | ISBN 9781108835725
    (hardback) | ISBN 9781108744829 (paperback) | ISBN 9781108888691 (epub)
Subjects: LCSH: International business enterprises–Environmental aspects. | Industrial management–
    Environmental aspects. | Climatic changes–Economic aspects. | Social responsibility of business. |
    BISAC: BUSINESS & ECONOMICS / Business Ethics
Classification: LCC HD30.255 .R58 2022 (print) | LCC HD30.255 (ebook) | DDC 658.1/8–dc23/
    eng/20220211
LC record available at https://lccn.loc.gov/2021063027
LC ebook record available at https://lccn.loc.gov/2021063028

ISBN 978-1-108-83572-5 Hardback
ISBN 978-1-108-74482-9 Paperback

To Caroline, the rainbow of my life. JR

To Hyun Jung and Adrian, for their love, support, and smiles. CHO

To Caroline, for all her love and happiness. JO

To Alex, Felix, and Leila, for being on this journey together. VC

And outside, the silent wilderness surrounding this cleared speck on the earth struck me as something great and invincible ... waiting patiently for the passing away of this fantastic [human] invasion.

Joseph Conrad, Hearth of Darkness, 1899

Contents

Figures

Tables

About the Authors

Jorge E. Rivera is a Professor of Strategic Management and Public Policy and Tucker Fellow at The George Washington University's School of Business. He received his Ph.D. from Duke University in 2001. Prof. Rivera's research studies how nature's adversity conditions, and other external context factors are associated with corporate environmental strategies. He has also examined how participation in domestic and international voluntary environmental certification programs is associated with business competitiveness and environmental performance. He has written over 50 manuscripts, including several dozen journal articles, and two books printed by top strategic management and public policy publications. His former book, *Business and Public Policy* by Cambridge University Press received the 2011 Outstanding Book Award by the Organizations and the Natural Environment Division of the Academy of Management. His publications' findings have been mentioned in more than 30 news stories by national and international newspapers including *New York Times* and *Financial Times*. Professor Rivera is founding Co-Editor of the Cambridge University Press's Book series on Organizations and the Natural Environment. In 2012, Professor Rivera was the Chair of the Academy of Management's Organizations and the Natural Environment Division.

Chang Hoon Oh is William and Judy Docking Professor of Strategy at the University of Kansas School of Business. He previously was the William Saywell Professor in Asia Pacific Business at the Beedie School of Business, Simon Fraser University, Vancouver, Canada. He was the Inaugural Alan Rugman Visiting Fellow at the University of Reading for 2015/2016. He was a marketing manager of Samsung Electronics and Samsung Corporation and served his military service as an instructor, first lieutenant ROTC, in South Korea. Professor Oh received his PhD degree (2007) from the Kelley School of Business at

Indiana University-Bloomington. His research centers on non-market strategy in challenging environments, business continuity and sustainability, and globalization versus regionalization. His research has been supported by the Social Sciences and Humanities Research Council of Canada (SSHRC), Canadian International Resources and Development Institute (CIRDI) and the National Research Foundation of Korea (NRF). He also collaborated with World Wildlife Fund of Nature (WWF) and United Nations Development Program (UNDP). He has published more than 55 papers in peer-reviewed journals. Currently, he is Co-Editor-in-Chief of *Multinational Business Review*, a senior editor of *Journal of World Business*, and serves *Journal of International Business Studies* and *Journal of International Business Policy* as a member of editorial review board.

Jennifer Oetzel is a Professor of Strategic Management in the Department of Management at American University's Kogod School of Business. Dr. Oetzel received her PhD in Strategic Management (2002) from the University of North Carolina at Chapel Hill. Her research focuses on understanding how firms manage risk and specifically on how businesses can best manage violent conflict, natural disasters, and other discontinuous risks. She also examines how promoting economic and social development, and, in some cases, peace building can minimize business risk and positively contribute to the local/regional community and the overall business environment. Her overall body of research includes more than 20 articles and book chapters. Her recent research work has appeared in the *Strategic Management Journal, Organization Science,* and the *Journal of International Business Studies,* among other outlets. In 2015, she won a Best Paper Award at the 2015 Academy of Management Meeting, was a finalist for the Haynes Prize for the Most Promising Scholar at the Academy of International Business (2009), and has been twice nominated at the Strategic Management Society (SMS) for best paper awards. She has also received funding from the Social Sciences and Humanities Research Council of Canada for two ongoing research projects. Professor Oetzel serves on the editorial boards for the *Strategic Management Journal, Journal of International Business Studies, Journal of World Business,* and *Business & Society.*

Viviane Clement is an expert on climate change adaptation and resilience working on climate policy, strategy, and analytics. She holds a PhD from The George Washington University School of Business. There, her research used an interdisciplinary approach, drawing from concepts in ecology and socioecology to examine how organizations manage climate-related risks while considering local ecosystem dynamics. Her work (with Jorge E. Rivera) has appeared in *Business Strategy and the Environment* and *Organization & Environment*.

Foreword

Imagine, for a moment, that we are writing in the year 2050. Many regions of the world are reporting exposure to severe climate change impacts. Megacities in South Asia and Africa are experiencing deadly heat waves; crop-producing regions in India and Pakistan suffer from substantial crop losses, flooding is severely impacting livelihoods, infrastructure and industries in coastal regions, and several regions in the US and in parts of Australia are experiencing severe droughts and wildfires. The most severely affected cities and regions have adopted permanent water and food rationing.

Current investments in mitigation efforts alongside green recovery plans and a heightened awareness of global risks after the impacts of the coronavirus pandemic give hope that the worst impacts of climate change can be avoided and that humanity will not experience such devastating outcomes. However, when examining the latest scientific evidence, it becomes clear that the above-mentioned scenarios are not unrealistic. Even if we collectively manage to mitigate the worst impacts of climate change, human activities have already led to about 1.0°C of warming above pre-industrial levels. As the warming trend continues, adverse impacts associated with climate change will become more noticeable, leading to substantial and varied impacts on businesses and industries in the future – with changes to the products we consume, the services available to us, and the expectations of how businesses address climate change.

Not long ago the impacts of climate change on firms and industries were considered a fringe topic in business research and practice. In fact, when presenting my initial dissertation work on organizational adaptation and resilience to climate change, a senior colleague remarked that this topic would not be suitable for a PhD in business. (Due to a courage of conviction and some stubbornness, I prevailed and fulfilled my doctorate in this area.) These days, an increased awareness of the adverse impacts of climate change, growing social movements, and popular dissatisfaction with political inaction, along with proactive examples of climate change policy implementation, have created a set of drivers that make it harder for business executives and policy makers (and perhaps also our colleagues in academia) to ignore the topic of climate change altogether, despite countervailing and vested interests aimed at preserving a "business-as-usual" scenario.

Given substantial debate about future impacts of climate change, the need for this book is obvious. The authors, Jorge Rivera, Chang Hoon Oh, Jennifer Oetzel, and Viviane Clement, have together drawn a timely and important contribution that examines the adaptation of businesses to the impacts of climate change. The acknowledgment that firms as well as various actors in society more generally need to adapt to climate change is not a fatalist admission that it is too late for climate change mitigation; rather, the consideration of adaptation means that businesses are aware of their own impacts on – and changing relationship with – their environment, which includes our climate system. Businesses are both part of the problem and part of the solution. Emissions from industrial activity have and continue to significantly contribute to climate change; however, businesses are uniquely positioned to support societal adaptation to climate change in terms of innovation, technology adoption, and business activities that generate positive societal impacts.

The main contribution of the book is that it advances our understanding of how businesses can adapt to climate change both in terms of gradual and slow-onset changes as well as changes in the frequency and intensity of extreme weather events attributed to and exacerbated by climate change. The authors draw together a convincing account of how businesses are impacted and can adapt, especially those operating in an international context and those in sectors directly impacted by climate change, such as winter tourism.

Scholars and practitioners will benefit from the rich material presented in the book that provides both conceptual foundations and empirical evidence for business adaptation to climate change. There is still little cross-disciplinary work that comprehensively integrates scientific findings into business thinking. I am therefore excited about the contribution of the book to the urgent debate on how businesses can adapt to climate change by developing conceptual ideas and propositions and providing illustrative examples. The book provides a solid foundation to inform this important area of research and to create awareness of the significant impacts of climate change that will occur if we do not act decisively and make substantial changes now.

Dr. Martina K. Linnenluecke
Professor of Environmental Finance
Director, Centre for Corporate Sustainability and
Environmental Finance
Macquarie University, Sydney, Australia

Preface and Acknowledgments

As the planet suffers increasingly from global warming's detrimental effects, our book provides a seminal global analysis of business adaptation to climate change. We focus on two general research questions: First, how do businesses adapt to chronic slow-onset nature adversity conditions linked to climate change? And second, how do firms adapt to weather-related natural disasters exacerbated by climate change? To answer these questions, we develop a conceptual framework that seeks to understand how businesses respond to climate change-related natural disasters and slow-onset adversity conditions. To test our conceptual ideas and propositions, in the second part of our book we rely on multiple empirical studies involving large data analyses of: a) the Western U.S. ski industry adaptation to warmer temperatures, and b) the effect of natural disasters on the foreign investment of multinational corporations around the world.

Business responses to natural disasters seem to involve a dynamic that initially involves denial, advancing through indifference, delay, avoidance, and other forms of resistance, on to proactive preparedness. Finally, when the catastrophic consequences of natural disasters are felt, the business response pattern is one of last-minute haphazard adaptation measures. If a company survives, managers either develop an arrogance about their ability to confront the next disaster or decide that such catastrophic events are flukes of nature. The obstinate nature of this dynamic is much stronger for slow-onset, climate change-induced adverse conditions whose negative effects are imperceptible in the short term.

The resistance to prepare for and recognize the importance of climate change adversity conditions by businesses is also pervasive among the most prestigious academic business management journals. Almost all top academic business journal editors and the leaders of business academic societies symbolically stress the need to study and address "grand challenges" like climate change. In reality, business response to climate change does not appear to be considered a legitimate area for business academic research given that very few papers addressing business responses (or lack of) to climate change actually get published in the premiere business research journals.

> For the 1998 to mid-2015 period, only 32 out of 22,903 (0.15 percent) articles published in the top 23 elite business academic journals mentioned "global warming," "climate change," "greenhouse," or "carbon" in the title, abstract, or key words.

The dearth of business and climate change articles in top academic business journals is of such magnitude that it has attracted attention by scholars specializing in examining academic publications trends. Diaz-Rainey et al.'s (2017) bibliographic study found that between 1998 to mid-2015, the top 23 elite business academic journals, by impact factor, published a total of 22,903 articles. Of those, only 32 (~0.15 percent) mentioned "global warming," "climate change," "greenhouse," or "carbon" in the title, abstract, or key words. For this period, the most elite general management journals by impact factor – *Academy of Management Journal* (AMJ), *Academy of Management Review* (AMR), and *Administrative Science Quarterly* (ASQ) published just two articles out of a total of 721 (0.28 percent) mentioning "global warming," "climate change," "greenhouse," or "carbon" in the title, abstract, or keywords (Diaz-Rainey, et al., 2017).

The tendency for climate change to be almost absent from discussion is even worse in other business academic disciplines for the same period. Within this timeframe, out of 8,737 articles published in the top three finance journals and top five marketing journals (by impact factor) zero mentioned "global warming," "climate change," "greenhouse," "carbon" in the title, abstract, or key words. To be sure, given that these bibliographic analyses focused on the title, abstract, and keywords, the actual number of publications that study topics related to climate change is likely to be higher. For instance, for the 2011–2020 period, we identified five additional manuscripts published in the top four empirical general management journals (*AMJ, ASQ, SMJ,* and *Organization Science*) examining how natural disasters affect business strategies. Yet, to illustrate the extent of disregard, even if the number of climate change-related manuscripts published by elite business academic journals were a thousand percent greater, the proportion of articles examining climate change-related topics would still be only 1.5 percent. Since 2015 there has been a small increase in the number of articles focusing on climate change related topics in top business academic journals, but the tendency to give marginal attention to this topic continues.

Acknowledgments. We appreciate the help of multiple people and organizations that allowed us to write this book. The support from George Washington University (GWU), American University, Simon Fraser University, and University of Kansas was critical for our research work. Professor Peter Tashman's research questions, work, and findings about business adaptation to climate change spurred our research on the ski industry included in this book. At GWU, the School of Business' Tucker Fellowship was key in allowing the extra time required to finish this book. Financial supports from Social Sciences and Humanities Research Council of Canada (SSHRC) were critical in conducting research on natural disasters and foreign investments. We thank Rui Wang for her support in editing the book's citations and references. We would also like to thank attendees at the Academy of International Business and Academy of Management Meetings for their feedback on earlier versions of our research manuscripts.

Publication Acknowledgments

This book extends the theory development and empirical analysis from our publications examining business adaptation to natural disasters and slow-onset nature adversity conditions exacerbated by climate change. Previous versions of this research have been published in the academic journal articles listed below and they are reproduced with the permission of publishers.

Clement, V., and Rivera, J. (2017). From adaptation to transformation: an extended research agenda for organizational resilience to adversity in the natural environment. *Organization & Environment*, 30(4), 346–365.

Oetzel, J., and Oh, C. H. (2014). Learning to carry the cat by the tail: firm experience, disasters, and multinational subsidiary entry and expansion. *Organization Science*, 25(3), 732–756.

Oh, C. H., and Oetzel, J. (2011). Multinationals' response to major disasters: how does subsidiary investment vary in response to the type of disaster and the quality of host country governance? *Strategic Management Journal*, 32(6), 658–681.

Rivera, J., and Clement, V. (2019). Business adaptation to climate change: American ski resorts and warmer temperatures. *Business Strategy and the Environment*, 28, 1285–1301.

PART I

Introduction

1 | *Introduction*
Why Adaptation to Climate Change?

The improvised power outages first implemented by Pacific Gas & Electric (PG&E), one of the largest utilities in the United States, in early October 2019, provide a stark example of the desperate low-tech adaptation measures enacted to respond to natural mega disasters (Fuller, 2019). The short-notice premeditated shutdown of power transmission lines to about 2 million people (roughly 700,000 households and/or businesses) in huge areas of Northern California was aimed at preventing catastrophic wildfires like those sparked by power lines in Napa and Sonoma counties in late 2017. Concurrently, Southern California Edison, another major electricity company in the state, shut down electricity to about 13,000 households in Central and Southern California.[1]

Moreover, at the end of October 2019, both California utilities again preemptively responded to forecasted extreme winds and dry conditions with additional and more wide-ranging precautionary blackouts, affecting several million California consumers (Serrano, Rubenstein, & Morris, 2019). At the same time these aggressive and widely unpopular adaptation tactics were implemented, PG&E's malfunctioning equipment was believed to have started another large and fast-growing wildfire (the Kincade wildfire), which affected California's wine country. In the fall of 2020, in the face of another record-breaking catastrophic wildfire season, which burned about 4.2 million acres (also severely affecting Oregon, Washington State, and Colorado), PG&E and other West Coast utilities were again preemptively shutting off power to millions of consumers for days at a time. Insurance companies were following suit with improvised low-tech adaptation by also preemptively revoking homeowners' insurance

---

[1] Both PG&E and Southern California Edison agreed to pay local California governments about 1.3 billion USD to settle lawsuits related to their liability in the 2019 and 2020 associated with wildfires sparked by their equipment.

policies (Fuller & Flavelle, 2020). And local governments, even in major cities like Portland, Oregon, were issuing state of emergency declarations that involved last-minute evacuation orders for a few suburban areas.

Also, in February 2021 a record-breaking snowstorm and historically frigid low temperatures triggered power outages across Texas,[2] which in turn forced the emergency shutdown of many power generation plants to keep the entire state's electricity generation system from collapsing into a statewide blackout, potentially lasting many weeks (Mulcahy, 2021). This improvised adaptation to a record-breaking weather-related disaster left 3–5 million Texans without power for almost a week (plus millions more without safe tap water for drinking for over 10 days) and resulted in at least 30 deaths (Mulcahy, 2021).

The frequency and severity of mega wildfires in California are aggravated by extremely dry and fast winds (known as El Diablo – "The Devil" in English – in Northern California and as the Santa Ana winds in Southern California) that damage electrical power lines, sparking flames. Such high-speed winds are not new, and their existence has not been linked to climate change (Nolte, 2019). Yet, warmer temperatures linked to climate change exacerbate other trends (e.g. scorching summers that generate overly dry vegetation, and millions of trees killed by drought and pine beetle infestations, which are triggered by warmer temperatures). These trends, combined with the winds and the aftermath of the unprecedented drought of 2011–2019, result in dangerous matchbox conditions that generate huge and rapidly spreading fires (Williams et al., 2019). Worsening mega wildfires amplified by climate change are not unique to California. Indeed, beginning in October 2019 Australia's east coast provinces were devastated by the severest wildfires in decades, blanketing Sydney and other major cities with dense smoke, destroying thousands of homes, and forcing the evacuation of tens of thousands of people (Cave, 2019).

Indeed, in 2019 PG&E sought to declare bankruptcy in the face of about 30 billion USD in liability damages associated with powerline-sparked fires in California's wine country in 2018. PG&E's drastic

---

[2] Particular extreme weather events cannot be linked to climate change. Yet, there is increasing evidence that the long term trend to more frequent and more extreme storms is related to climate change (IPCC, 2018).

actions were an improvised low-tech adaptation strategy by a company driven to declare bankruptcy, in part due to the increased frequency and severity of extreme weather events linked to climate change. Indeed, rolling blackouts are the most rudimentary low-tech reactive approach for adapting to California wildfire risks now understood to be exacerbated by climate change (Williams et al., 2019).[3]

PG&E has repeatedly failed for decades to implement basic proactive safety and fire prevention adaptation measures (such as tree trimming and transmission equipment inspections) to protect hundred-year-old power transmission installations (about 20,000 miles of power lines and almost 7000 transmission towers that have exceeded their useful life (Blunt & Gold, 2019). PG&E's lack of proactive adaptation and maintenance in the face of repeated record-breaking wildfire seasons speaks to extreme corporate negligence; the company apparently did not have knowledge of the exact age of thousands of transmission towers and power lines, which had not been inspected in decades (Blunt & Gold, 2019). Thus, stopping sales of electricity – PG&E's core product – could be deemed a desperate last-minute strategy to avoid more damage claims in the middle of bankruptcy proceedings, which were themselves originated by previous catastrophic wildfires.[4]

Do PG&E's response to wildfires – wildfires that year after year break historical records – illustrate problematic adaptation strategies adopted by companies to deal to natural disasters exacerbated by climate change trends? If so, how then might businesses adapt to adversity caused by climate change in a way that is less costly and disruptive? These are the core questions we explore in our book.

Core research questions of our book:

How do firms adapt to natural disasters exacerbated by climate change?

How do businesses adapt to chronic slow-onset nature adversity conditions linked to climate change?

---

[3] Well planned adaptation by other energy utilities to wildfire risk include the use of local microgrids that, when needed, can be isolated from long power transition lines prone to spark fires.

[4] These deliberate power outages are seen by some costumers and California government officials as a belligerent political strategy (one adopted after failing to influence politicians through lobbying and political donations). The perception is that the power outages are used to relax California's strict liability regulations that hold utilities responsible for wildfires sparked by their ageing equipment and extreme weather events (Blunt & Gold, 2019, WSJ).

Business school scholarship indifference to climate change.

Writ large, the response of business to natural disasters seems to involve a dynamic that begins with denial, advances through indifference, delay, avoidance, and other forms of resistance, then moves on to proactive preparedness. When catastrophic consequences of natural disasters first occur, the business response pattern is one of last-minute haphazard adaptation measures. If a company survives the event, its managers tend to develop an arrogance about their ability to confront the next disaster; or they may decide that catastrophic weather events are flukes of nature. The obstinacy of this dynamic is much stronger for slow-onset, climate-change–induced adverse conditions whose negative effects are imperceptible in the short term.

The resistance of businesses to prepare and recognize the importance of climate change adversity conditions is also pervasive among the most prestigious academic business management journals. Almost all top academic business journal editors as well as the leaders of business academic societies stress, in a pro forma way, the need to study and address "grand challenges" like climate change. In reality, they do not seem to view climate change and businesses' response/lack of response to it as a legitimate area for academic research, as evidenced in the very few papers addressing business responses (or lack thereof) to climate change actually get published in the premiere business research journals.

> For the 1998 to mid-2015 period, only 32 out of 22,903 (0.15 percent) articles published in the top 23 elite business academic journals mentioned "global warming," "climate change," "greenhouse," or "carbon" in the title, abstract, or keywords.

The dearth of business and climate change articles in top academic business journals has attracted the attention of scholars who specialize in examining academic publications trends. Goodall's (2008) bibliographic study found that between 1970 and 2006, the top 30 management journals (by impact factor) published a total of 31,000 articles. Of those, only 9 (~0.03 percent) mentioned "global warming" or "climate change" in the title, abstract, or keywords. This study also indicated that the top two cited management journals, *Academy of Management Journal* (*AMJ*) and *Academy of Management Review* (*AMR*) published no articles mentioning these terms in the title, abstract, or keywords from the mid-1970s to 2006.

This trend was also seen in the 1998 through mid-2015 period, with only 32 out of 22,903 (0.15 percent) articles published in the top 23 elite business academic journals mentioning "global warming," "climate change," "greenhouse," or "carbon" in the title, abstract, or keywords (Diaz-Rainey et al., 2017). For this period, the most elite (by impact factor) general management journals, *AMJ*, *AMR* and *Administrative Science Quarterly* (*ASQ*) published just two articles out of a total of 721 (0.28 percent) (Diaz-Rainey et al., 2017). The tendency to almost completely neglect climate change is worse in other business academic disciplines in the 1998 to mid-2015 period. For this timeframe, **out of 8,737 articles published in the top three finance journals[5] and top five marketing journals (by impact factor), *zero* mentioned "global warming," "climate change," "greenhouse," or "carbon" in the title, abstract, or keywords.[6]** To be sure, given that these bibliographic analyses focused on title, abstract, and keywords, the actual number of publications studying topics related to climate change is likely higher. For instance, in the 2011–2020 period, we identified five additional manuscripts published in the top four empirical general management journals (*AMJ*, *ASQ*, *SMJ*, and *Organization Science*) that examined how natural disasters affect business strategies. Yet, to illustrate the extent of disregard, even if climate change-related manuscripts published by elite business academic journals numbered a thousand percent greater, the proportion of articles examining climate change-related topics would still be only 1.5 percent. Since 2015, there has been a small increase in the number of articles focusing on climate change-related topics in top business academic journals, but the tendency to give marginal attention to this topic remains.

Strategic management theories and climate change adversity. The lack of attention to how businesses respond to climate change adversity is also reflected in the dominant *strategic management theory* frameworks. Understanding how firms change their strategies to fit the external environment is a foundational question in strategic management. A business' external context is widely understood to be a key driver of its strategic choices. Accordingly, multiple strategic management theories rely on an open systems perspective that gives prominence

---

[5] *Journal of Finance, Journal of Financial Economics*, and *Review of Financial Studies*.
[6] *Journal of Consumer Psychology, Journal of Consumer Research, Journal of Marketing, Journal of Marketing Research, Marketing Science*.

to a business' external contextual factors as key drivers of strategic choices and behavior (e.g. institutional theory, contingency theory, population ecology, resource dependency theory, stakeholder theory, and industrial organization framework). Yet, for these theories "external context" is usually constrained to industry, economy, and, to a lesser degree, government and non-profit actors. Seldom is the *natural environment* given more than lip service and in most cases it is assumed away.

Until recently, in the absence of visible harmful effects from climate change, the tendency to ignore these adverse conditions has made sense for strategic management scholars. To be sure, it is well understood that over the last 10,000 years, weather, climate, geological, and ecological conditions have been exceptionally steady, particularly when compared with other geological periods (Rockström et al., 2009; Whiteman & Cooper, 2011). Interestingly, the growing organization and natural environment literature has focused mainly on examining the negative impacts of organizations on nature, while paying relatively little attention to the reverse relationship: the effects of nature's adverse biophysical conditions on organization strategies and behavior (King, 1995; Linnenluecke & Griffiths, 2010; Winn et al., 2011). Notable exceptions to this trend involve seminal research done by Martina Linnenluecke, Monika Winn, Ans Kolk, Jonathan Pinkse, Andrew Hoffman, Peter Tashman, Tima Bansal, Gail Whiteman, and Nardia Haigh among others.

Natural scientists, however, have increasingly stressed the growing confidence in the global evidence that climate change trends are exacerbating slow-onset nature-adversity conditions and extreme weather events. Accelerating climate change trends and their associated detrimental effects are also receiving increased attention from top corporate managers, policymakers, the media, and international stakeholders. Despite the increasing understanding of – and agreement about how – climate change is linked to the worsening of weather-related natural disasters and slow-onset, adverse conditions in nature, fierce debate remains – particularly in the United States – among politicians and interest groups about the best ways to manage its effects. Debates over climate change causes and solutions have become a quintessential 'culture war' issues. These discussions include trade-offs between economic prosperity and environmental protection, as well as, competing ideological, political, and geopolitical factors and institutional logics.

In our book we contribute to the debate by developing conceptual ideas and propositions seeking to understand how businesses respond to climate change-related natural disasters and slow-onset adversity conditions. In particular, our book focuses on:

1. Examining how and why nature's adversity conditions and weather-related natural disasters linked to climate change affect different business adaptation strategies and performance.
2. Identifying how the relationships between climate change adversity conditions and business adaptation strategies are moderated by firm characteristics.

To examine our conceptual ideas and propositions, in the second part of our book we describe and discuss multiple empirical studies involving panel data analyses of: (a) Western U.S. ski industry adaptation to warmer temperatures, and (b) the effect of natural disasters on the foreign investment of European multinational corporations.

Challenges of Climate Change Mitigation and the Need for Adaptation

We use the term 'adaptation' to refer to business efforts and strategies that aim to achieve a better fit with a changed external environment. *Adaptation to climate change* is defined by the International Panel on Climate Change (IPCC) as: "Adjustment in natural or human systems in response to actual or expected climatic stimuli or their effects, which moderates harm or exploits beneficial opportunities" (IPCC, 2014b). Given that adaptation has just recently been embraced, examples of it tend to be limited to infrastructure and technological efforts adopted by vulnerable companies like ski resorts that produce artificial snow (Linnenluecke & Griffiths, 2015; Tashman & Rivera, 2016). However, business adaptation to climate change can include a wide variety of strategies such as: diversification at the product, service and/or geographic levels, mergers and acquisitions of competitor companies, government lobbying for friendlier adaptation restrictions and incentives, and purchasing of insurance and other financial hedging instruments.

Adaptation is distinguished from *mitigation of climate change*, the latter "[involving] actions that reduce the rate of climate change ... by limiting or preventing greenhouse gas (GHG) emissions and by enhancing activities that remove these gases from the atmosphere" (IPCC, 2014c). **Mitigation is, of course, the safer and more effective approach for dealing with the negative effects of climate change.** However, climate change adaptation efforts are fundamental and urgently needed to guarantee the well-being of humanity, even if at some point technological and political-economic breakthroughs allow us to implement dramatically successful climate change mitigation (Haigh, 2019). This urgent need for adaptation to climate change is justified for multiple reasons.

First, humanity has so far failed dismally in its efforts to reduce GHG emissions sufficiently to limit average earth warming to under 2 °C relative to preindustrial levels. A global average increase of 2 °C above preindustrial times (1850–1900) was in the past regarded as the maximum temperature increase humans could adapt to without risking dangerous climate change-related harm. More recently, the IPCC indicated that an average increase of 1.5 °C above preindustrial levels is a safer boundary, one that would allow humans to adequately cope with the harsh negative effects of climate change and avoid widespread high risk (IPCC, 2018). Even if all of the promises agreed to in the 2015 Paris Agreement were fully implemented, average earth temperatures are projected likely to rise by about 3.2 °C by the end of this century (UNEP, 2019).[7] To hold warming to below 2 °C starting from the year 2020, countries would have to triple their GHG reduction commitments under the Paris Agreement to about 2.7 percent per year on average (Christensen & Olthoff, 2019; UNEP, 2019). Staying within the safer 1.5 °C average increase range would require drastic reductions of GHG, allowing a net zero level to be achieved by 2050 (IPCC, 2018). Earth has experienced an average temperature increase of about 1 °C, as measured from preindustrial times (IPCC, 2018). Though many consider this amount of average warming insignificant, in fact, a 1 °C global average temperature increase over approximately 100 years is dramatic (IPCC, 2018).

Global emissions of GHG rose at an annual average rate of about 1.5 percent during the decade beginning in 2009. This rate puts us on pace for an increase of about 4 °C in global average warming by 2100 (UNEP, 2019).

[7] "Likely" in this sentence means, according to IPCC standards, to communicate the degree of certainty in assessment findings, "66–100 percent probability" (IPCC, 2014).

Worse, the United States and other countries (e.g. Australia, Brazil, China, and India) have been engaging in policies that not only exacerbate climate change but also explicitly and falsely deny that climate change even exists. To be sure, global emissions of GHG rose at an annual average rate of about 1.5 percent during the decade beginning in 2009, putting the planet on pace **for an increase of about 4°C** in global average warming by 2100 (UNEP, 2019). Moreover, even in the face of this worsening trend, after pulling out of the Paris Agreement, in 2017, the Trump administration continued to aggressively derail international efforts to agree on meaningful improvements in GHG reduction commitments and to create a regulated global carbon market.

President Joe Biden, on his first day in office, signed an executive order to have the United States rejoin the Paris climate agreement (Restuccia, 2021). He also initiated the multi-year process that would reestablish President Obama's climate change mitigation regulations and quickly reverse multiple climate change-aggravating presidential executive orders enacted by the Trump administration. Indeed, the new Biden administration aims to tackle climate change as a top priority and seeks to position the United States as a global leader in adopting stringent and legally binding rules to reduce greenhouse gases. However, President Biden's executive orders can quickly be wiped out with the stroke of a pen by a subsequent president's executive action. For more long-lasting regulations, the Biden administration needs the cooperation and approval of the U.S. Congress, which at this writing has a 50–50 divided Senate, with Democrats holding only the slightest majority, with Vice President Kamala Harris' authority to cast tie-breaking votes. Furthermore, opposition from Democratic senators from states like West Virginia with large fossil fuel industries has to be overcome. It is also important to note that cap-and-trade legislation to mitigate climate change failed to pass in the Senate during the early years of the Obama administration, even when Democrats had a 60-vote, filibuster-proof majority.

Second, adaptation is also fundamental to long-term global prosperity and survival because the cumulative negative effects of climate change will continue for many centuries, even if – what seems like a miracle now – humans could manage to completely stop emitting greenhouse gases today (IPCC, 2013). That is, even under this most optimistic climate change mitigation scenario, our distant descendants – many generations beyond our great grandchildren – will likely still experience adverse conditions from climate change such as an acceleration of slow-onset increased average temperatures, rising oceans, and desertification. Also, they will be more likely to experience frequent and severe climate-related extreme events like heat waves, hurricanes, floods, droughts, and wildfires.

These deteriorating nature-adversity conditions may accelerate and generate cascading disaster conditions resulting in record fatalities, economic loss, and other hardships for humanity. The year 2020 offered an illustration of such a cascading catastrophic dynamic, one that combined multiple natural disasters exacerbated by climate change (e.g. in the U.S. a record number of wildfires occurred, and the highest number of named hurricanes were recorded), along with other natural calamities not related to climate change (e.g. the COVID-19 pandemic).[8] To be sure, the actual amount of economic loss and the loss of human life lost due to climate change is currently very difficult to estimate (IPCC, 2014a). Yet, already observed examples include natural disaster-related fatalities, business bankruptcies, and damages to infrastructure (some reaching catastrophic levels) (Linnenluecke & Griffiths, 2015). Also, the forced displacement of large populations due to increased lack of fresh water, decline in crop yields, collapse of fisheries and coral reefs, spread of tropical diseases and pests to colder latitude countries, and the acceleration of massive biodiversity loss and extinction of animals and plants, among other factors, is on the rise (IPCC, 2014a; WRI, 2019).

Third, climate change mitigation is strongly opposed by multiple powerful actors in business and government. Some who oppose it are driven by conspiracy theories suggesting that mitigation is not needed because climate change is a "hoax." Others claim climate change

---

[8] Cascading disasters occur when an initial disaster sets off a sequence of events that "result in physical, social or economic disruption" and are, "associated more with the magnitude of vulnerability" than with the specific type of hazard involved (Pescaroli & Alexander). A classic example of a cascading disaster that affected multinational enterprises (MNEs) and their global supply chains was the earthquake off the coast of Japan in 2011. One hundred people died as a result of the earthquake. Another 18,000 people were killed after the earthquake triggered a tsunami. The tsunami then damaged the Fukushima Dai'ichi nuclear power plant's reactors, leading to the evacuation of 200,000 more people from the area (Pescaroli & Alexander). Overall, at least 32 million people in Japan are thought to have been affected by radioactive fallout (Smith, 2015).

mitigation is too costly in the short term and politically unfeasible because:

- Climate change effects are uncertain and long term;
- Mitigation costs mostly fall on economically key industries (e.g. oil companies, utilities, heavy manufacturing industries, and agriculture);
- Reliable alternative renewable energy sources and/or safe nuclear power are lacking;
- Companies and governments in developing countries benefit from potentially substantial free-riding;
- The 'public good' nature of mitigation benefits prevents companies from exclusively profiting from their mitigation efforts;
- Emerging market countries are not yet willing to reciprocate by proportionately matching the potential GHG reductions of industrialized countries.

Fourth, another reason that company managers oppose efforts to tackle the causes of climate change is a common belief – unfounded or not – that proposed mitigation regulations and carbon taxes imposed by politicians in Washington, or worse by international UN diplomats, are likely to increase their costs unfairly and dramatically, or even drive their businesses into bankruptcy. These managers ardently object to changing their core business strategies in response to climate change regulations and carbon taxes since these efforts are perceived to benefit other countries more than the U.S. (e.g. China and India) and/or future generations at the expense of present generations (Dolsak & Prakash, 2015, 2018).

Fifth, rationally or not, Republican politicians in the U.S. view climate change as the Democrat's excuse to enact – in the name of environmental protection – favored liberal policies that tend to burden key sectors of the economy that are major political supporters and donors primarily of the Republican party (e.g. oil, gas, and coal mining).

Sixth, geopolitically, climate change mitigation efforts also confront a very difficult political dynamic with challenges of a different kind. For the leaders of many developing countries, potential climate change mitigation regulations are seen as a throwback to colonial times. They fear that such regulations would allow former imperial powers to adopt draconian restrictions on developing countries self-management of domestic industries and exploitation of their own valuable natural resources. Additionally, developing countries would be asked to quickly transition to a carbon-free economy – one that replaces cheaper fossil fuels abundant in many non-industrialized nations in exchange for token promises of future financial aid.

Now, obviously many of these perceptions a are not based on the full facts liable to be driven by ideology and entrenched economic interests. However, these views are strongly held by many powerful actors whose support is fundamental if any meaningful global climate change mitigation policies are to be adopted by most actors (Dolsak & Prakash, 2015, 2018).

The benefits of adaptation to climate change. Initially, adaptation was opposed by both environmentalists and opponents of climate change mitigation (Linnenluecke & Griffiths, 2015). On the one hand, environmentalists saw adaptation efforts as a way of deflecting attention from climate change mitigation. On the other, opponents of climate change mitigation were afraid that embracing adaptation would signal an acceptance of human responsibility for climate change (Linnenluecke & Griffiths, 2015). Developing countries also took the view that emphasizing adaptation involved admitting a shared responsibility to deal with the negative effects of climate change. Additionally, in the late 1990s and the early 2000s there was limited initial scientific evidence linking climate change to deadly disasters (this is no longer the case). To be sure, adaptation did not receive much attention during the first 20 years of international negotiations under the UN Framework Convention on Climate Change (UNFCC) (Linnenluecke & Griffiths, 2015). It was only when the 2010 Conference of Parties (COP) in Cancún convened that a formal adaptation framework was approved.

> Both mitigation and adaptation strategies and policies are mutually reinforcing and necessary for confronting the enormous challenges involved in reducing the negative effects of climate change. Adaptation is not a panacea; it is a complement to climate change mitigation.

Over time, however, all camps have increasingly accepted that adaptation is an integral part of dealing with the challenges of climate change. Of course, as explained at the beginning of this chapter, the best adaptation strategy combines: (1) concerted global mitigation efforts to aggressively limit GHGs so that average temperatures do not exceed (1.5–2 °C) humanity's ability to cope; and (2) efforts that allow organizations and societies to cope with and be more resilient to climate change's long-term detrimental effects, effects that are likely to linger for many centuries to come (IPCC, 2014b). These points cannot be overstated. Both mitigation and adaptation are mutually reinforcing and necessary to confront the negative effects of climate change (Haigh, 2019). Adaptation is not a panacea; it is a complement to climate change mitigation.

The emerging realization that even drastic global efforts to reduce GHGs may not be able to forestall climate change's severe negative effects has begun to shift popular attention toward working out adaptation alternatives (IPCC, 2018). Additionally, given the difficult political and economic nature of climate change mitigation efforts, adaptation has begun to receive more attention by policy makers, environmentalists, and business managers. Shifting the focus of the climate change debate to also include adaptation has important advantages:

1. **Climate change adaptation benefits are shorter term and can be more directly and locally enjoyed by those engaged in it.** So, it can be adopted by individual companies, industries, communities, and countries without requiring the large collective action efforts necessary for mitigation (Dolsak & Prakash, 2015; Haigh, 2019).
2. **Adaptation's free riders** (those cheating on adaptation efforts and expecting to still enjoy its benefits) **can be more easily excluded from enjoying the direct benefits (and spillovers) of adaptation** implemented by others (Dolsak & Prakash, 2015).
3. **Engaging in climate change adaptation** brings increased attention to the negative consequences, costs, and some of the opportunities offered by climate change mitigation. As such, it **can help to soften the strong political and economic opposition to mitigation** (Dolsak & Prakash, 2015). Additionally, the greater interaction between business managers and environmentalists with expertise in climate change adaptation may increase mutual rapport and trust and lead to new political coalitions in favor of climate change action, including mitigation.
4. Some companies already have experience with risk management and preparedness that allows climate change adaptation to be reframed as part of routine risk management.

Contents of Book

Following this introduction, in Part II (Chapters 2–5) we develop a conceptual framework that contributes to understanding first, how business adaptation is shaped by slow-onset nature-adversity conditions;

and second, how weather-related natural disasters affect foreign subsidiary investment by multinational corporations (MNCs). Examining how MNC subsidiary foreign investment is affected by natural disasters can help provide an indication of how other businesses may adapt to future extreme events generated by climate change (Oh & Reuveny, 2010). About 75 percent of the natural disasters occurring since the year 2000 are weather-related disasters that were exacerbated by climate change (Oh, Oetzel, & Rivera, 2020). Additionally, given MNCs' high exposure to these disasters in multiple countries, their responses to these extreme events can guide other businesses as they adapt to climate change trends accelerate.

In Chapter 2 we build on resilience theory to provide a framework of analysis to illustrate how the intensity of nature adversity generated by climate change affects and limits business adaptation. Adaptation responses can span a broad range of strategies, beginning with unawareness to deliberate ignorance of nature-adversity conditions. Next, we examine protective adaptation – the quest to preserve the status quo of core business features – including substitution of nature's resources and services, buffering from negative conditions, government lobbying, and engaging in alliances or mergers and acquisitions. And then, at the highest levels of nature adversity, we look at adoption of diversification strategies (e.g. in terms of products/services, industry participation, and geographic location) or even the abandoning of businesses altogether.

In Chapter 3 we continue exploring how firms adapt to the intensity of chronic nature-adversity conditions. Our goal in this chapter is to contribute to the debate found in the strategic management literature on whether external adversity tends to be positively or negatively related to adaptation. We propose an inverted U-shaped relationship between nature-adversity intensity and protective adaptation, such that firms facing lower or higher than medium levels of nature-adversity intensity tend to adopt lower levels of protective adaptation. This is because of the interplay between latent counterbalancing mechanisms. First, at mild intensity levels of nature-adversity, organizational inertial forces constrain organizations' willingness to adapt. Second, at medium levels coalition-building and internal organizational politics allow managers to deploy adaptation resilience capabilities. Third, at severe levels of nature-adversity conditions, growing natural forces eventually impose limits beyond which protective adaptation becomes unviable. Additionally, we discuss how our proposed inverted U-shaped relationship between nature-adversity intensity and protective adaptation is likely to be moderated by several firm-level and institutional context-level characteristics (i.e. age, public ownership, slack resources, and stringency of regulations).

In Chapter 4 we shift the focus of our analytical framework to the effect of natural disasters on subsidiary-level foreign direct investments by multinational corporations. The question of where to compete internationally is one of the most fundamental questions in corporate strategy. In 2018, there were approximately 500,000 MNC subsidiaries operating around the world, generating about half of all international trade (European Commission, as cited in Kordos & Vojtovic, 2016; World Atlas of Global Issues, 2018). Given the very large number of MNC subsidiaries, it is critical to understand how MNCs adapt to extreme natural conditions that trigger more frequent and severe natural disasters. Thus, in this chapter we conceptually examine how natural disasters, compared to industrial disasters and terrorist attacks, shape MNCs' foreign market entry and expansion. We also investigate whether MNC subsidiary-level investment is more likely to decrease in response to the specific types of natural disasters that result in a higher number of fatalities. In addition, we also elaborate on how country governance characteristics (i.e. regulatory quality, rule of law, democratic freedoms, political stability, and corruption levels) moderate the relationship between disasters and MNC subsidiary-level investment. We examine these moderating effects because the quality of governance and the strength of the institutions in a country tend to have a significant impact on the ability and willingness of governments to respond to disasters within their borders.

In Chapter 5 we continue to develop our conceptual framework, describing how MNCs' foreign subsidiary investments are affected by natural disasters. We do so by examining whether MNCs are able to gain experiential advantages from managing through low or high impact natural disasters that enable them to enter and expand into countries experiencing similar risks. We also conceptually discuss whether advantages accruing from MNCs' subsidiary-level experience with natural disasters are greater than those gained as a result of terrorist attacks or technological disasters. Discontinuous risks, such as natural disasters, which are often difficult to anticipate or predict, have received little attention in the strategic management research.

Much of the research in this area has focused on firms' experience with continuous risks, risks that are steady and more predictable in a firm's operating environment.

In Part III, we detail and extensively discuss empirical research seeking to examine the research questions and test the propositions developed in the book's conceptual chapters. Chapter 6 focuses on two key research questions highlighted in Chapter 3: How does nature-adversity intensity affect the adoption of business protective adaptation strategies? And how do firm-level and institutional-level factors moderate the relationship between nature-adversity intensity and protective adaptation? In Chapter 6 we also test the propositions developed in Chapter 3. To do this, we study how the U.S. ski industry has adapted to warmer temperatures. The ski industry is highly vulnerable to nature adversity associated with changing climate conditions and reportedly lost around 1 billion USD in revenue from 1999 to 2010, attributable to lower demand for skiing because of warmer temperatures and uncertain snowfall (Burakowski & Magnusson, 2012; Zeng, Broxton, & Dawson, 2018). In Chapter 6 our quantitative analysis examines adaptation responses by large ski resorts in the Western United States from 2001 to 2013 (approximately 85 percent of the commercially open skiable acres in that region). Our data tracks snowfall and temperature conditions for Western U.S. ski resorts from 1995 to 2013 and includes an average of 75 ski resorts per year, resulting in panel data set of 850 firm-year observations over the 2001–2013 period. Our findings show that firms facing medium nature-adversity intensity levels (measured in terms of temperature) appear more likely to engage in higher adaptation while those experiencing low and high natural adversity intensity show a tendency for lower adaptation, yielding an inverted U-shaped relationship. Our findings also suggest that firm age, the stringency of the regulatory environment, and the presence of slack resources induce a flattening of this inverted U-shaped relationship. Public company status, however, induces a steepening of the inverted U-shaped relationship.

In Chapter 7 we empirically test the propositions and hypotheses developed in Chapter 4. Specifically, we examine whether natural disasters, compared to industrial disasters and terrorist attacks, affect multinational corporations' foreign subsidiary investment. We also analyze if this effect varies in response to the different subtypes of natural disasters that result in the highest number of fatalities.

Then, we test if stronger institutional environments and better country governance positively moderate the relationship between disasters and foreign subsidiary-level investment. We test our hypotheses using a panel dataset that includes 31,285 observations from 71 European Fortune Global 500 MNCs and their subsidiaries operating across 101 countries during the period 2001–2006. Our findings indicate that MNC foreign subsidiary investment is likely to decrease in response to severe terrorist attacks or technological disasters but not in response to natural disasters, except for the case of windstorms and related water surges, which are the deadliest weather-related natural disasters. For natural disasters, the likelihood of MNC subsidiary-level disinvestment increased with higher host country democratic freedoms and decreased with higher host country's regulatory enforcement quality.

In Chapter 8 we empirically examine the research questions and propositions conceptually discussed in Chapter 5: Are MNCs able to gain experiential advantages from managing during natural disasters – including disasters with both low and high impacts – that enable them to enter and expand into other countries experiencing similar risks? And how do MNCs' experiences with natural disasters compare to experience associated with terrorist attacks and technological disasters? We used a panel dataset with 57,500 observations from 106 European Global Fortune 500 MNCs and their subsidiaries operating across 109 countries during a seven-year period, 2001–2007. We find that experience with high-impact natural disasters (as well as terrorist attacks and technological disasters) can be leveraged for expansions into an existing host country, but not for initial entry into other countries experiencing similar high-impact disasters. We also find that experience with low-impact natural disasters does not appear to reduce the negative effect of disaster severity on expansion (or entry). Yet, experience with low-impact terrorist attacks and technological disasters does show a significant positive moderating effect on the relationship between disaster severity and expansion. A notable exception to the lack of significant moderating effects on the MNC entry models is the case of floods. Experience with high-impact floods does show a positive and significant moderating effect on the negative link between disaster severity and MNC entry.

Lastly, in the concluding part (Chapter 9) we discuss our main findings, contributions and research limitations, outline a future research agenda, and propose implications for business managers and policy makers.

PART II

Conceptual Framework

Understanding Business Adaptation to Climate Change

2 | Business Adaptation Limits and Resilience to Climate Change Adversity

Business strategy scholars have long been interested in the ability of firms to cope with adverse conditions in their operating environments. Previous research has considered both internal adversity such as structural and leadership changes or performance shortfalls, and external adversity such as competition, stakeholder demands, or other aspects of firms' regulatory and institutional environments (Linnenluecke, Griffiths, & Winn, 2013; Sutcliffe & Vogus, 2003). The concept of *organizational resilience* has been used more recently to describe firms' capabilities to maintain or regain functioning in spite of major mishaps or in the presence of continuous stress (Hollnagel, 2006; Sutcliffe & Vogus, 2003). Firms may build resilience through *adaptation*, defined by Levinthal (1994) as a "change in a significant organizational attribute, such as a basic business strategy or organizational structure in response to environmental change".

> *Organizational resilience:* **A firm's ability to maintain or regain functioning in the presence of continuous stress or despite a major mishap.**

Despite the extant research, there remain questions regarding how the nature and magnitude of adversity experienced by a firm may affect its ability to adapt and thereby maintain resilience. In particular, adaptation to adversity stemming from the natural environment, including from climate change, land use, and land cover change, or shifts in hydrological cycles, may be significantly limited (Adger & Barnett, 2009; IPCC, 2014a; Risky Business Project, 2014). We use the term *nature adversity intensity* to describe the *magnitude* of unfavorable chronic conditions generated by the natural environment that can hinder firm operations (U.S. Environmental Protection Agency, 1998). While firms may be able to cope with low to moderate

This chapter is a modified version of Clement and Rivera (2017), reproduced with permission of the journal publisher.

23

levels of nature adversity, their adaptive actions may become unfeasible and/or ineffective at higher levels of adversity. Firms may thus reach an *adaptation limit* (Dow et al., 2013), or a point at which available adaptation may no longer be sufficient to maintain their core business. Firms may therefore need to undertake more in depth or transformative change (Kates, Travis, & Wilbanks, 2012; Linnenluecke & Griffiths, 2010) or risk jeopardizing long-term survival. Yet the mechanisms by which they may reach adaptation limits and undergo potential transformation have not yet been adequately described in the organizational context (Beermann, 2010).

> *Nature adversity intensity*: The magnitude of unfavorable changes in natural environment conditions that can hinder a firm's operations.

> *Adaptation limit*: A point at which available adaptation may no longer be sufficient for a firm to maintain its core business.

There are also unanswered questions regarding how the interplay between adaptation and the wider resource contexts of a firm may affect resilience. In particular, we do not yet have a good understanding of the potential interdependencies between firm adaptation and the *nature* context in which actions are implemented (Starik & Kanashiro, 2013; Winn & Pogutz, 2013). Yet adaptation effectiveness may hinge upon the impacts that these very actions might have on resources within local ecosystems (ecosystem services), and firms might in turn *rely* on these resources for adaptation (Nelson, Adger, & Brown, 2007; Starik & Rands, 1995).

In examining these questions we draw on resilience theory from socioecology and develop several lines of inquiry. We first apply the theory's conceptualization of adaptation as a cyclical process regulated by external disturbances. We do this to consider how nature adversity intensity might drive firms to reach adaptation limits in different phases of their adaptive cycle. Nature adversity intensity at low to moderate levels may at first drive a firm to adapt through actions that attempt to sustain its core business. However, it may find that its ability to do so eventually becomes constrained as higher levels of adversity intensity start to undermine the viability of adaptive actions. We then consider how firms may have the opportunity to undertake more transformative change upon reaching adaptation limits. Through such change, they may be able to maintain and strengthen resilience despite heightened nature adversity intensity by adopting organizational forms that reduce vulnerability to adversity intensity. Finally, we also

Table 2.1. *Definitions of the main concepts used in Chapter 2*

Concept	Definition	Reference
Adaptation	Change in a significant organizational attribute, such as a basic business strategy or organizational structure in response to environmental change	Levinthal (1994)
Adaptation limit	Point at which available adaptation is no longer sufficient to maintain a firm's core business	Adapted from Dow et al. (2013)
Nature adversity intensity	Magnitude of unfavorable chronic conditions generated by the natural environment that can hinder a firm's operations	Adapted from U.S. EPA (1998)
Impoverished regime	A set of equilibrium states having persistently low potential, low connectedness, and low resilience, and that may be difficult to reverse	Gunderson and Holling (2002); Walker et al. (2009)
Regime shift	Persistent change in a system's structure and function	Stockholm Resilience Center (2015)
Resilience	Capacity of a system to absorb disturbance while undergoing change so as to retain essentially the same function, structure, identity, and feedbacks	Walker et al. (2004)
Equilibrium state	Stable combination of key attributes that constitute a system (e.g. components, functions, structures, and processes)	Beisner et al. (2003); Gunderson (2000)
Transformation	Process by which a system reorganizes itself with entirely new components, functions, structures, and processes	Folke et al. (2010); Walker et al. (2004)

seek to shed light on the potential interdependencies between firms and their local ecosystems. Organizational resilience may be contingent on how a company manages the broader ecosystems in which it operates because of the impacts its actions can have on those systems. This may be the case in particular for a firm that heavily depends on ecosystem services for its core business or for adaptation (see Table 2.1 for summary definitions of the chapter's main concepts).

We therefore propose to extend the budding literature on organizational resilience to nature adversity by incorporating key concepts from resilience theory in socioecology. First, we identify the mechanisms by which organizational resilience may fluctuate as a firm adapts to changing levels of nature adversity intensity. Second, we suggest that the existing conceptualization of organizational resilience could be expanded to include transformative change, which may allow a firm to mitigate the operational impacts of reaching adaptation limits. Finally, we explicitly draw out the relationship of "mutual impact and dependence" (Winn & Pogutz, 2013) that a company may share with its broader ecosystems and consider the implications that this interdependency might have for both organizational and ecosystem resilience.

Introducing Resilience Theory: Resilience and the Adaptive Cycle

While resilience is still a relatively new concept in the organizational literature, it has been explored in a number of other fields (Lengnick-Hall & Beck, 2005; Linnenluecke & Griffiths, 2013; Vogus & Sutcliffe, 2007; Yang, Bansal, & DesJardine, 2014). These include disaster risk and emergency management (Bruneau et al., 2003; Rose & Liao, 2005), supply chains (Fiksel, 2003), psychology (Luthar, Cicchetti, & Becker, 2000), and socioeconomic systems (Levin et al., 1998; O'Brien, Sygna, & Haugen, 2004) among others.

In business management literature, scholars have mainly examined resilience in the context of high-reliability organizations (Weick & Sutcliffe, 2001) or in the context of firm responses to quick-onset extreme weather events (Linnenluecke & Griffiths, 2012). As defined above, organizational resilience represents ability to maintain or recover (and even improve) functioning despite the presence of adverse conditions (Sutcliffe & Vogus, 2003; Weick & Sutcliffe, 2001). Resilience is therefore conceptualized as a relatively stable quality that is put to the test once a discontinuity occurs. Firms that adapt and return to their original equilibrium are deemed to exhibit resiliency.

This definition contrasts with the most recent developments on resilience theory in socioecology, which is distinct in its assumption that a given system may actually exist in multiple possible equilibriums (Gunderson, 2000). The field of socioecology studies the interdependencies and co-evolution of systems of people and nature (Stockholm Resilience Center, 2014). Systems may therefore include natural systems such as ecosystems, social systems such as organizations, or linked social and natural systems, termed "socioecological systems." As such, systems in socioecology are complex, open, and adaptive: they are made up of a large number of interacting components that collectively exchange resources with their external environment while constantly adjusting to changing external conditions (Frederick, 1998; Maguire et al., 2006; Valente, 2010).

In resilience theory, adaptation is conceptualized as a process or *adaptive cycle* along which a system progresses through different equilibrium states. Equilibrium states are stable combinations of the key attributes that constitute a system (e.g. components, functions, structures, and processes) (Beisner, Haydon, & Cuddington, 2003; Gunderson, 2000). In contrast to the current conceptualization of organizational resilience, a system's resilience in socioecology is therefore more dynamic: it is determined by the type and level of adaptation that the system is undergoing during a given phase of the adaptive cycle. Resilience in socioecology can formally be defined as "the capacity of a system to absorb disturbance while undergoing change so as to still retain essentially the same function, structure, identity, and feedbacks" (Walker, Holling, Carpenter, & Kinzig, 2004).

> Resilience in socioecology is defined as "the capacity of a system to absorb disturbance while undergoing change so as to still retain essentially the same function, structure, identity, and feedbacks."

A system's adaptive cycle is structured along four main phases: exploitation, conservation, release, and reorganization (see Table 2.2 for a summary of these phases) (Gunderson & Holling, 2002). The ecological example of mixed spruce and fir tree forests in the Eastern United States can serve to illustrate the different phases of the adaptive cycle (Holling, 2001). In these forests, long periods of growth and maturation are followed by rapid periods of destruction triggered by intense disturbances, which then lead to periods of revival and forest regrowth (Holling, 2001). In this example, wildfires and insect outbreaks play the role of disturbance agents (Holling, 2001). The dynamics in these ecosystems constitute a natural phenomenon that is an important part of forest renewal and regeneration (Holling, 2001).

Table 2.2. *Adaptive cycle's four main phases*

Phase	Main features and resilience level
Exploitation	Rapid growth and high susceptibility to external disturbance High resilience
Conservation	Gradual system expansion Medium resilience that can decline
Release	Rapid disbanding of resources accumulated in the system Low resilience
Reorganization	Reassembly of system components and resources Increasing resilience

Adaptation is a cyclical process that is regulated by external disturbances. A system's adaptive cycle is structured along four main phases: exploitation, conservation, release, and reorganization.

The **exploitation phase** of the adaptive cycle is characterized by rapid growth (Allen, Angeler, Garmestani, Gunderson, & Holling, 2014). In this initial phase, a system is highly influenced by external disturbances since it initially has low interconnectedness between its various components (Gunderson & Holling, 2002). Progressively, the system becomes dominated by components that have high adaptability to these disturbances (Gunderson & Holling, 2002). These components in turn collectively and rapidly expand the system by securing resources critical to system functioning (Allen et al., 2014). Resilience is high in this phase of the cycle thanks to the system's high adaptability and capacity to maintain functioning (Gunderson & Holling, 2002). During the exploitation phase in the forest example, the landscape is initially sparse and exposed. The ecosystem is then progressively colonized by highly adaptable species such as grasses and shrubs, which eventually pave the way for young, growing trees.

The **conservation phase** of the adaptive cycle is characterized by a more gradual expansion of the system (Allen et al., 2014). As interconnectedness within the system grows, functions and processes become more established and those components having greater adaptive efficiency are retained (Gunderson & Holling, 2002). The system as a whole is thus able to bring external disturbances under control and gradually continue accumulating resources (Gunderson & Holling, 2002). During the conservation phase in the forest example, the ecosystem evolves toward a denser mature forest (Holling, 2001). At first, the slow maturation rate of trees helps to control the amount of foliage in the forest (Holling, 2001). This reduces the amount of fuel available for fire in the forest. This also allows insectivorous birds to prey on insects, reducing their populations (Holling, 2001). As a system continues along this trajectory, however, it may also become less flexible, thus reexposing potential vulnerabilities to external disturbances (Holling, 2001). Resilience might be reduced in this phase, as the system may lose its ability to withstand new waves of increasing disturbances. In the forest example this rigidity becomes progressively manifest as the increasing density of the forest structure reduces the effectiveness of insect predation by birds and increases the fuel available for fire (Holling, 2001). As a result, the forest may no longer be able to suppress insect or fire outbreaks as effectively.

The **release phase** of the adaptive cycle is characterized by the rapid disbanding of resources accumulated in the system (Allen et al., 2014). This phase is triggered when external disturbances reach a high point of magnitude that overwhelms the system's capacity to maintain functioning (Holling, 2001). In other words, external disturbances cross a threshold that induces the system to reach an adaptation limit. During the release phase, adaptability collapses, functions and processes break down, and the system reaches its lowest level of resilience. In the forest example, the ecosystem eventually becomes limited in its ability to control insect populations and the potential fuel for wildfires (Holling, 2001). A release phase is then triggered when a significant insect outbreak or wildfire occurs, decimating the forest (Holling, 2001).

Finally, the **reorganization phase** of the adaptive cycle is characterized by a reassembly of system components and resources (Allen et al., 2014). Existing resources left over from previous exploitation and conservation phases consolidate, allowing the system to reset and transition to another exploitation phase as it closes the previous adaptive cycle (Allen et al., 2014; Holling, 2001). Resilience increases again in this phase, as the system is once again highly influenced by external disturbances, favoring high adaptability (Gunderson & Holling, 2002). In the forest example, reorganization leads to renewal and regrowth as the ecosystem enters a new cycle, with banks of residual seeds eventually enabling the regeneration of young, growing trees.

Resilience and Transformation

Rather than just resetting a system, however, the reorganization phase of
the adaptive cycle may also involve the association of entirely novel
components and resources (Gunderson & Holling, 2002). A system
may thus experience a regime shift, which fundamentally alters its nature
(Walker et al., 2004). The *transformation* of a system in this way can be
defined as the process by which a system reorganizes itself with entirely
new components, functions, structures, and processes (Adger, 2009;
Folke et al., 2010; Walker et al., 2004). A system may be driven to
undergo transformation particularly if external disturbances render a
return to its original regime untenable (Walker et al., 2004). As the system
enters the exploitation phase of a new adaptive cycle, it may therefore
begin building resilience to an entirely different set of external conditions.

> The *transformation* of a system is the process by which a system
> reorganizes itself with entirely new components, functions, structures,
> and processes.

Such transformations have been identified in a number of socio
systems, where strategic investments, divestments, and structural
changes have been implemented in order to transition a system toward
a new regime (Walker et al., 2004; Walker, Abel, & Anderies, 2009).
For example, Cumming (1999) describes how changes in land use
during the 1990s transformed the region of southeastern Zimbabwe
from an economy focused primarily on agriculture to one primarily
focused on wildlife. Extensive livestock production from both cattle
ranching and subsistence agriculture, complemented by marginal dry-
land crop production, originally constituted the predominant form
of land use in the region. From 1992 to 1994 an extended drought
decimated livestock and crop production. From there, many large
commercial ranches removed both remaining livestock and internal
fences to transform themselves into joint wildlife conservancies
(Cumming, 1999). Some subsistence farmers subsequently negotiated
to join their land to these conservancies (Cumming, 1999). As a result,
multiple uses of biodiversity services, including safari hunting, game
cropping, and ecotourism replaced livestock production as the
principle livelihood activity (Cumming, 1999).

Problems may arise, however, when external disturbances trigger
a release phase, but the system does not possess adequate residual

resilience to reorganize itself. The transition between the conservation and release phases or the point at which a system reaches an adaptation limit therefore represents a critical juncture. This is because a system's level of resilience at this point may determine the nature of the regime into which it can reorganize itself. In other words, if the system possesses adequate residual resilience, it may transition back into its original regime or into a novel one and begin rebuilding resilience. If not, the system risks losing its key attributes, collapsing its adaptive cycle, and potentially flipping into an *impoverished regime*. An impoverished regime can be defined as a set of equilibrium states that have persistently low potential, low connectedness, and low resilience, and thus may be difficult to reverse (Gunderson & Holling, 2002; Walker et al., 2009).

Catastrophic shifts in certain ecosystems – for example, coral reefs – illustrate this type of transformation (Scheffer et al., 2001). Coral reefs are characterized by their abundant biodiversity (Scheffer et al., 2001). However, they are vulnerable to irreversible shifts into impoverished algae-dominated ecosystems due to a combination of disturbance factors (Scheffer et al., 2001). These include warming ocean temperatures and increasing acidity, hurricanes, nutrient runoff from land-use change, and overfishing (Nyström & Folke, 2011; Scheffer et al., 2001). Such shifts have already been documented for coral reefs in parts of the Caribbean and elsewhere (Nyström & Folke, 2011; Scheffer et al., 2001).

Having introduced the main dimensions of resilience theory in socioecology, in the remining sections of this paper we build upon this theory to discuss how firms may be driven to reach potential adaptation limits, particularly when faced with growing nature adversity intensity. First, we highlight how firms and ecosystems share an open systems nature. Then, our discussion focuses on how the attributes of these core open systems drive a firm's adaptation dynamic to slow-onset nature adversity conditions.

Nature Adversity Intensity as a Driver of Business Adaptation Limits

We propose that resilience theory – taken from the field of socioecology, which views adaptation as a cycle driven by chronic disturbances – can help shed light on the mechanism by which the intensity of nature adversity drives a firm's adaptation. Resilience theory was first developed by ecologists to explain how ecological systems (ecosystems) adapt to external stressors (Holling, 1973). We borrow logics from resilience theory to explain how firms may respond to increasing nature adversity intensity. This use of analogical reasoning follows the tradition from management scholars – and those from other social sciences – to apply concepts and vocabulary from theories that model natural systems to understand patterns of managerial behavior and strategy-making (Cornelissen, 2005; Cornelissen & Durand, 2012; Okhuysen & Bonardi, 2011; Oswick, 2011; Poulis & Poulis, 2016; Weick, 1989).

Our analogical reasoning is based on fundamental structural similarities between firms and ecosystems that make the application of resilience theory useful in understanding organizational responses to ecological adversity intensity. First, both ecosystems and firms share an open systems structure in that they exchange resources with their external environment. Second, survival-seeking adaptation in response to external stressors takes place within both ecosystems and firms. Third, both ecosystems and firms may exhibit differences in their capacity to absorb varying levels of ecological adversity intensity. Additionally, our view of firms as open adaptive systems follows well-established perspectives in the organizational sciences (Frederick, 1998; Katz & Kahn, 1966; Maguire et al., 2006; Morel & Ramanujam, 1999; Valente, 2010). Firms differ from natural ecosystems, however, in possessing intentionality, foresight, the capacity to learn, and the ability to be governed by rules that are self-evolved (Holling, 2001; Lansing, 2003; Maguire et al., 2006; Valente, 2010). In contrast to ecosystems, firms may therefore have the agency to actively manage their adaptive responses to external stressors based on their perception of nature adversity intensity.

> Both ecosystems and firms share an open systems structure in that they exchange resources with their external environment. Survival-seeking adaptation in response to external stressors takes place within both ecosystems and firms. However, firms differ from natural ecosystems in possessing intentionality, foresight, capacity to learn, and ability to be governed by rules that are self-evolved.

Prior work in business strategy literature considered firms to be complex, open, and adaptive systems (Frederick, 1998; Maguire et al., 2006; Morel & Ramanujam, 1999; Valente, 2010). It is therefore plausible that firms may also progress through the different stages of their own adaptive cycles as they attempt to cope with changes in their operating environments. Linnenluecke and Griffiths (2010), in particular apply the adaptive cycle in the context of firm adaptation to rapid-onset extreme weather events. Under stable predisturbance conditions, a firm may go through exploitation and conservation phases, thus growing, expanding, and accumulating resources and capabilities geared toward achieving a certain level of core business performance (Linnenluecke & Griffiths, 2010). However, firms may become exposed to sudden and high-impact extreme weather events such as storms, droughts, or floods (Linnenluecke & Griffiths, 2010). Such natural disasters may overwhelm their coping capabilities by damaging physical capital, disrupting processes or supply chains, inducing hefty recovery costs, and creating a general climate of uncertainty.

Firm may thus experience a sudden decline in performance, akin to a rapid release phase (Linnenluecke & Griffiths, 2010). If resilience is high enough, the firm may nonetheless restore performance to predisturbance levels through reorganization (Linnenluecke & Griffiths, 2010). As a firm starts to re-accumulate resources and reestablish functions and structures, it may close its previous adaptive cycle and enter subsequent exploitation and conservation phases. In this example, external disturbance, in the form of a sudden crisis event, such as a natural disaster or economic meltdown, represents a punctuated and delimited moment in time. Firms build requisite coping capabilities *in the absence of* or *before* a disturbance event. Firm resilience is then put to the test in the aftermath of adverse events in enabling (or not) a return to initial equilibrium (see Chapters 4, 5, 8, and 9 for a detailed examination of business responses to natural disasters).

However, the mechanism by which firms may be driven to reach adaptation limits may be different when external disturbances are considered in the form of **slow-onset *continuous* stress**. Indeed, nature adversity intensity can also be characterized by *gradual* slow-onset changes in natural environment conditions that are both exogenous and unfavorable to the firm. For example, nature adversity intensity in the agriculture sector may take the form of changes in temperature and precipitation patterns (Risky Business Project, 2014). In the case of coastal industries, sea-level rise may constitute a salient indicator of nature adversity intensity (Risky Business Project, 2014). Nature adversity intensity may therefore be persistent and potentially impact firm performance at every stage of the adaptive cycle while also being out of a firm's immediate control. Managers may therefore need to adapt continuously to these conditions, without necessarily being certain that their efforts will be viable or yield requisite adaptive benefits at all levels of nature adversity intensity.

> Besides natural disaster-related adversity, nature adversity can also be characterized by the intensity of *gradual* slow-onset changes in the natural environment conditions both exogenous and unfavorable to a firm.

Low to moderate nature adversity intensity may at first drive a firm during the exploitation and conservation phases to select and then reinforce adaptation that attempts to sustain their core business. Such protective adaptation may enable a firm to continue pursuing its core business at the same or even extended levels (Busch, 2011; Hoffmann, Sprengel, Ziegler, Kolb, & Abegg, 2009), thus allowing it to grow and expand. Protective adaptation may also have the benefit of leveraging existing or familiar competencies. Adaptation can therefore rapidly become routine, allowing firms to be more effective in countering nature adversity intensity at low to moderate levels.

> Protective adaptation seeks to enable firms to continue pursuing their core business at the same or even extended levels. The need for protective adaptation may be stimulated when the reliability of ecological resources possibly critical to a firm's core business are threatened.

These arguments are consistent with prior research on organizational adaptation to climate change, which is one of the few areas where scholars have specifically considered how firms cope with natural environment dynamics. Prior work suggests that the need for protective adaptation may be stimulated when firms face increasingly unfavorable climate conditions (Berrang-Ford, Ford, & Paterson, 2011; Haigh & Griffiths, 2012; Tashman & Rivera, 2016). This especially might be the case if firms have a high dependency on their core business, have previously experienced unfavorable climate conditions, and are relatively certain of being exposed to such conditions in the future (Busch, 2011; Hoffmann et al., 2009). In particular, if the reliability of ecological resources that may be critical to a firm's core business is threatened, then the firm may focus protective adaptation on securing access to these resources (Tashman & Rivera, 2016). A good example of this adaptive strategy can be found in the ski industry, where variability in natural snowfall affects the length of

Table 2.3. *List of Chapter 2 propositions*

Proposition 1	As nature adversity intensity increases from low to moderate levels, firms are more likely to engage in increasing levels of protective adaptation.
Proposition 2	As nature adversity intensity increases from moderate to high levels, firms are more likely to engage in decreasing levels of protective adaptation.
Proposition 3	Firms experiencing or anticipating adaptation limits at moderate levels of nature adversity intensity are more likely to pursue transformation strategies.
Proposition 4	Firms responding to nature adversity intensity may undertake protective adaptation that has deleterious impacts on local ecosystem services.
Proposition 5	The degradation of local ecosystem services may feed back to constrain firms in their ability to continue pursuing protective adaptation and hasten their attainment of adaptation limits.

the ski season (Hoffmann et al., 2009; Tashman & Rivera, 2016). Ski resorts adapt to the unreliability of this key resource by implementing artificial snowmaking, which can supplement and even replace natural snow cover, or by developing ski runs in more climatically favorable areas, where resorts can capitalize on longer lasting snow cover (Scott & McBoyle, 2007; Tashman & Rivera, 2016). Overall, our previous discussion suggests the following proposition (see Table 2.3, at the end of this chapter, for a list of all the propositions developed from our discussion in this paper):

Proposition 1: As nature adversity intensity increases from low to moderate levels, firms are more likely to engage in increasing levels of protective adaptation.

However, as the intensity of nature adversity reaches a certain threshold, the ability of a firm to continue pursuing protective adaptation may start to reach its limits. Critical core business resources may continue to be threatened, but now the viability of the adaptation itself in terms of feasibility and effectiveness may start to be compromised as well. Rather than enabling firms to negate or avoid the threats of nature adversity intensity altogether (Busch, 2011; Weinhofer & Busch, 2013), protective adaptation may therefore only shield them temporarily from these threats.

In addition, fundamental uncertainties associated with the identification and interpretation of nature adversity intensity thresholds can induce adaptation limits (Dow et al., 2013). Indeed, nature adversity might exhibit variability in intensity, particularly at a local scale, that is difficult to predict (Linnenluecke & Griffiths, 2012; Winn, Kirchgeorg, Griffiths, Linnenluecke, & Gunther, 2011). Nature adversity intensity may also interact with other biophysical, socioeconomic, and technological constraints to shape the point at which adaptation limits are reached (IPCC, 2014a,b). Therefore, identifying a given adaptation as effective for a given level of nature adversity intensity might be contingent upon a large variety of different factors. Managers could thus find it difficult to perceive and anticipate corresponding adversity intensity thresholds until after the moment when these are actually crossed (Brozovic & Schlenker, 2010; Nelson et al., 2007).

As the intensity of nature adversity increases beyond this threshold, from moderate to high levels, firms may find their ability to adapt is more severely constrained, as protective adaptation reaches physical limits and starts to fail. Over time, business managers are also likely to show an increasing level of fatigue, which in turn limits their willingness to sustain a high level of adaptation efforts in the face of worsening nature adversity intensity conditions that show no end in sight. Additionally, since protective adaptation may have become routine, managers may also lack the flexibility or ability to implement the more in-depth adaptive changes needed to fit the severe level of adversity intensity being experienced. For these reasons, managers may be unable to effectively achieve adequate adaptive benefits at more intense levels of nature adversity and may be compelled to forgo protective adaptation.

> **Over time, business managers are also likely to show an increasing level of fatigue, limiting their willingness to sustain a high level of adaptation efforts in the face of worsening nature adversity intensity conditions that show no end in sight.**

An example of adaptation limits can be found in the impacts of the recent drought on agriculture firms in California's Central Valley. Agriculture firms in this area have traditionally coped with recurrent drought by using irrigation that relies on a complex network of reservoirs, canals, and aqueducts, which store spring snowmelt from high in the Sierra Nevada and Cascade mountain ranges and release it when it is needed most, during the summer months (Nijhuis, 2014). However, recent historic levels of drought intensity and prolongation coupled with shrinking snowpacks and earlier snowmelts due to warmer winters, have decimated water reserves and crippled the irrigation efforts used by these firms to adapt (Nijhuis, 2014). We therefore put forward the following proposition:

> **Proposition 2:** As nature adversity intensity increases from moderate to high levels, firms are more likely to engage in decreasing levels of protective adaptation.

Nature Adversity Intensity and the Potential for Organizational Transformation

As a firm reaches potential adaptation limits and forgoes protective adaptation, a release phase may be triggered in the adaptive cycle. As adaptation fails and/or is abandoned, a firm might begin to lose resources, processes, and functions, affecting core business performance. At this point, its level of residual resilience may determine how quickly it will be able to transition into a reorganization phase as well as the outcome of that phase.

Specifically, a firm may face three broad potential trajectories. Along the first, if residual resilience is high enough, the firm may recover and resume business as usual under its original operational regime. As it reenters the exploitation phase, however, now aware of the heightened risks posed by nature adversity intensity, it may need to modify selected adaptation strategies so as to build adequate resilience to this altered operating environment. Along the second potential trajectory, residual resilience might be so low, or nature adversity intensity so severe, as to preclude recovery to its original operational state. As a result, the firm could shift to a more impoverished operational regime, one that may be difficult to reverse; or it might be acquired by another company; or it might cease operations altogether.

Going back to the California drought example, with the failure of irrigation resources and systems from prolonged and more intense drought, some agriculture firms have been turning to alternative adaptation. These include supplementing water resources with groundwater, investing in water efficiency, or transitioning to more drought-resistant crops (Fishman, 2015). For others, however, irrigation failure has meant leaving fields fallow – even on the order of 430,000 acres, in 2014 (Nijhuis, 2014) – or going out of business altogether (Sahagun, 2015).

Along the third potential trajectory, a firm may undertake transformative change and shift to an entirely new operational regime, possibly enabling it to avoid the threats of future nature adversity intensity altogether. It would then re-enter the exploitation phase under a new regime, one in which it starts to build resilience to an entirely different set of external challenges. These new conditions might eventually push the firm to transform yet again, thus allowing for repeated and successive cycles of innovation and renewal.

Anecdotal evidence suggests that in certain industries some firms follow this third trajectory. In the ski industry for example, some resorts are diversifying their efforts toward rebranding as year-round tourism destinations or investing in real estate development (Branch, 2014; Scott & McBoyle, 2007; Tashman & Rivera, 2016). In the wine industry, which is dealing with drought and warmer temperatures in certain regions, some vintners are relocating to more northern latitudes or expanding their businesses into hoteling (Finz, 2013; Hannah et al., 2013). Finally, small farms being affected by adverse climate conditions are diversifying their revenue streams into agro-tourism and farm stay businesses.

The potential for firm transformation is seen in the application of resilience theory to organizational systems differs from its application to purely natural systems. As already mentioned, in contrast to natural systems, business organizations and other social systems possess agency (i.e. intentionality), foresight, the capacity to learn, and the ability to be governed by rules that are self-evolved (Holling, 2001; Lansing, 2003; Maguire et al., 2006; Valente, 2010). This means a firm can actively shape the outcomes of its reorganization phase, namely through transformation. A key point of tension is whether transformation happens predominantly in a reactive manner, after adaptation limits are reached, or potentially in a proactive manner, in anticipation of approaching limits.

> **The potential for firm transformation is seen in the application of resilience theory to organizational systems differs from its application to purely natural systems. Thanks to human agency, a firm may be able to actively shape the outcomes of its reorganization phase, namely through transformation.**

The strategic management literature supports multiple possibilities ranging from collapse to transformation. Under the *punctuated equilibrium model*, for instance, organizational transformation happens in short, discontinuous bursts as a result of significant changes in operating conditions or major declines in performance (Romanelli & Tushman, 1994; Tushman & O'Reilly, 1996). Rindova and Kotha (2001) show, for example, how Internet search engine firms were able to regenerate competitive advantage in response to changing market conditions over different periods by morphing their organizational forms. It is possible that firms may undertake transformation only when they experience an extreme need to do so. This is because transformation may involve complex and cascading changes that may be inherently difficult to implement, while also violating elements of organizational identity, which may engender internal resistance (Gavetti, 2012).

> Transformation is rare and very challenging because it involves complex and cascading changes that may be inherently difficult to implement, while also violating elements of organizational identity, which may engender strong internal resistance by managers.

> However, if firms can anticipate approaching adaptation limits and initiate transformation before these limits are reached, then firms may not need to actually experience a release phase triggered by nature adversity intensity.

Another school of thought regards organizations as potentially able to undertake transformative change in an anticipatory manner (Folke et al., 2010; Rickards, 2013). In particular, Tushman and O'Reilly (1996) define the idea of ambidexterity as "the ability to simultaneously pursue both incremental and discontinuous innovation and change". This means that firms may have a better fit with their operating environments in the short run, while also retaining the capacity to completely reevaluate and reinvent that alignment in the long run as needed (Tushman & O'Reilly, 1996).

> A firm's pursuit of an ambidextrous strategy in the face of worsening nature adversity intensity is likely to be more favorable than if it were to persist in attempts to protect core business activities for which viability limits may be approaching.

In response to growing nature adversity intensity, ambidextrous firms may be able to leverage existing processes and resources to adapt in the shorter term, while also developing capabilities to innovate and transform toward potentially novel states in the longer term. For instance, managers can encourage the creation of entirely new business lines and diversify away from the core business being affected (Hoffmann et al., 2009). This may be more favorable than persisting in attempts to protect core business activities for which viability limits may be approaching. Ambidextrous firms may therefore have the ability to actively manage their adaptive cycles. If a firm can anticipate approaching adaptation limits and initiate transformation before these are reached, then it might not need to actually experience a release phase triggered by nature adversity intensity. Instead, they may be able to manage the transition directly from the conservation phase to the reorganization phase. Then through transformation, firms may enter a new exploitation phase using a novel set of resources and capabilities without having undergone major declines in performance. Such firms may retain high resilience throughout their adaptive cycles. We therefore put forward the following proposition:

> **Proposition 3:** Firms experiencing or anticipating adaptation limits at moderate levels of nature adversity intensity are more likely to pursue transformation strategies.

Interdependencies between Organizational and Ecosystem Resilience

Having discussed the processes by which a firm maintains or renews resilience in response to nature adversity intensity, we now consider how its embeddedness in wider ecosystems can affect its resilience. This interconnectedness may be particularly salient for a firm having a high dependence on ecosystem services for its core business or for adaptation. Ecosystem services can be formally defined as those services which people obtain from nature: the provisioning (e.g. water resources), regulating (e.g. climate regulation, water quality), cultural (e.g. aesthetic), and supporting (e.g. soil formation) benefits (Millennium Ecosystem Assessment, 2005).

Firms not only rely on ecosystem services but also affect the provisioning of these services (Nelson et al., 2007; Starik & Rands, 1995). In particular, as mentioned above, when reliability of critical ecological resources becomes compromised, a firm may respond by seeking to maintain or augment its usage of these resources (Hoffmann et al.,

2009; Tashman & Rivera, 2016). A firm may find this a cost-effective and expedient strategy, especially if it is able to externalize the costs of consuming these resources (Tashman & Rivera, 2016). In particular, this may be the case if it owns or controls its surrounding ecosystems or if ecosystem services are treated and regulated as public goods (Ostrom, 2010; Tashman & Rivera, 2016). However, at least since Hardin's (1968) *Tragedy of the Commons*, scholars have argued that ecosystem services are rarely infinite. Ecosystem services can be diminished by overexploitation, particularly when access and use by multiple users is difficult or costly to restrict (Ostrom, 2010). Therefore, while ecosystems may possess a certain capacity to sustain services, overconsumption by one or multiple users may eventually lead to deteriorating productivity and function (Folke et al., 2010; Nelson et al., 2007).

> A firm responding to pressures from nature adversity intensity tends to end up utilizing ecosystem services in a way that exceeds the ecosystems' capacity to sustain it. However, because observable ecosystem change tends to be nonlinear or delayed, managers may find it difficult to make sense of the link between their actions, ecosystem service degradation impacts, and how these impacts may, in turn, feed back to affect them.

It follows that a firm may not be able to continuously carry out an adaptation that increases its usage of ecosystem services without having potential negative spillover effects on the provisioning of these services. Firms responding to pressures from nature adversity intensity may therefore end up utilizing ecosystem services in a way that exceeds the ecosystems' capacity to sustain them. More specifically, as a firm draws on local ecosystems during the exploitation and conservation phases of its adaptive cycle, it may be progressively depleting the stored-up potential in these ecosystems. However, due to the ambiguous nature of ecosystem change, managers may not be able to immediately perceive deleterious changes occurring in ecosystems (Bansal & Knox-Hayes, 2013; Linnenluecke & Griffiths, 2013). Some ecosystems may change in a smooth, continuous manner, while others may remain unchanged until impacts reach a critical threshold, while still others may exhibit abrupt shifts from one state of functioning to another (Scheffer et al., 2001). Observable ecosystem change may thus be nonlinear or delayed and managers find it difficult to make sense of the link between their actions, ecosystem service impacts, and how these impacts may in turn feed back to affect them (Holling, 2001; Whiteman & Cooper, 2011; Winn et al., 2011).

In addition, even if managers are able to perceive the harmful impacts of their actions, they may still be prone to short-termism (Bansal & DesJardine, 2014). Managers myopically tend to focus on short-run adaptive gains over more long-term and uncertain impacts on ecosystems. They may therefore more easily misinterpret or ignore threats to or declines in ecosystem services and persist in their adaptive efforts (Bansal & Knox-Hayes, 2013; Starik & Rands, 1995). We therefore put forward the following proposition:

> **Proposition 4:** A firm responding to nature adversity intensity may undertake protective adaptation that has deleterious impacts on local ecosystem services.

However, a persistent degradation of local ecosystem services may in turn feed back to affect firm resilience in later phases of the adaptive cycle. When firm impacts are compounded by other types of stress, ecosystem service provisioning may completely collapse. Now, unable to continue drawing on ecosystem services for adaptation, the firm may more rapidly reach adaptation limits and enter a release phase. Furthermore, if it is unequipped to cope with such severe or rapid ecosystem service collapse, its residual resilience may be too low upon entering the reorganization phase. As a result, the firm may be precluded from returning to its original operational regime or from opting for more transformative change, with potential survival consequences. For firms with a high dependence on ecosystem services, adaptation that may appear successful in building resilience in the short term may actually prove to be maladaptive in the long run by unintentionally sabotaging future resilience pathways.

> For firms with a high dependence on ecosystem services, adaptation that may appear successful in building resilience in the short term may actually prove to be maladaptive in the long run by unintentionally sabotaging future resilience pathways.

Cascading breakdowns have been described for a number of socioecological systems, including in agriculture, forestry, and fisheries. In all of these, managers fail to take into account the dynamics of adaptive cycles at the ecosystem level, resulting in maladaptive management decisions and the collapse of the socioecological system (Barnett & O'Neill, 2010; Gunderson & Holling, 2002; Walker & Abel, 2002).

The example of arid rangelands threatened by drought and overgrazing in many parts of the world can serve to illustrate how such collapses might occur (Scheffer et al., 2001). Rangeland managers may at first respond to drought conditions by increasing the grazing of grasslands in order to maintain livestock numbers (Walker & Abel, 2002). However, grasslands may become progressively impoverished, less productive, and more eroded as a result of the compounded impacts of drought and overgrazing (Walker & Abel, 2002). If drought conditions and overgrazing become prolonged, resilience in grassland ecosystems may become so deteriorated as to induce a complete collapse in livestock production (Walk & Abel, 2002). If residual resilience has become too degraded, then the entire rangeland system may be unable to regenerate and shift into an impoverished regime of desertification (Holling, 2001). We therefore put forward the following proposition:

> **Proposition 5:** The degradation of local ecosystem services may feed back to constrain a firm's ability to continue pursuing protective adaptation and hasten its attainment of adaptation limits.

Conclusion

From an organizational perspective, certain industries, especially those which directly depend on natural systems, appear to already be at the forefront of the resilience challenges posed by nature adversity intensity; business strategy scholars are well positioned to tackle and anticipate future research avenues in this area and their potential implications for strategy and management.

In this chapter, we offered our view on two ways in which the research on firms and their natural environment can address these challenges: by building interdisciplinary bridges and by expanding a research agenda on organizational resilience. Specifically, we have sought to propose an extension to the previous literature by encouraging scholars to continue to think about organizational resilience as a dynamic property of a firm, one that integrates processes of both adaptation and transformation and that is longer term and intersystemic in nature.

> **Firms operating in industries that that directly depend on natural systems (e.g. agriculture, forestry, tourism, fisheries, coastal real state, energy production and supply, or food and beverage industries, among others) appear to already be at the forefront of the resilience challenges posed by nature adversity intensity.**

3 | Adaptation to Slow-Onset Nature Adversity Intensity

In this chapter we continue exploring how firms adapt to the intensity of adverse chronic conditions stemming from the natural environment (see Table 3.1 for a list of this chapter's propositions). Our goal is to contribute to the debate in the strategic management literature on the question of whether external adversity tends to be positively or negatively related to adaptation. Building on the resilience theory ideas discussed on Chapter 2, we propose that diverging perspectives tend to predict part of firm adaptation to nature adversity intensity. This is because of the interplay among latent counterbalancing mechanisms. First, at mild levels of nature adversity intensity, organizational inertial forces constrain organization willingness to adapt. Second, at medium levels of nature adversity intensity, coalition building and internal organizational politics allow managers to deploy adaptation resilience capabilities. Third, at severe levels, growing natural forces eventually impose limits beyond which protective adaptation becomes unviable.

In general, multiple literatures examining organizational responses to unfavorable environmental conditions can be divided into two broad diverging perspectives (Levinthal, 1991). The first perspective views organizational adaptation as likely to be constrained by inertial forces, attributing variation in organizations to their birth and death resulting from selection processes in the external environment (Hannan & Freeman, 1984; Staw, Sandelands, & Dutton, 1981). Alternatively, the second perspective tends to view competitive firms as more likely to be able to deliberately adapt to changing external demands (Chakravarthy, 1982; March, 1991).

Scholars have suggested that these broad organizational adaptation perspectives may be partially reconciled and have called for research to

This chapter is a modified and updated (for moderating effects of context and firms characteristics) version of the conceptual part of Rivera and Clement (2019), reproduced with permission of the journal publisher.

Table 3.1. *List of propositions developed in Chapter 3*

Proposition 1	The relationship between nature adversity intensity and protective adaptation follows an inverted U-shape, such that firms facing either lower or higher levels of nature adversity intensity are more likely to engage in lower levels of protective adaptation than those facing medium levels.
Proposition 2	The inverted U-shaped relationship between nature adversity intensity and protective adaptation is less pronounced for older firms than for younger firms.
Proposition 3	The inverted U-shaped relationship between nature adversity intensity and protective adaptation is less pronounced for firms operating in more stringent regulatory environments than for firms operating in less stringent regulatory environments.
Proposition 4	The inverted U-shaped relationship between nature adversity intensity and protective adaptation is less pronounced for firms with more slack resources than for firms with less slack resources.
Proposition 5	The inverted U-shaped relationship between nature adversity intensity and protective adaptation is more pronounced for publicly owned firms than for privately owned firms.

identify the different conditions under which each may be validated (Dobrev, Kim, & Carroll, 2002; Levinthal, 1991). Research has since identified potential drivers and inhibitors of adaptation including firm attributes and characteristics of a firm's operating environments (Chattopadhyay, Glick, & Huber, 2001; Dobrev et al., 2003). Prior work on adverse external environmental conditions has focused on firm competitive, economic, political, and institutional contexts. This work has provided empirical support to both views of organizational adaptation (Lewin, Weigelt, & Emery, 2004). However, examining unfavorable external conditions that go beyond these contexts may constitute an avenue for identifying when the relationship between external adversity and adaptation is likely to be positive or negative.

In this chapter, we focus on conceptually examining how nature adversity intensity affects a firm's *protective adaptation*. Unfavorable natural conditions can vary along distinct dimensions such as *intensity* (i.e. temperature magnitude), *uncertainty* (i.e. unpredictability of temperature magnitude) and *speed* (i.e. rate of change of intensity) (Linnenluecke et al., 2012; Winn et al., 2011). **Protective adaptation involves organizational adjustment efforts aimed at reducing the vulnerability of a firm's core features to adverse operating conditions and allowing it to maintain these features at the same or extended levels** (Adger, 2006; Hannan & Freeman, 1984; Hoffmann et al., 2009).

As we discussed in Chapter 2, growing nature adversity intensity may pose an important strategic problem as increasing evidence suggests adaptation limits for firms facing severe adverse conditions in their natural environment (Halkos et al., 2018; Winn et al., 2011). For example, businesses appear to be increasingly impacted by unfavorable nature conditions linked to global climate change such as higher temperatures, greater variations in the amount and timing of rainfall and snowfall, sea level rise, and more frequent and intense weather-related disasters (IPCC, 2014; Linnenluecke et al., 2012; Weinhofer & Busch, 2013).

> *Protective adaptation* involves organizational adjustment efforts aimed at reducing the vulnerability of a firm's core features to adverse operating conditions and at allowing it to maintain these features at the same or extended levels.

We posit that a firm's protective adaptation to nature adversity intensity is shaped by an interplay of latent counterbalancing mechanisms. First, at lower than medium levels of nature adversity intensity, organizational inertial forces constrain an organization's willingness to adapt, despite the low and slowly growing costs of protective adaptation. Second, at medium levels of nature adversity intensity, the interplay between natural adversity signals and constraints – internal organizational inertial forces, and business resilience capabilities – makes firms more willing and able to implement greater protective adaptation. Third, at severe levels, growing natural forces eventually impose limits beyond which protective adaptation becomes unviable. Accordingly, we suggest an inverted U-shaped relationship between nature adversity intensity and protective adaptation, such that firms facing lower or higher than medium levels of nature adversity intensity tend to adopt lower levels of protective adaptation.

> A firm's *protective adaptation* to nature adversity intensity is shaped by an interplay of multiple counterbalancing factors such as organizational inertial forces, adaptation costs and benefits, business resilience capabilities, biophysical limits.

We suggest an inverted U-shaped relationship between nature adversity intensity and protective adaptation, such that firms facing lower or higher than medium levels of nature adversity intensity tend to adopt lower levels of protective adaptation.

Nature Adversity Dimensions as a Distinct Aspect of Firms' Operating Environment

In the management and strategy literatures, the traditional external context has mostly reflected competitive, economic, social, and to a lesser degree political environments. Even the growing literature on corporate environmental management strategy has focused on examining the impacts of firm strategies on the natural environment, but it has paid scant attention to the reverse relationship (King, 1995; Weinhofer & Busch, 2013; Winn et al., 2011). Compared to other aspects of a firm's external contexts, nature adversity is generally exogenous (Rockström et al., 2009; Winn et al., 2011). Firm managers tend to perceive these unfavorable conditions as "acts of God" for which little can be done (Linnenluecke et al., 2012; Slovic, 2000). Additionally, in contrast to other traditional external context dimensions, the spatial and temporal scope and severity of nature adversity conditions are perceived as highly uncertain and more likely to occur in distant locations and time (Gasbarro, Rizzi, & Frey, 2016; Weinhofer & Busch, 2013; Winn et al., 2011). Thus, firms are less likely to respond to nature adversity even when its negative consequences are higher than those resulting from other external context dimensions traditionally considered by strategy scholars (Oh & Oetzel, 2011).

A firm's response to nature adversity intensity can be divided into two general categories: *adaptation* and *mitigation*. As we described earlier, protective adaptation involves adjusting to adverse conditions to reduce the susceptibility of business core activities to harm. In contrast, mitigation involves efforts aimed at addressing the root causes of nature adversity. Mitigation of nature adversity intensity generates global, long-term public goods. That is, the diffused benefits of mitigation are not only long term but also cannot be exclusively enjoyed by those implementing employing the effort, thus resulting in extensive free riding. Conversely, adaptation's benefits are more short term, can be directly enjoyed by those engaging in it, and require much less collective action than mitigation (Dolsak & Prakash, 2018;

Gasbarro, Rizzi, & Frey, 2016). Additionally, free riders can be more easily excluded from enjoying the spillover benefits of adaptation that is implemented by others (Dolsak & Prakash, 2018). Hence, firms tend to see nature adversity mitigation as a costly endeavor – characterized by strong political divisions and collective action challenges – that should be the responsibility of governments and international organizations (Oh & Oetzel, 2011; Slovic, 2000).

> **Firms' responses to nature adversity intensity can be divided into two general categories: *adaptation* and *mitigation*.**

> **Mitigation involves efforts aimed at addressing the root causes of nature adversity.**

Dimensions of Nature Adversity

Unfavorable natural conditions can vary along distinct basic dimensions such as *intensity* (i.e. magnitude), *uncertainty* (i.e. unpredictability of magnitude) and *speed* (i.e. rate of change of intensity) (Linnenluecke et al., 2012; Winn et al., 2011). These adverse conditions may involve chronic stress from gradual and persistent changes in biophysical conditions (e.g. rising oceans, decreasing rain levels), or they may be the result of extreme and sudden disruptions such as natural disasters (Linnenluecke, Griffiths, & Winn, 2012; Weinhofer & Busch, 2013).

> **Unfavorable natural conditions can vary along distinct basic dimensions such as *intensity, uncertainty, speed*, and *geographic* and *temporal scope*.**

Business strategy scholars have paid scant attention to how chronic slow-onset nature adversity stressors affect business adaptation efforts. These chronic slow-onset conditions, although less dramatic than natural disasters, are also very important for businesses because they may build up to generate hefty negative impacts that are longer lasting and cover larger geographic areas (Linnenluecke et al., 2012; Weinhofer & Busch, 2013; Winn et al., 2011). For example, American ski areas – although relatively less confronted with natural disasters – often have been experiencing higher temperature intensity levels and greater snowfall uncertainty.

The seminal strategy research that has examined the effects of chronic slow-onset nature adversity suggest that protective adaptation is positively related to *uncertainty* in climate conditions, such as temperature and precipitation, that directly affect core organizational activities (Gasbarro, Rizzi, & Frey, 2016; Haigh & Griffiths, 2012; Hoffmann et al., 2009; Pinkse & Gasbarro, 2017; Weinhofer & Busch, 2013). For instance, previous research that one of the authors co-authored with Peter Tashman (Tashman & Rivera, 2016) found that ski resorts experiencing greater uncertainty in snowfall levels are significantly more likely to increase adaptation efforts like snowmaking. In general, this small number of seminal empirical studies tends to support the deliberate view of organizational adaptation.

However, as we discussed in Chapter 2, the effect of the *intensity* of chronic nature adversity on firm adaptation may be different. Increasing nature adversity intensity may eventually limit a firm's ability to continue protecting its core business through adaptation. When considering uncertainty, conditions may change such that firms may either benefit from, or be disadvantaged by, fluctuations that are often difficult to predict. Ski resorts for instance, may benefit from above average natural snowpack levels early in the ski season to then be disadvantaged by below average snowpack in January and February. They can thus implement adaptive practices that ensure an adequate availability of slack resources to buffer them as needed when uncertainty increases (Tashman & Rivera, 2016). In contrast, biophysical constraints on a firm's core business activities become more difficult to overcome as nature adversity intensity increases to upper bound levels, even as the willingness to adapt may continue to increase.

Diverging Perspectives on Organizational Adaptation

Broadly, two general perspectives exist in the strategic management literature regarding how firms tend to respond to external change. One view describes the adaptive process as "beneficial" while the other describes it as "difficult and perilous" (Delacroix & Swaminathan, 1991). Under the first perspective, organizations tend to purposefully improve their resources and competencies to fit changing external conditions (Chakravarthy, 1982; McKendrick, Wade, & Jaffee, 2009). The dynamic capabilities literature in particular views some highly innovative firms as able to develop higher order competencies that modify, reconfigure, and even transform their existing resource and capability base to sustain competitive advantage (Eisenhardt & Martin 2000; Teece, Pisano, & Shuen, 1997). This literature further suggests that depending on the pace of change and/or the magnitude of the adverse conditions in firm environments, adaptation may take on different forms, from incremental to more radical (Teece et al., 1997). Research building on Cyert and March's *Behavioral Theory of the Firm* is aligned with this perspective, but emphasizes that incremental adaptation may constitute the preferred approach. While firms will be stimulated to search for alternatives upon experiencing adverse conditions, this search will tend to be local and focused on the familiar characteristics of a problem and potential solutions (Gavetti, 2012). Hence, firms preferentially respond to immediate and certain adversity rather than longer term ambiguous events for which the consequences of potential actions may be more uncertain (Gavetti, Greve, Levinthal, & Ocasio, 2012). Firms may also favor actions with local, rather than distant, benefits in terms of both time and space (Slawinski & Bansal, 2015). Resulting solutions will thus tend to be short run, incremental and rely on previously established routines (Cyert & March, 1963; Kraatz & Zajac, 2001; Shimizu, 2007). Overall, the first perspective suggests that firms tend to undertake deliberate adaptation in response to external adversity.

> Broadly, two general perspectives exist in the strategic management literature regarding how firms tend to respond to external change. One view describes the adaptive process as "beneficial," while the other describes it as very "difficult and perilous."
>
> Under the first perspective, organizations tend to purposefully improve their resources and competencies to fit changing external conditions. Under the second broad perspective, firms tend to be largely constrained in deliberately coping with significant external adversity due to internal and external inertial forces.

Under the second broad perspective, firms tend to be largely constrained in terms of deliberately coping with significant external adversity due to internal and external inertial forces (Hannan & Freeman, 1984). Under the structural inertia view, external contextual forces reward organizational reproducibility, reliability, and accountability, and thus tend to enhance the survival of more inert firms with well-established routines (Amburgey, Kelly, & Barnett, 1993; Hannan & Freeman, 1984). Inertia, in turn, makes firms resistant to new adaptation, precluding them from timely and effective realignment when environmental conditions change (Haveman, 1992; McKendrick et al., 2009). The threat-rigidity hypothesis also echoes this view in suggesting that firms, "behave rigidly in threatening situations" (Staw et al., 1981). When facing adverse environmental conditions, firms may restrict information processing, concentrate control, and focus on resource conservation, which may result in practices that are less varied and flexible (Staw et al., 1981). The structural inertia perspective does allow, however, for some degree of incremental adjustment to peripheral organizational features to occur in relatively stable environments (Amburgey et al., 1993; McKendrick et al., 2009). Inertia will tend to set in especially when environmental change is rapid, demanding equally rapid or in-depth transformation of core organizational features (Hannan & Freeman, 1984; McKendrick et al., 2009). Under this second perspective, firms will therefore tend to refrain from novel adaptation in response to adversity.

> Organizational inertia tends to set in especially when environmental change is rapid, demanding equally rapid or in-depth transformation of core organizational features.

In sum, these broad diverging views suggest that adverse external operating conditions tend to be either positively or negatively related to firm adaptation. This results in an apparent paradoxical understanding, since these proposed relationships seem mutually exclusive (Pierce & Aguinis, 2013). Taking on more contingent views, scholars have attempted to identify when and how firm behavior becomes consistent with each perspective. Scholars have, for example, examined how firms respond to variability in their operating environments, including changes in frequency, uncertainty and magnitude (Dess & Beard, 1984; Tashman & Rivera, 2016; Wholey & Brittain, 1989). Other studies have examined how the munificence of firms' operating environment may affect firm adaptation with conclusions that support both positive and negative effects (Aragon-Correa & Sharma, 2003; Delacroix & Swaminathan, 1991; Dess & Beard, 1984). With regard to firm attributes, network embeddedness, research and development capabilities, presence of slack, firm age, experience, and size may differentially enhance or inhibit adaptation (Chattopadhyay et al., 2001; Kapoor & Klueter, 2014; Le Mens, Hannan, & Pólos, 2011).

> In sum, these broad diverging views suggest that adverse external operating conditions tend to be either positively or negatively related to firm adaptation. This results in an apparent paradoxical understanding because these proposed relationships seem mutually exclusive.

Nature Adversity Intensity as a Driver and Inhibitor of Protective Adaptation

Building on the resilience theory ideas discussed in Chapter 2, we suggest that the variance in firm adaptation to nature adversity intensity is partially explained by the organizational processes highlighted in the broad diverging perspectives on organizational adaptation discussed above. In particular, we propose that protective adaptation is simultaneously shaped by an interplay of counterbalancing latent mechanisms. First, organizational inertial forces constrain organizations' willingness to adapt. Second, coalition building and internal political processes allow managers to deploy adaptation resilience capabilities (Ortiz-de-Mandojana & Bansal, 2016; Winn et al., 2011). Third, growing natural forces eventually impose limits beyond which protective adaptation becomes unviable. This combination of mechanisms leads us to suggest a general proposition positing that:

> **Proposition 1:** The relationship between nature adversity intensity and protective adaptation follows an inverted U-shape, such that firms facing either lower or higher levels of nature adversity intensity are more likely to engage in lower levels of protective adaptation than those facing medium levels.

That is, an initially positive relationship between nature adversity intensity and firm protective adaptation reaches an inflection point, after which it becomes negative (Clement & Rivera, 2017).

Lower than medium levels of nature adversity intensity. Firms experiencing modest levels of nature adversity intensity tend to show less willingness to adopt protective adaptation compared to those facing medium levels. On the one hand, at lower levels of nature adversity intensity, firms are likely to find it easier to implement protective adaptation by leveraging familiar capabilities requiring modest investments and learning (Kraatz & Zajac, 2001; Le Mens et al., 2011; Levinthal, 1991). From a classical economics point of view, at mild levels of nature adversity intensity, the costs of protective adaptation are low. As adversity intensity begins to rise, the costs tend to increase at a slower rate than the benefits. Thus, it may seem that firms would show greater levels of protective adaptation at lower rather than medium levels of nature adversity intensity.

However, considering sensemaking, organizational inertia, and organizational politics, allows us to go beyond the narrower economic cost-benefit account to posit that: at lower levels of natural adversity intensity, a firm tends to forgo or delay protective adaptation despite its relatively low and slower growing costs. Consistent with an organizational inertia lens, we argue that lacking a stronger nature adversity intensity signal (e.g. ski resorts experiencing daily average temperatures below freezing levels), it is difficult for managers to overcome internal forces that favor the status quo (Hannan & Freeman, 1984). Also, from a sensemaking perspective, modest levels of nature adversity intensity may go unnoticed by firm managers, as they tend to take for granted that natural environmental conditions are relatively stable (Tisch & Galbreath, 2018; Weick, 1995; Whiteman & Cooper, 2011). Accordingly, managers are less likely to transcend identity, collective understanding, and learning barriers that make them unaware of slow-onset nature adversity intensity cues (Bansal, Kim, & Wood, 2017; Whiteman & Cooper, 2011). Instead, managers pay more attention to changes in external competitive, technological, and social contexts (Rockström et al., 2009; Whiteman & Cooper, 2011). Even if detected, however, these slow-onset levels of nature adversity intensity may not pose a strong enough threat to organizational core activities and aspired levels of performance to gain enough managerial attention and catalyze protective adaptation (Berkhout, Hertin, & Gann, 2006; Pinkse & Gasbarro, 2017; Shapira, 2017; Weinhofer & Busch, 2013). Managers may thus experience a lower sense of need and urgency to adapt (Hoffman, 2011; Tisch & Galbreath, 2018).

A consideration of sensemaking, organizational inertia, and organizational politics allows us to go beyond the narrower cost-benefit analysis of economics to posit that: at lower levels of natural adversity intensity, firms tend to forgo or delay protective adaptation despite relatively slight and slower growing costs.

Additionally, the complexity and ambiguity generated by lower bound levels of nature adversity intensity may make it difficult to identify its causes and future trends. Thus, engaging in protective adaptation to deal with lower levels of nature adversity intensity tends to generate sensitivity to lower nature adversity intensity cues and may be more likely to put the focus on adaptation efforts that do not involve changes to business strategies and operations. Instead, managers may seek to enhance their understanding of nature adversity intensity and/or explore financial and insurance risk management instruments (Berkhout et al., 2006; Hoffmann et al., 2009).

Higher than medium levels of nature adversity intensity. Although it may initially seem counterintuitive, we posit that firms facing higher levels of nature adversity intensity also tend to adopt lower levels of protective adaptation. On the one hand, at higher levels of adversity, signals from major chronic stressors in the natural environment pose a clearer threat to core business strategies and operations that are harder to ignore (e.g. ski resorts experiencing daily minimum temperatures above freezing during most of the winter) (Berkhout et al., 2006; Pinkse & Gasbarro, 2017). This is likely to generate a heightened perceived vulnerability that enhances internal support for protective adaptation and bolsters a sense of urgency to act (Kelly & Amburgey, 1991; Kraatz & Zajac, 2001; Pinkse & Gasbarro, 2017). Also, the higher perceived vulnerability weakens internal inertial forces and barriers to organizational learning.

> Although it may initially seem counterintuitive, we posit that firms facing higher levels of nature adversity intensity also tend to adopt lower levels of protective adaptation.

> This is because more in-depth, longer-term oriented, and innovative adaptive efforts – beyond routine protective adaptation measures – are needed to develop advanced resilience capabilities that allow firms to effectively counter more extreme constraints from a higher nature adversity intensity. Developing such advanced strategic resilience capabilities involves complex and cascading change processes and breakthrough innovations that are more transformative and harder to develop and implement.

Yet, despite this increased sense of vulnerability, we argue that firms are less likely to implement greater levels of protective adaptation when facing higher nature adversity intensity. This is because firms are likely to continue relying on established protective adaptation practices similar to those implemented at medium levels of nature adversity intensity. The effectiveness of these practices becomes significantly undermined as increasing nature adversity intensity progressively imposes stiffer biophysical constraints (DesJardine et al., 2017; Gavetti, 2012; Hannan & Freeman, 1984; Repenning & Sterman, 2002). Instead, more in-depth, longer-term oriented, and innovative adaptive efforts – beyond routine protective adaptation measures – are needed to develop advanced resilience capabilities that allow firms to effectively counter more extreme constraints from a higher nature adversity intensity (Clement & Rivera, 2017; Gunderson & Holling, 2002; Ortiz-de-Mandojana & Bansal, 2016). Resilience capabilities involve increased resources and competencies to understand, anticipate, and flexibly counter external adversity cues and signals in a timely manner (Ortiz-de-Mandojana & Bansal, 2016). These more advanced resilience capabilities make it possible for firms to overcome the tendency to rely on practices that have become maladaptive (Ortiz-de-Mandojana & Bansal, 2016).

Developing such advanced strategic resilience capabilities involves complex and cascading change processes and breakthrough innovations that are more transformative and more difficult to develop and implement (DesJardine et al., 2017; Gasbarro, Rizzi, & Frey, 2016; Halkos et al., 2018; Tisch & Galbreath, 2018). The risk of failure for transformative change is greater because it tends to challenge organizational identity, routines, and well-established relationships engendering renewed internal inertial forces (DesJardine et al., 2017; Gavetti, 2012; Hannan & Freeman, 1984; Repenning & Sterman, 2002).

From a traditional economics perspective, growing levels of severe nature adversity intensity make the costs of protective adaptation escalate at a faster rate than the benefits resulting in an accelerating decline of protective adaptation. This onset of a quicker increase in costs relative to benefits is due to rapidly approaching physical limits imposed by the severe intensity of nature adversity conditions. For instance, a ski resort frequently experiencing above freezing temperatures during the winter may consider expanding to higher altitudes and increasing night-time snowmaking (because it is colder at a higher elevation and during the night) as more effective for sustaining its core business than adopting potentially more expensive transformative adaptation strategies to cope with nature adversity. Nevertheless, frequent above freezing temperatures during the day render accumulation of snow financially unfeasible, even at elevated terrain altitudes.

Additionally, firms may face stronger political and legal opposition from external stakeholders (e.g. environmental activists and local community groups) that may delay or block government permits needed to implement more transformative protective adaptation strategies required to cope with higher levels of nature adversity intensity (Le Mens et al., 2011; Rivera, 2010). Overall, the arguments above suggest that firms exposed to higher than medium levels of nature adversity intensity are less likely to implement greater levels of protective adaptation.

Medium levels of nature adversity intensity. At medium levels of nature adversity intensity, the interplay between natural adversity signals and constraints, internal organizational inertial forces, and business resilience capabilities makes firms more willing and able to implement greater protective adaptation than those experiencing lower or higher levels. Medium nature adversity intensity constraints are not so stiff as to render protective adaptation efforts too costly. Concurrently, managers collectively begin to fully internalize a higher sense of vulnerability because it becomes difficult to miss, ignore, deny, or misinterpret the increasing threats posed by nature adversity intensity as it reaches medium levels (Bansal et al., 2017; Tisch & Galbreath, 2018; Weinhofer & Busch, 2013). This higher sense of vulnerability enhances the positive assessment of the net economic benefits of protective adaptation. It also leads, in turn, to the decline of internal organizational inertial forces that initially diminished a firm's willingness to develop and deploy protective adaptation practices at lower levels of nature adversity intensity (Kelly & Amburgey, 1991; Kraatz & Zajac, 2001; Pinkse & Gasbarro, 2017). This increased willingness to adapt may also be reinforced by other external factors such as shareholder pressure, stakeholder demands, and/or exemplary protective adaptation efforts developed by competitors (Berkhout et al., 2006; Tashman & Rivera, 2016).

Additionally, at medium levels of nature adversity intensity, internal coalitions of managers favoring protective adaptation may generate enough internal political support to take advantage of already developed resilience capabilities and resources (Armenakis & Bedeian, 1999; Tisch & Galbreath, 2018). These growing internal coalitions may also allow pro-adaptation managers to gain enough influence to neutralize or bargain with opposing top-level managers (Rivera, 2010). Higher internal political support can also increase the tendency to create managerial positions aimed at addressing adaptation to nature adversity intensity that favor language, plans, reports, and budgets consistent with greater implementation of protective adaptation practices (Rivera, 2010).

Although a firm's resilience capabilities and resources needed to develop and implement protective adaptation may begin to be challenged by these medium levels of nature adversity intensity, they will be adequate to address the negative impacts on core business activities. The increased cost effectiveness of firms' resilience capabilities and resources at intermediate nature adversity intensity levels, may be due to learning curve benefits obtained from its earlier sensemaking efforts to detect, understand, and confront growing stress signals (Kraatz & Zajac, 2001; Levinthal, 1991; Ortiz-de-Mandojana & Bansal, 2016). It may also arise from opportunities to imitate or collaborate on successful and innovative monitoring approaches for nature adversity intensity and protective adaptation strategies developed by stakeholders and other firms, and/or from taking advantage of government adaptation incentives and technical assistance (Ortiz-de-Mandojana & Bansal, 2016). In sum, firms facing medium levels of nature adversity intensity are more likely to display greater levels of protective adaptation than firms experiencing lower and higher levels. That is, protective adaptation first increases with nature adversity intensity at a decreasing rate to reach a turning point, after which protective adaptation decreases at an increasing rate.

> At medium levels of nature adversity intensity, firms are more willing and able to implement greater protective adaptation than those experiencing lower or higher levels.

> Although firm resilience capabilities and resources needed to develop and implement protective adaptation may begin to be challenged by medium levels of nature adversity intensity, they will still be adequate for addressing the negative impacts on core business activities.

Moderating Effects on the Protective Adaptation and Nature Adversity Intensity Relationship

The way in which firms adopt and implement protective adaptation in response to nature adversity intensity is likely to be contingent on several firm-level and institutional environment-level factors. In this section, we examine how these factors may moderate our proposed inverted U-shape relationship between nature adversity intensity and protective adaptation. In terms of firm level factors, we investigate how firm age, public ownership, and the presence of slack resources may moderate this relationship. In terms of institutional environment level factors, we examine how firm operation in more stringent regulatory environments may moderate this relationship.

Firm Age

We first examine how firm age may influence the inverted U-shaped relationship posited in Proposition 1. As nature adversity intensity levels move from low to medium, the commensurate increase in the need to adapt may be attenuated in older firms as compared with younger firms. Older firms may have built cultural resistance to change (Le Mens et al., 2015) and may therefore need a stronger threat signal to overcome the inertial forces that favor the status quo. In addition, older firms may be accustomed to experiencing and assuming beneficial conditions in the natural environment, making them less sensitive to conditions that may be in the process of becoming deleterious.

> Older firms may be accustomed to experiencing and assuming beneficial conditions in the natural environment, making them less sensitive to emerging slow-onset nature adversity conditions. Older firms may also need stronger nature adversity signals to accept that their protective adaptation practices may have reached biophysical limits.

Older firms may thus act more cautiously and be slower to invest in protective adaptation, perhaps preferring instead to adopt other "softer" types of risk-spreading strategies. As nature adversity intensity levels move from medium to high, older firms may also be slower in foregoing protective adaptation. Once older firms have invested in and routinized protective adaptation practices, older firms may in turn need a stronger signal to indicate that protective adaptation practices have reached their limits of effectiveness and that more in depth adaptive changes are needed. Internal inertial forces may therefore induce a stronger persistence and slower decline of protective adaption practices in older firms. Taking these arguments together, we would therefore expect that the slopes of the inverted U-shaped relationship between nature adversity intensity and protective adaptation are flatter in older firms than they are in younger firms.

> **Proposition 2:** The inverted U-shaped relationship between nature adversity intensity and protective adaptation is less pronounced for older firms than for younger firms.

Regulatory Environment Stringency

We then examine how firm operation within a more stringent regulatory environment may influence the inverted U-shaped relationship posited in Proposition 1. As nature adversity intensity levels move from low to medium, a firm's ability to adapt may be attenuated by a more stringent regulatory environment. More stringent regulations may restrict firms in their ability to implement preferred protective adaptation practices due to the added costs, time, and resources needed for compliance. For example, firms with core business activities that are dependent upon operations within natural landscapes or upon natural resources may be closely scrutinized before they are able to implement adaptive practices that may impact these landscapes or resources. Thus, even though firms operating in more stringent regulatory environments may be aware of the need for protective adaptation, they may be slower in being able to implement it.

More stringent regulations may restrict firms in their ability to implement preferred protective adaptation practices that exacerbate environmental degradation.

As nature adversity intensity levels move from medium to high, these firms may also be slower in foregoing protective adaptation. Once firms have made the upfront investment to be granted the permits to implement protective adaptation practices, they may be reluctant to give these up. These firms may be waiting for a stronger nature adversity intensity signal to indicate that protective adaptation limits have been reached. These firms might also be locked into protective adaptation practices because of higher initial upfront investments. Firms in more stringent regulatory environments may thus see a stronger persistence and slower decline in hard-earned protective adaption practices. Taking these arguments together, we would therefore expect that the slopes of the inverted U-shaped relationship between nature adversity intensity and protective adaptation are less steep in firms operating in more stringent regulatory environments.

Proposition 3: The inverted U-shaped relationship between nature adversity intensity and protective adaptation is less pronounced for firms operating in more stringent regulatory environments than for firms operating in less stringent regulatory environments.

Slack Resources

We then examine how the presence of slack resources may influence the inverted U-shaped relationship posited in Proposition 1. As nature adversity intensity levels move from low to medium, a firm's need to adapt may be attenuated by the presence of more slack resources. Firms with more slack resources may have an added buffer against increasingly intense nature adversity conditions. These firms may also be able to devote investments and focus efforts on other types of adaptation practices with different strategic objectives, such as diversifying away from affected core business activities.

> **With their added buffer, firms with more slack resources may have the added ability and flexibility to adopt more of a "wait and see approach," in case nature adversity intensity eases off or is heightened even more.**

Such firms could thereby delay protective adaptation even further or implement it at a slower pace. As nature adversity intensity levels move from medium to high, these firms may also be slower in foregoing protective adaptation. With their added buffer, firms with more slack resources may have the added ability and flexibility to adopt more of a "wait and see approach," in case nature adversity intensity eases off or is heightened even more. Taking these arguments together, we would therefore expect that the slopes of the inverted U-shaped relationship between nature adversity intensity and protective adaptation are flatter in firms with more slack resources.

> **Proposition 4:** The inverted U-shaped relationship between nature adversity intensity and protective adaptation is less pronounced for firms with more slack resources than for firms with less slack resources.

Public Company

Finally, we also examine how firm status as a public company may influence the inverted U-shaped relationship posited in Proposition 1. As nature adversity intensity levels move from low to medium, the need for publicly owned firms to adapt may be accentuated. As nature adversity intensity starts to pose a threat to core business strategies and revenue, shareholder pressure to respond to this threat may spur a firm into more quickly implementing protective adaptation measures. Such pressure may more rapidly overturn internal inertial forces and political opposition that favor the status quo and make managers more sensitive to nature adversity.

As nature adversity intensity starts to pose a threat to core business strategies and revenue, shareholder pressure to respond to this threat may spur a firm into more quickly implementing protective adaptation measures.

As nature adversity intensity levels move from medium to high, publicly owned firms may also be quicker to forego protective adaptation. Shareholders may once again pressure firms to drop adaption practices that are proving ineffective or too costly to maintain. The ability of firms to continue pursuing protective adaptation may thus be more sharply reduced by such pressures. Taking these arguments together, we would therefore expect the slopes of the inverted U-shaped relationship between nature adversity intensity and protective adaptation to be steeper in publicly owned firms.

Proposition 5: The inverted U-shaped relationship between nature adversity intensity and protective adaptation is more pronounced for publicly owned firms than for privately owned firms.

Conclusion

Multiple strategic management literatures prominently highlight the importance of the external environment for firm strategy, but limit their attention to economic, competitive, political, and institutional contexts, overlooking adverse conditions stemming from the natural environment. In this chapter, we conceptually examined the effect of nature adversity intensity on firm tendency to adopt protective adaptation measures that seek to preserve core organizational activities. This research area is increasingly critical for managers and public policymakers as the detrimental slow-onset effects of climate change may become more pronounced and prevalent (Bansal et al., 2017; IPCC, 2014). Considering the way in which adaptation may be affected by nature adversity intensity also contributes to the debate between broad diverging views of organizational adaptation that respectively suggest that environmental adversity tends to be either positively or negatively related to adaptation (Astley & Van de Ven, 1983; Levinthal, 1991). We posit **an inverted U-shaped relationship between nature adversity intensity and protective adaptation.** That is, firms tend to exhibit lower degrees of protective adaptation at both the lower and upper ranges of nature adversity intensity, while displaying greater levels of protective adaptation at medium levels of nature adversity intensity.

4 | Can You Learn from the Second Kick of a Mule?

MNCs Foreign Investment, Natural Disasters, and Country Governance

There is nothing to be learned from the second kick of a mule.

Mark Twain

This chapter shifts the focus of our analytical framework, from slow-onset nature adversity conditions, to the effect of natural disasters on subsidiary-level foreign investments by multinational corporations (MNCs). In 2018, there were approximately 500,000 MNC subsidiaries operating around the world, generating about half of all international trade (Kordos & Vojtovic, 2016; World Atlas of Global Issues, 2018). Given this very large number of MNC subsidiaries, understanding how MNCs adapt to extreme natural conditions that are triggering more frequent and severe natural disasters is critically important. The question of where to compete internationally is one of the most fundamental questions of corporate strategy. Until very recently, business managers rarely considered natural disasters risk when making this key corporate strategy decision. However, in part due to climate change trends, the frequency and severity of weather-related disasters increased significantly over the past couple of decades, making natural disaster risk a more important factor to consider when making foreign subsidiary investment decisions. Accordingly, in this chapter we conceptually examine how natural disasters, compared to industrial disasters and terrorist attacks, shape MNCs' foreign market entry and expansion. We also investigate whether or not MNC subsidiary-level investment is more likely to decrease in response to specific types of natural disasters that result in a higher number of fatalities. In addition, we elaborate on how country governance characteristics moderate the relationship between disasters and MNC

This chapter is a modified and updated (for individual sub-types of natural disasters) version of the conceptual part of Oh and Oetzel (2011), reproduced with permission of the journal publisher.

Table 4.1. *List of propositions developed in Chapter 4*

Proposition 1	In response to disasters, MNC investment at the subsidiary level varies depending upon disaster type. MNC subsidiary-level investment will be more likely to decrease in response to technological disasters and terrorist attacks than in response to natural disasters.
Proposition 2	Natural disaster types that show a pattern of significantly deadlier consequences, year after year, become hard to ignore and underestimate as one-time historical anomalies. MNC subsidiary-level investment is more likely to decrease in response to the natural disasters showing the highest levels of fatalities.
Proposition 3	Governance quality in the host country will moderate the relationship between disasters and subsidiary-level investment in such a way that major disasters will be less likely to lead to foreign subsidiary disinvestment.

subsidiary-level investment (see Table 4.1 for a list of this chapter's propositions).

Over the course of any given year, various disasters – not only natural ones, but also terrorist attacks and technological disasters – are likely to occur in multiple locations around the world. In the past several decades, global populations have witnessed cyclones and tsunamis that ravaged Southeast Asia, hurricanes that repeatedly devastated the United States Gulf and East coasts (e.g. Stan, Katrina, Sandy), and record-breaking mega wildfires gravely affecting California and Australia. Although loss of life is the most difficult and tragic aspect to any disaster, such natural hazards also have the potential to threaten legal systems, worsen political instability, disrupt economic life, lower firm profits, threaten business survival, and discourage new foreign investment.

While catastrophic natural disasters can devastate businesses, the impact of these hazards varies across countries and by type of disaster. Governments in some countries may be better equipped to handle the aftermath of disasters than others (Davis & Seitz, 1982). Investigations after the hurricanes in the Caribbean and earthquakes in Turkey, in 1999, and China, in 2008, revealed that the great loss of life and a significant portion of property damage were due to a lack of effective government oversight, which led to the shoddy construction of homes, schools, offices, and other structures (Kinzer, 2001; Transparency International, 2008). Given these issues and concerns, the research questions we seek to address are:

(1) How do natural disasters, compared to other calamity hazards, shape multinational corporation (MNC) foreign subsidiary investment?[1]
(2) Is MNC subsidiary-level investment more likely to decrease in response to the natural disasters that result in a higher number of fatalities?
(3) Do stronger institutional environments and better country governance positively moderate the relationship between exogenous disasters and subsidiary-level investment?

To conceptually investigate these issues, we develop propositions that build on two streams of literature: the research on firm response to external risk and the literature on country governance and its relationship to firm location and investment. Understanding the role that country context and institutional quality play in mitigating (or exacerbating) risk is critical for managers who seek to formulate effective business strategies in case of emergency, particularly since there is evidence that most companies have neither a detailed plan for addressing major disaster risk nor a person in charge of managing disasters that firms face (Oetzel, 2005).

Answers to these questions will also provide managers with a more nuanced understanding of major disasters and when they are more or less likely to pose a risk to the firm. An awareness of exactly how country governance can mitigate or exacerbate the effect of major disasters on a foreign subsidiary can help managers of MNCs better calculate investment risk when formulating their location strategy. Also, ex post disaster, managers will be better able to analyze a host country's ability to rebound from natural and other types of disasters and thus determine whether disinvestment is an appropriate strategic response.

In terms of theoretical contributions, we seek to contribute to understanding how host country governance can mitigate or exacerbate the

---

[1] Throughout the paper we use the terms MNC subsidiary-level investment and investment at the subsidiary level to refer to the presence of MNCs' subsidiaries in a particular host country. The change in subsidiary-level investment is the MNC's response to disaster(s) and reflects an increase or decrease in the number of subsidiaries in a host country.

impact of major disasters on MNC investment at the subsidiary level (e.g. García-Canal & Guillén, 2008; Meyer et al., 2009). We also seek to contribute to research on risk management by gaining insights into how firms respond to different types of natural disasters.

Disaster Categories

A wide variety of disasters can befall businesses in their normal course of operations. Three major categories include natural disasters, technological disasters, and terrorist attacks. We examined these categories of risk for several reasons. First, a significant body of research has looked at the threat that policy uncertainty and other types of political events pose for firms (Delios & Henisz, 2003; Tallman, 1988) as well as the impact of institutional transitions on firm strategy (Hoskisson et al., 2000). Little research, however, has been done on the effects of natural disasters, technological disasters, and terrorist attacks on business.

Second, the lack of research on natural disasters is troubling since there is a strong and growing body of evidence provided by climate change researchers suggesting that the threat posed by weather-related natural disasters is growing, both in terms of event frequency and severity (Benson & Clay, 2004; IPCC, 2012; NAS, 2016; World Bank, 2004; Wahlstrom & Guha-Sapir, 2016). Greater understanding of these threats is needed for effective firm response.

Finally, a third reason we focus on comparing natural disasters to technological accidents and terrorist attacks is that similar forces affect a country's vulnerability to natural and human made disasters. A country's governance structures and economic and social arrangements can make firms simultaneously more or less vulnerable to all three types of threats, arguably making it important for strategists to consider potential parallels between natural and human-made disasters (Kennedy, 2002; Zanini, 2009). Thus, the context in which a major disaster occurs is critical in the assessment of its impact on business.

Natural disasters. These are disasters triggered by natural conditions that result in widespread human and economic loss. The causes of natural disasters include not only hazards caused by geophysical, meteorological, hydrological, climatological, and biological forces but also human involvement such as urbanization, industrialization, population growth, overfishing and over farming, among others

(Perrow, 2007; Slovic, 2000). These disasters include, but are not limited to, droughts, earthquakes, epidemics, extreme temperatures, floods, insect infestations, mudslides, volcanic eruptions, tsunamis, and wildfires. Examples include Cyclone Nargis, which devastated Myanmar in May of 2008 and left over 130,000 people dead (Lin et al., 2009), and the tsunami that hit Southeast Asia on December 26, 2004, and resulted in more than 220,000 deaths throughout the region (Stone, 2006). Researchers have noted that natural hazards take a greater toll on property and life in developing countries than they do in developed nations. In the mid-1980s, statistics showed that in developing countries, geophysical hazards (i.e. floods, droughts, earthquakes, tsunamis, etc.) were responsible for 250,000 deaths per year, on average, and $15 billion in damage and mitigation costs (Kasperson & Pijawka, 1985). During the same period, deaths from geophysical hazards in the United States were fewer than 1,000 per year (Kasperson & Pijawka, 1985).

Natural disasters are generally tracked and classified by international agencies into broad general categories based on the type of natural hazard causing the disaster. For example, geological disasters include earthquakes and volcanic activities. Hydrological, meteorological, and climatological disasters are jointly referred to as *weather-related disasters* (Bergholt & Lujala, 2012; CRED, 2016). Floods, storms, slides, extreme temperatures, droughts, and wildfires are the most common weather-related disasters.[2] These disasters have attracted the most international attention because of the acute increase in their frequency and severity as well as an exponential growth in fatalities and economic damage in many areas of the world. Indeed, since 1995, 90 percent of the recorded natural disasters involved weather-related events. Floods and storms are the fastest growing weather-related disasters in terms of their number; they involved over 70 percent of the 6457 weather-related disasters that occurred between 1995 and 2015 (Wahlstrom & Guha-Sapir, 2016).

> **Weather-related disasters have attracted the most international attention of governments, business managers, and the media because of the acute increase in their frequency and severity as well as the exponential growth of their related fatalities and economic damage.**

---

[2] Wave actions, fogs, and glacial lake outburst floods (floods that occur when a dam containing a glacial lake fails) are other rarer weather-related disasters.

Storms and their related surges are the deadliest weather-related natural disasters; they accounted for about 40 percent of the 606,000 deaths caused by weather-related disasters between 1995 and 2015 (Wahlstrom & Guha-Sapir, 2016). In the same period, floods came second, causing about 27 percent of all fatalities related to weather related disasters (Wahlstrom & Guha-Sapir, 2016). Storms were also the costliest natural disasters, generating around 38 percent of the reported $1,900 billion in economic losses generated by all natural disasters (including earthquakes and volcano eruptions) between 1995 and 2015 (Wahlstrom & Guha-Sapir, 2016). Heatwaves, although rarer, have also become significantly more intense and accounted for about 25 percent (148,000) of all deaths generated by natural disasters in that period (Wahlstrom & Guha-Sapir, 2016). Despite the high causal complexity of weather-related disasters, natural scientists increasingly agree that climate change is one of the key factors contributing to the increased intensity, frequency, and duration of these calamitous events (IPCC, 2017; NAS, 2016).

> **Storms were the most deadly and costly weather-related natural disasters from 1995 to 2015.**

Terrorist attacks. Terrorist attacks have been defined as the use of violence or the threat of violence to attain political or ideological goals and the willingness to attack noncombatants (Wernick, 2006). Terrorism may be domestic in origin, or it may result from international groups or networks of individuals. Spain has dealt with domestic terrorism from ETA, the Basque separatist group, which was active between 1960 and 2010 and dissolved in 2018. ETA specifically targeted Basque entrepreneurs and corporations, exacerbating the impact of terrorism on the business sector (Abadie & Gardeazabal, 2003). Al Qaeda, the international terrorist network, attacked the World Trade Center and the Pentagon in the United States on September 11, 2001, causing the death of more than 2900 people (National Consortium for the Study of Terrorism and Responses to Terrorism, 2008). In 2002, Jemaah Islamiyah, a violent Islamist group, was convicted of the terrorist bombing in Bali that killed 202 people – the majority of whom were foreign nationals – and injuring over 200 people, devastating the island's economy for several years afterward (Baker & Coulter, 2007). In the months following the bombing, hotel occupancy rates fell to 14 percent, down from an occupancy rate of 75 percent prior to the attack (Baker & Coulter, 2007).

Technological disasters. The third category of disasters under our consideration involves technological disasters. Although modern technologies have led to dramatic improvements in labor productivity during recent decades, breakdowns of technological systems, or accidents associated with the processing, storage, and transportation of explosive or toxic chemicals, radioisotopes, and other hazardous materials have the potential to cause massive loss of life and property. Such disasters can also endanger the wider social environment in which an incident occurs (England, 1988; Evan & Manion, 2002). Examples of technological disasters include transportation accidents such as airplane, train, or large-scale automobile crashes, and industrial accidents such as the disaster at a Union Carbide pesticide plant in Bhopal, India, in 1984. In that incident, the Union Carbide plant released 40 tons of methyl isocyanate gas that resulted in 16,000 deaths in the first 10 years after the event. In addition, over 200,000 people who were exposed to the gas suffered long-term health effects (Sarangi, 1995). Another devastating example is the Exxon Valdez oil spill in 1989, which exacted a heavy environmental toll across 1500 miles of noncontinuous Alaskan coastline. Economists estimated the cost of the spill in terms of lost tourism, recreational sport fishing losses, replacement of birds and mammals, and the public value of a pristine Prince William Sound to be in the billions of dollars (Miller, 1999).

MNC Foreign Subsidiary Investment and Disaster Categories

Although strategy research has traditionally focused more on terrorism risk (particularly as a type of political risk) than on natural or technological hazards, all three types of disasters can result in lost revenues through a direct impact on the operations of MNCs or their key value chain partners, and/or indirect effects on critical infrastructure and the wider economy (Suder, 2004; Wernick, 2006). As discussed earlier, natural disasters are vastly more frequent, deadly, and costly than terrorist attacks and technological disasters (Wahlstrom & Guha-Sapir, 2016).

Despite their severe negative effects, it is also important to highlight the fact that disasters may also lead to business opportunities that result in new foreign investment. The potential benefits of entering into a country under uncertainty and complexity could be higher than under safety and stability (Miller, 1998). New foreign investment may take place because firms expect to participate in large government recovery projects after disasters and because consumers are likely to demand new products and services as they return to their normal lives (Vigdor, 2008). Determining where and whether firms should make new investments post-disaster is therefore critical for effective strategy formulation.

To assess how disasters may influence a firm's strategic decisions regarding its subsidiary activity and structure, managers may employ an initial risk calculus where the firm's response would be in proportion to the loss of life and the duration and severity of the disaster. Following this logic, natural disasters would receive the greatest levels of attention. Yet, individuals tend to pay more attention to disasters that are perceived to be more controllable and to some degree preventable, such as terrorist attacks and technological disasters.

In a study of Turkey, Israel, and Greece, researchers found that the intensity and geographic location of terrorist incidents had a significant effect on tourist arrivals (Drakos & Kutan, 2003). Other scholars have found similar results. In a study of tourism from the G-7 countries (Canada, France, Germany, Italy, Japan, United Kingdom, and United States) to 134 locations over three years, Llorca-Vivero (2008) found that tourists considered the number of both domestic victims and international terrorist attacks when making destination decisions. In another study, Nitsch and Schumacher (2004) demonstrated that terrorism reduced bilateral international trade by about 4 percent.

Although there is evidence that tourists and investors may consider the number of casualties and the severity of the disasters before traveling or investing into affected areas. Research on risk suggests that responses to disasters can only be imperfectly understood within a classical conception of risk, wherein a risk calculus is utilized to assess threats (March & Shapira, 1987). For instance, studies have shown that responses to risks may not be consistent with the actual probability or severity of the threat. When asked to rate disasters based on likelihood of occurrence, respondents frequently rate the risk of airplane crashes, nuclear disasters, and terrorist attacks to be much greater than car crashes, despite statistical evidence to the contrary (Slovic, Fischhoff, & Lichtenstein, 2000). Individuals tend to overestimate the risks associated with dramatic and sensational disasters they perceive as more controllable and preventable. Alternatively, they tend to underestimate the risks associated with natural disasters, which despite being much more deadly are considered more ordinary, unspectacular, and outside of human control (Slovic et al., 2000).

> Natural disasters are vastly more frequent, deadly, and costly than terrorist attacks and industrial disasters. Yet, the risks of natural disasters are regularly underestimated by business managers and policy makers.

Social amplification of risk is another factor that can influence how individuals respond to different types of disasters (Kasperson et al., 1988). Social, psychological, and institutional mechanisms can interact in ways that cause individuals to magnify the impact of terrorist attacks and industrial accidents and downplay natural disasters, resulting in potentially distorted responses to the events (Kasperson, 1992). When disasters are socially amplified, people's biased responses can generate exaggerated social or economic consequences that extend far beyond direct harm to human health or the environment (Okuyama & Chang, 2004). Compared to natural disasters, the fear and anxiety associated with terrorist attacks and industrial accidents is often socially amplified, and firms tend to disinvest or take other dramatic steps regardless of the actual threat to the firm or its investments. Research analyzing investor response to terrorism supports these arguments. In a study of options trading in London, scholars found that markets are highly sensitive to terrorist attacks even when the actual attack causes extremely low levels of damage (Garvey & Mullins, 2008).

The regular tendency to underestimate the risks of natural disasters is not uniform for the different types of natural hazards. Natural disaster types that show a pattern of significantly deadlier consequences, year after year, become hard to ignore and underestimate as if they were one-time historical anomalies. We argue this may be that case for the most deadly weather-related disasters that over the last few decades have shown a trend of increased frequency and severity linked to climate change trends (IPCC, 2017; NAS, 2016; Wahlstrom & Guha-Sapir, 2016).

In sum, MNCs would be more likely to disinvest in response to terrorist attacks and technological disasters – disasters that are seen as dramatic, sensational, and perceived to be more controllable, and to some degree preventable – than they would be in response to natural disasters considered "acts of God." Thus, we suggest the following propositions:

> **Proposition 1:** In response to disasters, MNC investment at the subsidiary level varies depending upon the disaster type. MNC subsidiary-level investment will be more likely to decrease in response to technological disasters and terrorist attacks than in response to natural disasters.

> **Proposition 2:** Natural disaster types that show a pattern of significantly deadlier consequences, year after year, become hard to ignore and underestimate as one-time historical anomalies. MNC subsidiary-level investment is more likely to decrease in response to those natural disasters showing the highest levels of fatalities.

Country Governance and Subsidiary-Level Investment in Response to Major Disasters

Understanding the external forces that can affect firm performance and survival is central to the study of corporate international strategy. Neo-institutional theorists have argued that formal and informal institutions establish the "rules of the game" and structure economic, legal, and political relationships in a country (North, 1990). In turn, these institutions affect the quality of governance, the overall environment of business, and the attractiveness of a particular market to foreign firms (Banerjee, Oetzel, & Ranganathan, 2006; North, 1990). Strong and effective governance is expected to lower the costs of doing business and attract foreign investment.

Social scientists studying perceptions and responses to risk have known – and empirically demonstrated for several decades now – that nature, technology, and society interact in fundamental ways that influence a region or country's vulnerability and resilience to disasters (Burton, Kates, & White, 1978; Slovic, 1992). The impact of disasters on a country is considered socially dependent, where social processes influence the incidence and vulnerability to disasters, and institutions determine – at least partially – a society's ex post response (Slovic, 1992). Presumably, governments that are prepared for disasters and have the capacity to respond to them are better able to minimize the economic and human costs of a catastrophe as well as the time it takes to recover.

The impact of disasters on a country is considered socially dependent where social processes influence the incidence and vulnerability to disasters, and institutions determine – at least partially – a society's post-response.

Failure to effectively respond to a major disaster can also send a signal that a government lacks the capacity or willingness to respond, thus increasing anxiety about the impact of future disasters. An accident that takes many lives may produce relatively little social disturbance if it occurs as part of a familiar and well-understood system, such as a train accident, and if the government effectively responds to the disaster and signals that future accidents of the same kind will be prevented (Slovic, 1992). In contrast, even a disaster that results in a relatively small loss of human life can have immense social consequences if the disaster is perceived as a harbinger of future catastrophic mishaps (Slovic, 1992).

Given their importance to business, researchers have focused on the relationships between certain aspects of the institutional environment and country governance and their impact on firm strategy and investment (Dunning, 1998; García-Canal & Guillén, 2008; Henisz & Delios, 2001). Because of the added costs of doing business abroad (Eden & Miller, 2004), a key aspect of any location decision is the consideration of whether the advantages of doing business in a particular location will outweigh the costs (Dunning, 1998). A firm's location decision becomes financially more significant as the depth and level of its investment in another country increases. An MNC's wholly owned subsidiary engaged in higher-order activities such as research and development (R&D), or one that must make large asset-specific investments, may be particularly sensitive to potential hazards in the operating environment.

Research has shown that the institutional environment plays a significant role in MNC subsidiary location decisions (Henisz & Macher, 2004; Woodward & Rolfe, 1993), even outweighing other factors such as market growth and access (Hatem, 1997). Significant advances have been made in our understanding of how political uncertainty and policy environments (Henisz, 2000), the legal and regulatory environment (La Porta et al., 1998; North, 1990), and corruption (Doh et al., 2003; Henisz & Williamson, 1999), affect firm location and entry mode decisions. Other factors that influence a firm's response to disasters are less understood. One reason is that research on the effect of the institutional environment on firm location has tended to focus on the relationship between the external country context and firm decision making. While the institutional context is known to influence firm entry mode and location choice, less attention has been given to the examination of how the institutional context may moderate the relationship between disasters that occur post-investment and MNC subsidiary-level investment.

The quality of governance and the strength of institutions in a country are assumed to have a significant impact on the ability and willingness of governments to respond to disasters within their borders (Cuervo-Cazurra & Genc, 2008; Kaufmann, Kraay, & Mastruzzi, 2008). Governments that lack basic organizational capabilities and sufficient resources and that are plagued by high levels of political instability are likely to be less effective at responding to major disasters than better-prepared governments. While a large and growing body of literature has focused on the direct effects of country governance characteristics on firm behavior (Cuervo-Cazurra & Genc, 2008; Globerman & Shapiro, 2003; Rivera et al., 2009), fewer empirical studies have focused on the moderating role that governance characteristics may play, particularly in terms of the relationship between risk and firm level response.

> The quality of governance and the strength of institutions in a country are assumed to have a significant impact on the ability and willingness of governments to respond to disasters within their borders.

Governance characteristics. A government's ability to effectively respond to a major disaster within its national borders is a function of its capacity to formulate appropriate responses to crises and its willingness and ability to implement them. The formulation of effective responses depends on the availability of technically skilled and knowledgeable individuals with the authority to design appropriate responses and the power to implement them. A nation's economic wealth is positively associated with its ability to develop the human capital required to minimize the damage associated with major disasters before they occur, and to formulate and implement post-disaster responses, but financial resources are not synonymous with government effectiveness (North, 1990).

The U.S. government's gross mismanagement of disaster relief after Hurricane Katrina in August 2005 demonstrates that economic resources are necessary but not sufficient determinants of government effectiveness in the face of crisis. In the years prior to Hurricane Katrina, the U.S. Army Corps of Engineers arguably failed to adequately maintain the levee system in New Orleans and to establish appropriate flood control mechanisms. In the days, weeks, and months after Hurricane Katrina, federal, state, and local governments were criticized for their lack of preparation (despite advance warning of the storm), mismanagement of the disaster, and corruption and favoritism in the allocation of government funds related to the cleanup.

Stronger regulatory quality and rule of law. These are two additional aspects of country governance that are expected to reduce the impact of major disasters. By "regulatory quality" we mean the ability of governments to formulate and implement sound policies and regulations (Kaufmann et al., 2008). "Rule of law" refers to the extent to which citizens abide by the rules of society, the ability to enforce contracts and property rights, and the degree to which police and courts fairly and capably enforce the law (Kaufmann et al., 2008; La Porta et al., 1998). With respect to regulatory quality, governments often enact various types of regulations to prevent or minimize the risk of disasters before they occur. For example, in the United States, there are a wide variety of regulations aimed at preventing industrial accidents such as those dealing with industrial codes of conduct, the proper labeling of chemicals, and the safe transportation of hazardous materials (Zimmerman, 1985). To be effective, however, regulations must be properly implemented and effectively enforced by government. It is the latter – effective government enforcement – that is generally the most problematic part of the regulatory process.

The 1999 earthquake in Turkey illustrates the importance of regulatory quality and rule of law in reducing the impact of a major disaster. In the aftermath of the quake, it quickly became evident that the government had allowed unscrupulous contractors to build housing developments directly above fault lines. The government also issued building permits to unqualified architects and builders who constructed shoddy structures with low-grade materials that quickly turned to rubble in the quake (Kinzer, 2001). The lack of effective regulation and oversight in construction became obvious after the quake, when people were shocked to see that while some buildings were decimated by the quake, others right next door were intact and had sustained little or no damage.

Regulatory quality and rule of law also have indirect effects on the disaster-firm response relationship. If a country has more effective regulation and controls the legitimate use of force (which helps manage potential internal challengers in the aftermath of disasters), the country is more likely to effectively mediate impending conflicts before they turn violent (Barnett, 2003). Thus, better regulatory quality and effective rule of law enable a country to better cope with the damage of disasters in the short term.

Another characteristic of governance is the degree of **democratic freedoms** that allow individuals to select their government, freely associate and express their views, and demand responsible action of those in power – either through the courts, the ballot box, the media, or other institutional mechanisms. This is another critical quality of a favorable institutional environment. Civil society groups across the United States held federal, state, and local governments accountable for their mishandling of disaster relief after Katrina. The pressure exerted by these groups led the U.S. House of Representatives to create the Select Bipartisan Committee to Investigate the Preparation for and Response to Hurricane Katrina. The Committee's work led to a report detailing the failure to respond at all levels of government, despite adequate advance warning of Katrina and longstanding knowledge that the region was vulnerable to natural disasters.

The stronger the democratic freedoms are in a country, the less likely that a major disaster will negatively affect businesses.

Other scholars have examined the relationship between civil liberties and government response to natural disasters. In countries with stronger civil liberties, citizens are able to freely voice their pleasure or displeasure with government, hold officials accountable for their actions, and participate in the process by which government officials are selected and replaced (Kaufmann et al., 2008).

We argue that in countries with more institutionalized democratic traditions, businesses are more likely to display greater cooperation during the process of enacting and implementing disaster prevention, preparedness, and recovery than in authoritarian regimes (Rivera, 2010). This is because *free speech traditions* make it easier to publicly and timely convey concerns and demands to business managers, the media, and government officials about the consequences of problematic business practices that enhance the vulnerability to disasters (Rivera, Oetzel, de Leon, & Starik, 2010).

Additionally, *freedom of association* rights inherent to more democratic nations expedite the organization of advocacy groups and coalitions that are better able to debate, promote, and politically mobilize to sustain demands for disaster prevention and response (Rivera & Oh, 2013). *Freedom of political participation* and *the right to vote* also play a key role promoting adequate disaster prevention and recovery regulations because groups advocating for them can support the election of like-minded politicians (Rivera, 2010).

For example, a team of environmental scientists and geoscientists at Princeton University determined that the number of deaths associated with natural disasters is lower for nations with democratic forms of government and higher national income (measured by gross domestic product [GDP]) (Van der Vink et al., 2007). According to the researchers, "the World Bank's Democracy Index, a measure of how strong a democracy is, and a nation's GDP are stronger predictors of a natural disaster's humanitarian impact (as measured by deaths) than either the size of the event or the population density in the area of the disaster" (Van der Vink et al., 2007). Research also shows that the less democratic a country is, the more likely its trade flows will be reduced by a major disaster (Gassebner, Keck, & Teh, 2006). Thus, we argue that the loss of life and the economic devastation wrought by major disasters are a function of the interaction between the disaster and voice and accountability in the host country. The stronger voice and accountability, the less likely a major disaster will negatively affect businesses.

Another relevant governance characteristic is the degree of *political stability* in a country. Research on political risk management has noted for several decades now that managers cite political instability as one of the most important factors influencing their foreign direct investment (FDI) decisions (Fatehi-Sadeh & Safizadeh, 1989). Although it is generally recognized that political instability is not necessarily equated with political risk, instability – manifested in the form of coups d'état, civil strife, threats to the peaceful transfer of power, expropriation of assets, unstable policies and regulations, or other forms of social and political turmoil – may directly affect the profitability and survival of firms (Root, 1972). Managers of MNCs must assess the risk posed by political institutions in potential host countries when they decide whether to establish a subsidiary abroad or expand an existing one. In stable political environments, the risk of arbitrary changes in government policy and other forms of political turmoil are lower. Thus, it is expected that foreign firms will be more willing to operate in politically stable countries (Morrow, Siverson, & Tabares, 1998).

We suggest that political instability not only directly affects firm location and investment decisions but also has an indirect effect on the disaster-firm response relationship; a government in turmoil is assumed to be less capable of formulating and implementing effective relief plans. Power struggles can leave governments incapable of effectively responding to disasters when they occur. In this way, political instability may also moderate the relationship between a major disaster and firm location decisions because it can exacerbate the impact of disasters. Thus, as political uncertainty and instability increase, the impact of a major disaster on a firm is also likely to increase.

Corruption is also expected to affect the quality of governance and the ability of the host country government to respond to major disasters. It has been argued that 75 percent of all earthquake deaths can be attributed to corruption (Lewis, 2005), often related to shoddy building construction. After both the 1999 earthquake in Turkey and the 2008 earthquake in China, investigators found that corruption was associated with the issuance of building permits to unqualified architects and a lack of enforcement of building codes. In countries with high levels of corruption, victims of major disasters may find it difficult to receive aid and assistance. Relief supplies may be diverted into private hands and sold on the black market. In sum, based on our discussion above, we suggest that:

Proposition 3: Governance quality in the host country will moderate the relationship between disasters and subsidiary-level investment in such a way that major disasters will be less likely to lead to foreign subsidiary disinvestment.

Conclusion

Natural disasters are not rare occurrences. To be sure, the large majority of countries experience natural disasters, and they are vastly more deadly than industrial disasters and terrorist attacks. In this chapter, we challenged the commonly accepted wisdom that managers employ a risk calculus where the firm's response would be in proportion to the loss of life and the duration and severity of the disaster. Instead, we argued that business managers tend to ignore natural disasters and pay more attention to those types of disasters perceived to be more "controllable" and to some degree more preventable, such as terrorist attacks and technological disasters (Slovic et al., 2000). We also posit that despite the typical tendency to dismiss natural disasters as uncontrollable "acts of God," the most severe weather-related natural hazards, like windstorms, become hard to ignore and underestimate as one-time historical anomalies. Accordingly, MNC subsidiary-level investment is more likely to decrease in response to natural disasters showing the highest levels of fatalities. Additionally, we propose that the likelihood of MNC subsidiary disinvestment after disasters decreases as regulatory quality, political stability, and/or corruption control in a host country government increase.

5 | Disaster Experience and MNC Subsidiary Entry and Expansion

A man who carries a cat by the tail learns something he can learn in no other way.

Mark Twain

In this chapter we continue developing our conceptual framework about how MNCs foreign subsidiary investments are affected by natural disasters. The following questions are the focus of our examination:

(1) Are MNCs able to gain experiential advantages from managing through low or high impact natural disasters that enable them to enter and expand into countries experiencing similar risks?
(2) Are foreign direct investment (FDI) experiential advantages associated with natural disasters greater than those resulting from terrorist attacks or technological disasters?

For decades now, an important issue in strategic management has been to better understand how risk and uncertainty affect firm decisions. Scholars across the spectrum of management studies have examined the role of risk and its effect on managerial decisions and organizational performance (e.g. Bloom & Milkovich, 1998; March & Shapira, 1987; McNamara & Bromiley, 1999; Shapira, 1995; Singh, 1986; Vaaler, 2008; Vaaler & McNamara, 2004). In this broad research area, a key issue in corporate strategy is to understand the effect of external sources of risk and uncertainty on multinational corporations' (MNCs) investment choices. Specifically, to know which markets a firm should enter (foreign entry); and to know whether or not a firm should increase its level of investment (expansion) in a particular country (e.g., Chung & Beamish, 2005; Delios & Henisz, 2003; Holburn & Zelner, 2010; Miller, 1993).

This chapter is a modified and updated (for individual subtypes of natural disasters) version of the conceptual part of Oetzel and Oh (2014), reproduced with permission of the journal publisher.

Although the accumulated research on firm response to risk is substantial, it is notable that much of it has focused on the experience of firms with continuous risks – risks that are steady and more predictable within a firm's operating environment. An example of continuous risk, particularly for foreign firms operating or expanding abroad, may be corruption in the host country environment. In emerging markets and developing countries, corruption is a continuous risk in a firm's day-to-day operations.

Alternatively, discontinuous risks such as natural disasters are episodic occurrences that are often difficult to anticipate or predict. These types of risks have received much less attention in the strategic management research (Lampel et al., 2009; Ramanujam, 2003; Slovic et al., 2000; Perrow, 2007). Filling the gap in the research on risk management and organization studies is important for two main reasons. First, in terms of theoretical implications, if natural disasters are generally outside the control of managers and their firms, they may be able to develop capabilities and experiential advantages enabling them to respond to these risks and possibly gain a competitive advantage over other firms (Mitroff et al., 1987)? Second, research in this area is also vital because while natural disasters tend to be episodic, they are not rare or isolated occurrences. To be sure, as we discussed earlier, due in part to climate change trends, natural disaster severity and frequency has significantly increased over the last few decades (IPCC, 2012; NAS, 2016; Wahlstrom & Guha-Sapir, 2016). The trend is geographically dispersed: natural disasters affect any country, developed or developing.

Additionally, growing evidence shows that cost and prevalence of natural disasters is on the rise (Alexander, 2006; IPCC, 2012; NAS, 2016; Wahlstrom & Guha-Sapir, 2016). Therefore, analyzing this gap in the literature and developing a better understanding of how natural disasters compare to other discontinuous risks (i.e. terrorist attacks and technological disasters) should provide managers and practitioners with valuable guidance in responding to them. Although there is an important body of scholarly work that has reviewed and integrated studies on different types of risks and strategies for responding to them (Fitzpatrick, 1983; Miller, 1992), as well as proposed new approaches for identifying the relationship between specific risks and risk-taking behavior (Baird & Thomas, 1985), much of this work was published two decades ago (and in other areas of the social sciences). Serious attention has not been given to the study of major discontinuous risks in the context of strategic management and organization study.

This chapter aims to contribute to strategic management research in two ways. First, utilizing insights from the *resource-based view* (RBV) of the firm, we extend the research on the RBV by examining whether there are limits to the value of firm experience with natural disasters. We also examine whether this experience is a potential source of competitive advantage to enable foreign entry and expansion. Our second contribution is to extend the research on strategic risk management by examining discontinuous rather than continuous risk, which is more commonly studied. It may be difficult for firms to gain experience managing discontinuous risks, but if this experience is effective in the decision-making process of MNC subsidiary entry and expansion, it may constitute an intangible asset that is a source of competitive advantage.

Natural Disasters, Discontinuous Risk, and Firm Entry and Expansion

Discontinuous risk is defined here as the possibility that a disaster, which is episodic and often difficult to anticipate or predict, might occur and may have a substantial impact on a firm and its operating environment (Ramanujam, 2003; Slovic et al., 2000). This definition results from an integration of two conceptualizations of discontinuous risk. Ramanujam (2003) explicitly applies the concepts of discontinuous change and discontinuous risk to describe shifts in organizational domains that are infrequent and episodic as opposed to incremental changes that are ongoing. This notion of risk closely parallels research on discontinuities that are external to a firm, occurring in the wider operating environment (Slovic et al., 2000). Natural disasters, terrorist attacks, and technological disasters are types of discontinuous and unpredictable risk (Perrow, 2007).

While the impact of both continuous and discontinuous risks can be assessed and measured, there are notable distinctions between the two. Scholars studying the relationship between continuous risk and firm entry and expansion have generally concluded that higher levels of risk deter foreign entry and expansion by MNCs (Henisz & Delios, 2001), except in the case of regulated industries where firms may actually seek out policy discretion at the entry stage of an investment

(García-Canal & Guillén, 2008). Poor quality governance, weak institutions, and high levels of corruption have all been associated with lower levels of foreign direct investment (FDI) (Daude & Stein, 2007). Researchers have also examined the effect of policy shifts and the threat of expropriation of foreign assets on foreign entry and expansion decisions (Henisz & Delios, 2001; Williamson, 1996). Policy uncertainty, which arises when a government's ability to commit to a given set of policies is in question, may be ever present but never result in a major discontinuity. Likewise, governments may threaten expropriation but not follow through.

> Scholars studying the relationship between continuous risks (such as poor quality governance, weak institutions, and high levels of corruption) and firm entry and expansion have generally concluded that higher levels of risk deter foreign entry and expansion by MNCs.

Unlike continuous risks in the host country's political or institutional environment, discontinuous risks like natural disasters, terrorist attacks, and technological disasters are more difficult to predict, anticipate, and thus avoid.[1] In addition, such discontinuous risks do not necessarily have serial correlations between prior risks and present risks. These threats can cause injury or death to a significant number of people. Examples of technological disasters include transportation accidents such as airplane, train, or large-scale automobile crashes, and industrial accidents such as oil spills, chemical explosions, or biological infections. In these examples, there exists the potential for major discontinuous change at the level of the host country.

In particular, businesses are increasingly more vulnerable to natural disasters. These natural disaster risks are not necessarily confined to the immediate area affected by a disaster. In some cases, the effects are national in scope (IPCC, 2012; Perrow, 2007). Obviously, some countries and/or regions may be more (or less) susceptible to weather-related natural disasters or earthquakes.

---

[1] In Chapter 3, we defined terrorism as the willingness to use violence or the threat of violence to attain political or ideological goals. Terrorists that attack noncombatants may be domestic in origin or may result from international groups or networks of individuals (Wernick, 2006). Natural disasters are generally defined as the result of a natural hazard and can cause human and financial losses, business disruption, and/or environmental damage (Alexander, 2000). Technological hazards are human-made threats that arise from the breakdown of technologies and systems.

Our question in this chapter is whether, compared to other calamities, manifest natural disasters – not the threat or potential of – result in decreased entry into foreign markets and limited expansion. We know that the threat of expropriation creates a deterrent to FDI and is associated with lower levels of resource commitment (Henisz & Delios, 2001; Williamson, 1996). In addition, sociopolitical stability, broadly speaking, is reportedly a key consideration for MNCs in allocating funds to foreign projects, with greater instability decreasing the likelihood of entry and expansion (Buckley & Casson, 1998; Vernon, 1983).

The direct and indirect cost of major natural disasters is substantial – both for society and for business continuity and profitability. The reported global cost of natural disasters rose 15-fold between the 1950s and the 1990s (Benson & Clay, 2004). The World Bank reported that between 1990 and 2000 natural disasters resulted in damages constituting between 2 and 15 percent of an exposed country's annual GDP (2004). Between 1995 and 2015, natural disaster caused about 600,000 deaths and produced about $2 trillion in economic loses, with weather-related disasters accounting for the vast majority of damages from 1995 to 2015 (Wahlstrom & Guha-Sapir, 2016).

For businesses, this translates into damage to facilities, disconnection with their supply chains, disruptions to business, lost revenues, and in the case of particularly severe disasters, firm failure. The Congressional Research Service reported that property insurance premiums increased by 5 percent in the United States, that shipping costs subsequently totaled 1–3 percent of shipment value just for covering security, and that terrorist attacks resulted in a decline in global economic growth in 2001 and 2002, totaling up to $300 billion (Nanto, 2004). In the case of technological disasters, there is evidence that the stocks of all petrochemical firms may suffer a decline after a chemical disaster (nearly 1 percent the day of the disaster and 1.4 percent over the course of the first week following it), regardless of whether or not they were involved in the disaster or directly affected by it (Capelle-Blancard & Laguna, 2010).

Businesses are more vulnerable to more severe and frequent natural disasters that cause damage to firm facilities, disconnection with their supply chains, lost revenues, and in the case of particularly severe disasters, firm failure. Between 1995 and 2015, natural disasters

caused about 600,000 deaths and produced about $2 trillion in economic losses. Weather-related disasters accounted for the vast majority of damages from 1995 to 2015 (Wahlstrom & Guha-Sapir, 2016).

Given the risks and costs involved, many corporations increasingly view natural disasters as important considerations when making investment and expansion decisions. The French multinational Groupe Danone, for example, states on its corporate website that it calculates these risks prior to making a new investment:

"The Company's main industrial sites have a limited exposure to major natural hazards (floods, earthquakes and hurricanes). These risks are evaluated in advance of each major investment, and the Company's new industrial installations are designed with all applicable safety standards. However, the Company's international development makes it necessary for the Company to set up businesses in areas that are occasionally exposed to the risk of natural disasters, in particular earthquakes (Japan, Indonesia, Turkey, Mexico and Algeria)." (Danone, 2011)

Echoing this sentiment, the President and CEO of the Greater Phoenix Economic Development Council, is quoted in one academic study, as saying that natural disasters are "very top-of-mind issues for companies" and with regard to disasters, "site selection isn't really 'site selection' so much as 'site elimination'" (Escaleras & Register, 2011). In the same study, the authors examined the impact of natural disasters on FDI in 94 countries between 1984 and 2004. They found that natural disasters had a negative impact on FDI, and furthermore, that those which occurred toward the end of the period – from 1999–2004 – had the greatest negative effect on foreign direct investment. Thus, overall we argue that natural disasters may be increasingly more likely to deter *foreign firm entry and expansion* (Escaleras & Register, 2011).

Natural Disaster Experience and Firm Entry and Expansion

From the perspective of RBV scholars, through the integration, construction, and reconfiguration of internal and external competencies, firms can develop dynamic capabilities to address rapidly changing environments (Barney, 1991, 1996; Teece et al., 1997; Wernerfelt, 1984; Zollo & Winter, 2002). One of the key factors that contribute to the development of dynamic capabilities is experience (Zollo & Winter, 2002). As a firm develops new capabilities through its experience it can leverage this intangible asset in foreign markets (Kogut & Zander, 1993). For example, scholars building on these ideas have studied the role of MNC host country experience on subsidiary survival and profitability (Delios & Beamish, 2001). Others have examined whether relevant international experience might minimize the effect of policy uncertainty on investment (Delios & Henisz, 2003).

> One of the factors that contributes to the development of dynamic capabilities is experience. International experience may be helpful because managers to navigate and obtain resources in non-home country environments.

Although in this chapter we focus on experiential learning across a large number of firms rather than on the process of organizational learning *within* a single firm (see Levinthal & Rerup, 2006; Weick & Sutcliffe, 2006, for examples), we want to recognize this closely related body of literature that examines how individual firms learn from unusual events. This research has important implications for our research and these articles constitute some of the most significant contributions to managing unexpected events. Specifically, research at the organizational level has contributed substantially to our understanding of how managers learn from events such as coal mining disasters (Madsen, 2009), organizational crises (Rerup, 2009), corporate acquisitions (Zollo, 2009), and unique customer requests (Starbuck, 2009), among others (Baum & Dahlin, 2007; Christianson et al., 2009). Madsen (2009), for instance, shows how the process of aggregating data on rare coal mining accidents can enhance the detection of problems and facilitate learning from others in the industry.

In another paper, Christianson et al. (2009) show how a rare event – the collapse of the roof at the Baltimore and Ohio Museum Roundhouse – led to a transformation of the institution. Problems with the roof started a learning process that led to a change in organizational focus and identity. These are examples of the internal organizational processes that might be occurring within firms and ultimately lead to the development of new capabilities around managing disaster risk.

In terms of managing risk, international experience may be helpful simply because managers have previously learned how to navigate and obtain resources in non-home country environments. In turn, these prior experiences may enable firms to quickly switch to undamaged suppliers, alternative logistic channels and distributors, and identify appropriate public and private services such as medical professionals and other emergency support resources. With greater international experience, cultural understanding, and at times, knowledge of the local language, it is expected that managers will face fewer cultural barriers and have an easier time communicating with local individuals and organizations (Barkema et al., 1996). In addition, international experience is likely to give managers confidence in managing challenges, in spite of their awareness of risks and threats (Sönmez & Graefe, 1998). For these reasons, we expect that firms with international experience may be more willing to enter and expand in foreign markets that are experiencing discontinuous risks.

Although the importance of experience – particularly international and host country-specific experience – and its relationship to new market entry and expansion decisions is well documented, researchers have also argued that some types of experience are not necessarily transferable across borders (Barkema et al., 1996; Johanson & Vahlne, 1977; Kogut & Zander, 1993). These findings pose serious questions for firms seeking to develop valuable, firm-specific capabilities around disaster management. For instance, it is not unreasonable to assume that firms can develop valuable, difficult to imitate, capabilities for managing disasters. Yet, to some extent, the impact of disasters and the appropriate disaster response is likely to vary by country and by type of disaster. Thus, while firms may not be able to leverage host country specific knowledge across borders, the knowledge and capabilities relevant to managing during and after disasters in different country contexts may be a valuable, transferable resource.

> Firms with international experience may be more willing to enter and expand in foreign markets that are experiencing natural disasters. Yet, some types of natural disaster experience are not necessarily transferable across borders because the appropriate disaster response is likely to vary by country and by type of disaster.

Indeed, although research on firm experience with discontinuous risks, particularly as defined here, is limited, there has been a substantial body of research on firm experience with continuous risks, particularly political and other country-level hazards (hazards that are often, although not exclusively, continuous risks). Findings from this research indicate that firms with more extensive international experience in countries with high political hazards have higher entry rates into other high-risk countries (Delios & Henisz, 2000, 2003; Holburn & Zelner, 2010). Experience is assumed to be valuable for managing risk because it may enable a firm to obtain "information on local factors and political markets that may aid in the implementation of safeguards" against host country risks (Delios & Henisz, 2000). Delios and Henisz (2000) further found that firms with greater experience in environments prone to policy and political hazards were less likely to be deterred by these same risks.

Experience with previous natural disasters may lead to improved preparedness of firms and individuals against disasters. Firms with natural disaster experience are likely to develop business recovery plans, discover how to obtain various sources of recovery aid, or take other steps to cope with disasters (Webb et al., 2002). For example, despite the size and intensity of Hurricane Andrew, one of the most destructive storms ever to have affected the United States (National Hurricane Center, 2010), very few offshore oil and gas platforms were damaged by its force. Positive outcomes like Andrew's have arisen because of advances in knowledge about preparing for such disasters – knowledge that is based on marine environments, design standards, building materials and construction practices, platform installation procedures, and continuous improvements in operations and maintenance (Hayes, 1992). This example of improved offshore oil and gas platforms can be denoted a "social learning model of disaster management" (Mitchell, 1996). The 2010 BP oil spill in the Gulf of Mexico reinforces the notion that organizational learning is firm-specific and that not all firms achieve experience advantage.

> **Firms with natural disaster experience may be more likely to develop business recovery plans, discover how to obtain various sources of recovery aid, or take other steps to cope with disasters.**

According to reports from Continental Airlines, the company developed an emergency plan in 2006 after barely avoiding Hurricane Rita, in 2005 (which hit soon after Hurricane Katrina) (Worthington et al., 2009). In 2008, when Hurricane Ike threatened the Houston area (Continental's hub), the airline temporarily transfered its business operations in Houston, Texas, to an underground bunker in Conroe, Texas, to maintain business continuity (Continental Magazine, 2008). The bunker reportedly enables Continental to conduct airline operations in any region where airports are operational.

As Pete Fahrenthold, the managing director of Risk Management at Continental Airlines, stated:

"The key to our emergency preparedness is getting ready for events you pray will never occur. We knew Houston is in a hurricane corridor, so we felt – particularly when we digested Katrina's impact on New Orleans – we had to develop a business continuity plan that would let us operate no matter what the weather brought us." (Continental Magazine, 2008)

The learning process typically starts with reactive strategies intended to lower the impacts of disasters and work toward creating anticipatory strategies. Through repeated and traumatic catastrophic experience, natural disasters move to the center of the strategy-making process, and top managers are able to acquire knowledge about alternative coping mechanisms. In fact, experience with previous disasters is associated with higher levels of responsiveness and preparedness, which eventually improves a firm's capability to recover from disasters (Dahlhamer & D'Souza, 1997). Managers may make plans to temporarily relocate businesses and use alternative supply chains. At a minimum, they are more familiar with various sources of recovery assistance in a country. These findings are consistent with the notion that firms can gain experiential knowledge related to risk management; knowledge that is difficult for foreign firms to acquire in any other way (Barkema et al., 1996; Chang, 1995; Johanson & Vahlne, 1977). Given the importance of experience for future entry and expansion across a variety of issues and contexts, we argue that firm experience with discontinuous risks is relevant for firms deciding whether or not to expand into countries experiencing similar risks. Even where risks are infrequent and difficult to predict, experience managing during sudden and devastating disasters is likely to generate important lessons that can only be attained from learning-by-doing.

> The disaster learning process typically starts with reactive strategies intended to lower the impacts of disasters and work toward creating anticipatory strategies.
>
> Through repeated and traumatic catastrophic experience, natural disasters are more likely to move to the center of the strategy-making process, and top managers are able to acquire knowledge about alternative coping mechanisms.

Thus, based on prior research we argue that experiential knowledge that is difficult to codify can be transfered through wholly owned subsidiaries and leveraged in new or subsequent investments (Kogut & Zander, 1993; Teece et al., 1997). If this knowledge proves valuable, it may serve as a source of competitive advantage in subsequent ventures. For these reasons, aside from more general international experience, we would expect that firm experience specifically related to managing during natural disasters would be valuable in subsequent entry and expansion into markets experiencing similar disasters. Therefore, we posit that:

> **Proposition 1:** Firm experience with natural disaster risk moderates the negative relationship between natural disaster risk and firm entry and expansion in such a way that firms with greater levels of experience operating in countries with natural disaster risk are more likely to enter and expand into other countries experiencing similar disasters.

Experience with High- (Low-) Impact Natural Disasters and Firm Entry and Expansion

While experience with specific types of natural disaster risk is expected to be valuable for firms entering and expanding into other countries, the severity of the risk is also expected to matter. Prior research has shown that people tend to overestimate the risks associated with dramatic and sensational events perceived to be under greater human control, such as terrorist attacks and technological accidents, and they underestimate the risks associated with more deadly natural disasters seen as unavoidable "acts of God" (Slovic et al., 2000). This, at least partly, explains why respondents frequently rate the perceived risk of airplane crashes and nuclear disasters as carrying a greater risk of death than natural disasters, despite statistical evidence to the contrary (Slovic et al., 2000). To be sure, as we discussed in Chapter 3, since 1995, on average natural disasters have been vastly more frequent, deadly, and costly than terrorist attacks and industrial disasters. Yet, the risks of natural disasters are regularly underestimated by business managers and policy makers (Wahlstrom & Guha-Sapir, 2016).

Scholars studying organizational responses to unusual events note similar reactions. According to Lampel et al. (2009), when unusual or atypical events have a major impact on an organization, "there is clear motivation to draw lessons and make the necessary operational and cognitive adjustments." In contrast, when unusual events have a minor impact, "learning is kept to a minimum and the experience is seldom transformed into implementable lessons" (Lampel et al., 2009).

Thus, experience with low-impact disasters is likely to have only a transitory effect on the firm. In contrast, firms that experience severe, high-impact events may have a transformative experience that translates into the development of experientially based capabilities for managing future disasters (Lampel et al., 2009). For these reasons, we would expect that, all else being equal, the more dramatic and severe the disaster the more likely it is to be a deterrent to future investment. Low-impact disasters – disasters that result in little loss or damage – may cause minor disruptions to business, but they rarely induce major organizational or strategic changes. Thus, firms will likely deem these risks to be as great a deterrent to new market entry and expansion as more serious disasters. In contrast, the most severe disasters are generally dramatic and highly publicized discontinuities.

> **Experience with low-impact natural disasters is likely to have only a transitory effect on the firm. In contrast, firms that experience severe, high impact events may have a transformative experience that translates into the development of experientially based capabilities for managing future disasters.**

Although the direct effect of high-impact disasters may deter market entry and expansion, we argue that a firm that experiences high-impact disasters will be more likely to enter and expand into countries experiencing similar disasters than one with low-impact disaster experience. Experiential learning may provide valuable tacit knowledge that can be applied to future ventures (Kogut & Zander, 1993). Frederick W. Smith, chairman, president, and chief executive officer of FedEx Corporation, alluded to such in a statement about terrorism and the threat of disaster, in 2008:

"The security challenges in the post-9/11 era require new thinking and new approaches that go far beyond traditional physical security models. Companies need to embed security in all aspects of their business processes and operations." (Business Roundtable, 2008)

In contrast, firms with experience in low-impact disasters are likely to ignore and overlook the possibility of deadly disasters and are less likely to understand how to manage through – and overcome – a major natural catastrophe. Those firms that have experienced low-impact natural disasters may see them as a minor threat until such time when they experience high-impact disasters.

While it is unlikely that firms would intentionally seek out high-risk environments in which to operate, firms with experience with high-risk/high-impact disasters may be better prepared to overcome future ones. Managers of these firms may also be willing to enter or expand in markets, in spite of major natural disasters there, if their experience capabilities allow them to more competitively respond and adapt to such calamities. Firms with prior experience with major disasters would presumably be more willing to invest than firms will little or no experience with them. In fact, if a firm holds valuable tacit knowledge that is difficult for other firms to imitate, it may even take advantage of the business opportunities created by a high-threat disasters.

This notion is supported by research on continuous risks showing that firms with greater experience in high-risk political environments are more likely to expand to other risky countries. Delios and Henisz (2003), found, for example, that firms with experience operating in countries with high degrees of political risk were more likely to enter another country facing similarly high risks. Companies with experience in high-risk countries were also more likely to enter countries at mean or low levels of political risk (Delios & Henisz, 2003). The authors of that study found that experience with low-severity risks was associated with significantly higher entry rates into other countries facing low-severity risks. Indeed, the entry rate into low-risk countries (for companies with low-risk experience) was almost three times larger than the entry rate into high-risk countries. A key implication of this study is that firm experience with both risk type and risk severity is relevant to its entry into other markets. That is, firm experience with risk can be leveraged across borders.

Thus, for new entries, firms will tend to enter countries with risk levels that match their prior experiences in other countries. In terms of firm expansions in countries where firms already operate, research suggests that country-specific experience may be valuable, above and beyond that of the firm's experience with a specific risk and its intensity (Johanson & Vahlne, 1977; Kogut & Zander, 1993). Doz (1986) emphasizes that each nonmarket environment generates distinct problems and responses. Given the heterogeneity of problems and responses, every subsidiary has to create some degree of unique knowledge to manage risks and exploit opportunities in a host country (Gupta et al., 2001).

Experiencing high-impact disasters in foreign countries may help MNCs gain general knowledge and preparedness measures against disasters that can apply to other countries the firms newly enter. A firm can develop its corporate-level framework and practices against catastrophic disasters. At the same time, firms that gain experience managing high-impact risks in a particular country will also gain country-specific knowledge that may further enhance the value of experience. Although it is possible that in some cases increased "local" knowledge could deter further investment if managers perceive structural weaknesses in a country's ability to manage a disaster, generally the research suggests that country-specific experience would enhance risk-specific knowledge. Overall, based on this reasoning, we posit:

Proposition 2: Firm experience with high-impact natural disasters will moderate the negative relationship between natural disaster severity and firm entry and expansion in such a way that firms with greater levels of experience with high-impact natural disasters will be more likely to enter and expand into other countries experiencing the same type of high-impact natural disaster than firms with experience with low-impact impact natural disasters.

Proposition 3: Compared to experience with *low-impact terrorist attacks and industrial disasters*, experience with *low-impact natural disasters* is less likely to show a positive moderating effect on the relation between disaster severity and entry and expansion.

Conclusion

After nearly every disaster anecdotal stories abound about firms that survive and even expand after a crisis, thus suggesting some firms may develop unique capabilities or response strategies for managing risk. In this chapter, we argued that MNCs may reap benefits from experience with high-impact natural disasters. We posited that firms having experience with high-impact natural disasters are more likely to expand into host countries experiencing natural disasters. We believe that the source of this experiential advantage arises from a greater understanding of high-impact discontinuous natural disasters. This experience enables firms to more accurately assess potential risk to the firm and perhaps manage that risk more effectively.

We also highlighted limits to this experiential advantage with high-impact natural disasters. In particular, we posited that that experience with high-impact natural disasters positively moderates the negative link between natural disaster severity and expansion into current host countries, but not entry into new ones. That is, we proposed that experience with high-impact natural disasters can be leveraged in a MNC's existing host country *but not for entering* into new countries experiencing similar high-impact disasters. Disaster experience needs to be accompanied by country-specific knowledge to be valuable. Contrary to previous research on political risk, experience with natural disaster risks does not appear to be transferable across borders.

PART III

Empirical Studies of Business Adaptation to Nature Adversity

6 | *Canary in the Coal Mine*

Western U.S. Ski Industry Adaptation to Warmer Temperatures

Prior strategic management research on adverse external environmental conditions has tended to ignore the natural environment, instead traditionally focusing on firm competitive, economic, political, and institutional contexts. Seldom is the *natural environment* given more than lip service. Interestingly, the narrower corporate environmental management literature has also paid little attention to the adverse effects of nature on business strategies, focusing instead on examining the negative impacts of business on nature. In the absence – until recently – of the harmful effects of severe climate change, this tendency to ignore nature's adverse conditions has made sense for business executives and management scholars.

As we discussed in the conceptual chapters of the book, business managers tend to perceive adverse natural phenomena in terms of "acts of God," for which little could be done (see Chapters 2 and 4). To be sure, it is well understood that during the last 10,000 years, weather, climate, geological, and ecological conditions have been exceptionally steady, particularly when compared to the earth's earlier geological periods. Yet, in the case of vulnerable industries like the ski industry, accelerating slow-onset climate change trends, and their associated detrimental effects, are already generating increased attention from top corporate managers around the world. Two key questions are highlighted by this increased attention: (1) How does nature adversity intensity affect the adoption of business protective adaptation strategies? (2) How do firm-level and institutional-level factors moderate the relationship between nature adversity intensity and protective adaptation? To answer these questions we describe and discuss

This chapter is a modified and updated (for moderating effects of context and firm characteristics) version of the conceptual segment of Rivera and Clement (2019), reproduced with permission of the journal publisher.

an empirical study that tested hypotheses developed as propositions in Chapter 3:

Hypothesis 1: The relationship between nature adversity intensity and protective adaptation follows an inverted U-shape, such that firms facing lower and higher levels of nature adversity intensity are more likely to engage in lower levels of protective adaptation than those facing medium levels.

Hypothesis 2: The inverted U-shaped relationship between nature adversity intensity and protective adaptation is less pronounced for older firms than for younger firms.

Hypothesis 3: The inverted U-shaped relationship between nature adversity intensity and protective adaptation is less pronounced for firms operating in more stringent regulatory environments than for firms operating in less stringent regulatory environments.

Hypothesis 4: The inverted U-shaped relationship between nature adversity intensity and protective adaptation is less pronounced for firms with more slack resources than for firms with less slack resources.

Hypothesis 5: The inverted U-shaped relationship between nature adversity intensity and protective adaptation is more pronounced for publicly owned firms than for privately owned firms.

Specifically, in this chapter we examine the adaptation responses by large ski resorts in the Western U.S. between 2001 and 2013 (approximately 85 percent of the commercially open skiable acres in the Western U.S.). To do this, we build on earlier empirical research that one of us co-authored with professors Peter de Leon and Peter Tashman examining the Western U.S. ski industry (Rivera & de Leon, 2004; Rivera, de Leon, & Koerber, 2006; Tashman & Rivera, 2017). Our data tracks 1995–2013 snowfall and temperature conditions for these ski resorts and it includes an average of 75 ski resorts per year, resulting in an unbalanced panel dataset of 850 firm-year observations over the 2001–2013 period. The findings show that firms facing medium nature adversity intensity levels (measured as temperature) appear more likely to engage in higher adaptation, whereas those experiencing low and high natural adversity intensity show a tendency for lower adaptation, yielding an inverted U-shaped relationship. Our findings also suggest that firm age, the stringency of the regulatory environment, and the presence of slack resources, induce a flattening of this inverted U-shaped relationship. Status as a public company, however, induces a steepening of the inverted U-shaped relationship.

Research Methodology

Research Context: Western U.S. Ski Industry

The ski industry is highly vulnerable to nature adversity intensity associated with changing climate conditions. The U.S. ski industry reportedly lost around $1 billion in revenue between 1999 and 2010, attributable to lower demand for skiing because of deteriorating snowfall conditions (Burakowski & Magnusson, 2012; Zeng, Broxton, & Dawson, 2018). This industry has been focusing on undertaking protective adaptation practices such as slope expansion and snowmaking in response to declining snowfall. Before 2014, adaptation in the form of diversification to summer outdoor recreation activities was seldom implemented because it was legally restricted for ski resorts located on national forest lands (the vast majority of most Western ski resorts).[1] Slope expansion to more climatically favorable areas, such as higher elevations or north-facing mountainsides, attempts to capitalize on longer-lasting snow cover, while snowmaking enables ski resorts to supplement and even replace natural snow cover (Hoffmann et al., 2009; Scott & McBoyle, 2007). Both actions are meant to help ski resorts maintain or extend the ski season (Pickering, 2011; Scott & McBoyle, 2007). The main challenge, however, is that the projected trend toward warming temperatures yielding decreasing natural snowfall may affect the degree to which these adaptation measures will remain effective (Burakowski & Magnusson, 2012; Scott & McBoyle, 2007).

> The ski industry is highly vulnerable to nature adversity intensity associated with changing climate conditions. The U.S. ski industry reportedly lost around $1 billion in revenue between 1999 and 2010, attributable to lower demand for skiing because of increasingly poorer snow conditions.

Data and Sampling

Our population of interest includes ski resorts in the Western U.S. located in the Pacific Northwest, Southwest, and Rocky Mountain

---

[1] In 2014, The U.S. Forest Service published new regulations allowing ski areas to market year-round outdoor recreating activities at ski areas and resorts located in national forest lands as part of the implementation of the Ski Area Recreational Opportunity Enhancement Act of 2011.

regions, and covers the period 2001–2013. We initiated our data collection on protective adaptation practices, such as ski areas' slope expansion and snowmaking capacity, by relying on figures collected by the Ski Area Citizens Coalition (SACC) from official environmental impact assessments and development plan proposals to federal and state government agencies (Tashman & Rivera, 2016). SACC is an alliance of nonprofit conservation organizations that monitored and rated Western U.S. ski resorts on their environmental policies and practices between 2001 and 2013 (SACC, 2014). SACC included more Western ski resorts over the years starting with the largest 57 resorts in 2001, covering 70 in 2003, and as of 2011 it had rated 85 (out of 153 ski resorts in the Western U.S.).

> **Our population of interest includes ski resorts in the Western U.S. located in the Pacific Northwest, Southwest, and Rocky Mountain regions and covers the period from 2001 to 2013.**

We collected data on nature adversity intensity from the PRISM Climate Group at Oregon State University. PRISM gathers climate observations from a wide range of monitoring networks including the National Weather Service Cooperative Observer Program (COOP) and Weather Bureau Army Navy (WBAN) stations, among others. The organization also applies quality control measures and develops climate datasets available at multiple spatial and temporal resolutions covering the period from 1895 to the present (PRISM Climate Group, 2004). These datasets were commissioned by the U.S. Department of Agriculture through the Natural Resources Conservation Service (USDA NRCS) to serve as the official spatial climate datasets of the USDA. Using PRISM's Data Explorer tool, time series climate observations can be determined for any individual location (PRISM Climate Group, 2016). We collected climate data for ski resorts using their geographic coordinates.

Final sample. Once we merged the data from our different sources, our final sample included an average of 75 ski resorts per year, resulting in an unbalanced panel dataset of 850 firm-year observations over the 2001–2013 timeframe with a mean of 11.3 observations per ski resort. This sample excludes some of the smallest Western U.S. ski areas.[2]

---

[2] Very small ski areas often include just ski runs and ski lift systems, are usually owned by local communities, have no accommodation facilities, and are rarely visited by non-local tourists. In contrast ski resorts include accommodation facilities and other attractions, and attract a wider clientele.

However, it accounts for about 85 percent of the skiable acres in the Western U.S. and thus the large majority of ski resort economic activity in this region (e.g. number of customers, revenue, and regional development).[3] For this reason, it enables us to capture the vast majority of the Western U.S. ski industry's adaptation dynamics. After adding the data related to the moderating variables, our final sample size consisted of 75 ski resorts, resulting in a panel dataset of 749 firm-year observations over the 2001–2013 timeframe with an average of 10.0 observations per ski resort.

> Our sample excludes some of the smallest Western U.S. ski areas. However, it accounts for about 85 percent of the skiable acres in the Western U.S. and thus the large majority of ski resort economic activity in this region.

Measures

Protective adaptation (dependent variable). We measured the level of protective adaptation using annual acres of slope terrain expansion over the 2001–2013 period (Hoffmann et al., 2009; Scott & McBoyle, 2007). Our analysis in this chapter improves on the recent work by Tashman and Rivera (2016) by compiling the actual physical measures of protective adaptation (i.e. acres of slope expansion) used by SACC to develop its ratings. The SACC rating scores may reflect planned expansion that a ski resort may have announced but not necessarily implemented. Tashman and Rivera highlight this as one of the main limitations of their study.

> We measured the level of protective adaptation using annual acres of slope terrain expansion and – for robustness tests – we also used annual acres of added snowmaking capacity.

Prior studies have established that slope expansion to more climatically favorable areas is one of the main protective adaptation practices used in the ski industry (Hoffmann et al., 2009; Scott & McBoyle, 2007; Tashman & Rivera, 2016). There is evidence that ski resorts specifically implement expansion as a buffer to decreasing snow availability as opposed to other factors such as market demand (Hoffmann

---

[3] For comparison, the average ski resort size in our sample is 1613 acres, while the average size for Western U.S. ski areas and resorts that are not included in our sample is 721 acres.

et al., 2009; Tashman & Rivera, 2016). In the U.S., market demand has been relatively stagnant over the last decade or so. For this period, according to the National Ski Areas Association (NSAA), the U.S. ski industry trade association, the total active number of snow sport participants has remained flat at about 9 million for an annual average of 56.5 million snow sport visits (that is one-person skiing/snowboarding per day) (NSAA, 2016). In addition, slope expansion is an adaptation that requires important up-front and long-term investments on the part of ski resorts. The scale of projects is often large. Completing such projects requires lengthy permit application processes to federal and local regulatory authorities. These processes are characterized by frequent opposition from civil society groups, increasing the time and effort needed for approval (Scott & McBoyle, 2007). For these reasons, it represents a strong signal of ski resorts' commitment to protect their core business activities.

Nature adversity intensity (independent variable). For each ski resort we measured nature adversity intensity using the *daily minimum temperature average for the ski season* from October 1 to April 30 of the following year (i.e. the mean of 211 daily minimum temperatures readings for each ski season year). We chose daily minimum temperature because it is a necessary condition for ski areas' protective adaptation to be effective at sustaining accumulation of high quality snow for skiing (i.e. dry, powdery snow). Above freezing temperatures – greater than $0\,°C$, or $32\,°F$ – indicate progressively higher nature adversity intensity, with snowfall melting altogether at temperatures of $5\,°C$ or warmer (National Snow and Ice Data Center, 2015). Conversely, colder temperatures beginning at $0\,°C$ indicate lower nature adversity intensity (National Snow and Ice Data Center, 2015).[4]

> For each ski resort, we measured nature adversity intensity using the *daily minimum temperature average for the ski season* from October 1 to April 30 of the following year.

> We also relied on the following alternative proxies for nature adversity intensity to test the robustness of our regression analysis: average ski season temperature, number of days with average temperatures above $-5\,°C$, number of days with average temperatures above $-2\,°C$, and number of days with minimum temperatures above $-5\,°C$.

---

[4] Favorable conditions for snowfall accumulation also involve air humidity (National Snow and Ice Data Center, 2015).

Our October to April ski season timeframe includes the months early in the season when ski resorts start building snowpack depth prior to opening. Managers consider temperature conditions during these early months when considering the effectiveness of slope expansion in maintaining and/or extending the length of the ski season. The inclusion of these early season months also constitutes an improvement on Tashman and Rivera (2016), where snowpack variability is measured over the November–April time frame.

Since we examined one-to-five year lags, our data collection period for the temperature measure was from 1995 to 2013 rather than the 2001–2013 period covered by the protective adaptation measure. Because slope expansion constitutes a long-term investment, we suspected that the process of perception and evaluation of climate conditions and subsequent decision-making to implement this adaptation could take several years. In addition, for ski resorts operating on public land, the permit application process for slope expansion to regulatory authorities can take several years. Therefore, we chose a four-year lag for our nature adversity intensity measure in our primary model.

Besides the ski season's daily minimum temperature average, we also relied on the following alternative proxies for nature adversity intensity to test the robustness of our regression analysis: average ski season temperature, number of days with average temperatures above $-5\,°C$, number of days with average temperatures above $-2\,°C$, and number of days with minimum temperatures above $-5\,°C$.

Control and moderating test variables. We included additional time-variant control variables to complement other time-invariant factors already captured in our fixed-effects models. These controls follow previous studies on the ski industry (Rivera & de Leon, 2004; Rivera et al., 2006; Tashman & Rivera, 2016) and also include factors previously found to be associated with adaptation. All data for our controls were collected on an annual basis, and each variable was lagged one year. We used acres as a proxy for ski resort *Size* And measured *Ski Resort Age* using years since establishment (this variable was also used in an interaction term with nature adversity intensity to test its moderating effect). We created a dummy variable to capture whether ski resorts were *Subsidiaries* of a company managing multiple ski areas. We included this control to capture another type of adaptation strategy, one where firms seek to share the risks of potential financial impacts from adverse conditions through acquisitions of other ski resorts (Hoffmann et al., 2009; Scott & McBoyle, 2007; Tashman & Rivera, 2016).

We also controlled for the status of a ski resort as a *Public Company* using a dummy variable. Publicly traded companies may have greater access to financial capital to devote to adaptation, or potential share-holder pressure to implement adaptation (Rivera & de Leon, 2004). We also proxied *Ski Resorts' slack resources* using their posted season pass price in a given year.[5] Season pass prices capture the revenue needed to cover operating costs (e.g. ski lifts, base lodges, grooming equipment, energy needs, labor) as well as protective adaptation costs. Prices also capture ski resort quality along different dimensions, which may be indicative of available slack resources. (The public company dummy variable and ski resort season pass prices were also used in an interaction term with nature adversity intensity to test its moderating effect.)

With regard to ski resort operating and institutional environments, we controlled for *Membership in the Sustainable Slopes Program (SSP)* using a dummy variable. The SSP is a voluntary program sponsored by the NSAA, which is meant to promote enhanced environmental per-formance through sharing of technical assistance with member ski resorts. We also controlled for ski resort operation on *Public Land* and *Private Land* using dummy variables, with the reference group including ski resorts operating on a combination of both. This was done to account for typically higher oversight by federal government agencies on public land (this dummy variables was also used in an interaction term with nature adversity intensity to test its moderating effect) (Rivera & de Leon, 2004). We also controlled for *State Environmentalism* by including the Sierra Club's number of annual state memberships per 1,000 inhabitants. This accounts for potential normative pressures from environmental activist stakeholders (Fremeth & Shaver, 2014). We also included the annual *State Population* to serve as a proxy for the size of ski resorts' local market (U.S. Census Bureau, 2012). Additionally, we controlled for *County Population Density* to serve as an indicator of ski resort land availabil-ity for potential slope expansion.

---

[5] To obtain a ski resort's season pass price, we used a web archive tool (web .archive.org) to consult the webpages for each ski resort for each year in our sample and retrieve the posted annual season pass price.

We also controlled for *Average Snowpack* during the ski season to capture additional climate conditions that may affect ski resorts' adaptation implementation. To do this, we used *Snow Water Equivalent*, a common snowpack measurement. We collected data for this control measure from the USDA NRCS' Snow Telemetry (SNOTEL) network. Finally, we controlled for *Ecological Uncertainty* to account for the effect natural adversity variability examined by Tashman and Rivera (2016). To do this, we measured nature adversity as the coefficient of variation (standard deviation divided by the mean) of the average ski season snowpack (using *Snow Water Equivalent*) at each resort over the previous 10 years. For the moderating effects tests, we also included an additional control variable reflecting *Ownership Change*, measured as the number of times during the period from 1995 to 2013 a ski resort changed owners. We did this in order to capture how changes in leadership may affect a ski resort's adoption and implementation of protective adaptation.

Analytical Approach

To test our hypotheses, we relied on a panel regression approach with firm and year fixed-effects to control for unobserved heterogeneity across firms and years. Hausman tests indicated that fixed-effects models were more appropriate for our data than random effects. To account for serial correlation within each firm, we also use clustered standard errors by ski resorts.

$$PA_{it} = c + aNAI_{i,t-4} + bNAI^2_{i,t-4} + \Sigma cX_{i,t-1} + F_i + T_t + \varepsilon_{it} \qquad (1)$$

where:

PA_{it} = protective adaptation for firm i in period t (acres of slope expansion)

$NAI_{i,t-4}$ = nature adversity intensity for firm i in period $t - 4$ (average minimum temperature during the ski season)

$NAI^2_{i,t-4}$ = nature adversity intensity squared for firm i in period $t - 4$

$\Sigma X_{i,t-1}$ = vector of control variables for firm i in period $t - 1$

F_i = firm fixed effects

T_t = year fixed effects

ε_{it} = error term for firm I in period t.

To identify the inverted U-shaped relationship suggested by Hypothesis 1, we followed a more stringent multitest methodology developed by Lind and Mehlum (2010) and recommended for use in organizational and management research (Haans, Pieters, & He, 2016). First, as has been done traditionally by previous management researchers, we needed to confirm that the b coefficient for $NAI^2_{i,t-4}$ the squared term of the nature adversity intensity measure, included in equation (1), was negative and significant.[6] This standard initial test is a necessary but not a sufficient condition to identify an inverted U-shaped relationship (Haans et al., 2016; Lind & Mehlum, 2010). Second, we needed to verify that the nature adversity intensity slope was positive and statistically significant at the lower bound of the nature adversity intensity measure range, and negative and significant at the upper bound (Haans et al., 2016). Third, we needed to confirm that the 95 percent confidence interval turning point of our curvilinear relationship fell within our nature adversity intensity measure data range.[7]

To test for the proposed moderation of the inverted U-shape suggested by Hypotheses 2–5, we continued to follow the more stringent approach outlined in Haans et al. (2016). As these hypotheses posit a flattening or steepening of the inverted U-shaped curve, we needed to confirm that the interaction term consisting of the moderator and the square term of the nature adversity intensity measure was significant (see equation (4)). A flattening occurs when the coefficient is positive and a steepening occurs when the coefficient is negative (Haans et al., 2016). We also included the interaction term consisting of the

---

[6] We did not mean center the nature adversity intensity measure before taking its square, as doing so does not increase the power to detect quadratic effects but instead can result in confusion in the interpretation of results by complicating the computation of the turning point (Haans, Pieters, & He, 2016).

[7] The nature adversity intensity slope is obtained by taking the first partial derivative with respect to *NAI* in equation (1):

Nature adversity intensity slope : $\partial PA/\partial NAI = a + 2bNAI$ (2)

The turning point expression is calculated by making equation (3) above equal to zero and then solving for *NAI*. We performed all the Lind and Mehlum (2010) tests using the *utest* command in Stata.

Turning point $= a/2b$ (3)

moderator and the unsquared term of the nature adversity measure in order to formally eliminate the possibility of a turning point shift in the inverted U-shaped curve induced by the moderator (Haans et al., 2016). This also prevents bias in the estimated coefficients due to exclusion of either interaction term (Haans et al., 2016):

$$PA_{it} = a + \beta_1 EA_{i,t-4} + \beta_2 E + \beta_3 EA_{i,t-4} M_{i,t} + \beta_4 EA_{i,t-4}^2 M_{it} \\ + \beta_5 M_{it} + \beta_6 X_{i,t-1} + \beta_4 F_{i,t-1} + \beta_5 T_{i,t-1} + \varepsilon_{it} \tag{4}$$

where:

PA_{it} = protective adaptation for firm i in period t
$EA_{i,t-4}$ = nature adversity intensity for firm i in period $t - 4$
$EA_{i,t-4}^2$ = nature adversity intensity squared for firm i in period $t - 4$
M_{it} = moderating variable for firm i in period t
$X_{i,t-1}$ = control variables for firm i in period $t - 1$
$F_{i,t-1}$ = firm dummies for firm i in period $t - 1$
$T_{i,t-1}$ = year dummies, with 2001 as base year for firm i in period $t - 1$
ε_{it} = error term for firm i in period t.

Results

Table 6.1 reports descriptive statistics and correlations for our variables. Between 2001 and 2013, ski resort annual slope expansion ranged between 0 and 783 acres at an average 134.96 acres/year. With regard to nature adversity intensity, the average daily minimum ski season temperature was –5.74°C for a range of –13.67 to 4.07°C. Figure 6.1 includes a map that shows the average minimum ski season temperatures experienced by ski resorts in our sample together with the level of implemented slope expansion across our sample period.

> From 2001 to 2013, ski resort annual slope expansion ranged between 0 and 783 acres, at an average 134.96 acres/year. With regard to nature adversity intensity, the average daily minimum ski season temperature was –5.74°C for a range of –13.67 to 4.07°C.

Table 6.2 presents the results for our main regression models. Hypothesis 1 posited an inverted U-shaped relationship between nature adversity intensity and the level of protective adaptation undertaken by firms. Following the Lind and Mehlum (2010) procedure, we first confirmed that the coefficient for the squared term of the nature

Table 6.1. *Descriptives and correlations*

	1	2	3	4	5	6
1 Slope expansion	1.00					
2 Nature adversity intensity	−0.25[*]	1.00				
3 Sustainability program	−0.00	−0.16[*]	1.00			
4 Size	0.18[*]	−0.19[*]	0.12[*]	1.00		
5 Age	−0.19[*]	0.17[*]	−0.14[*]	−0.05	1.00	
6 Public land	−0.04	0.01	0.06	−0.14[*]	0.35[*]	1.00
7 Private land	0.02	0.02	−0.05	0.21[*]	−0.36[*]	−0.49[*]
8 Subsidiary	0.10[*]	−0.12[*]	0.08[*]	0.29[*]	−0.03	0.00
9 Public company	0.25[*]	−0.31[*]	0.09[*]	0.38[*]	−0.14[*]	−0.02
10 State environ-mental-ism	−0.12[*]	0.09[*]	0.12[*]	−0.09[*]	0.02	0.21[*]
11 State population	−0.23[*]	0.38[*]	−0.05	−0.01	0.01	0.09[*]
12 County population density	−0.06[*]	0.33[*]	0.09[*]	-0.09[*]	0.20[*]	0.17[*]
13 Snowpack	0.09[*]	0.36[*]	0.03	0.04	0.05	0.05
14 Ecological uncertainty	−0.23[*]	0.26[*]	−0.00	−0.05	−0.05	0.05
15 Artificial snowmaking	0.28[*]	−0.28[*]	0.04	0.47[*]	−0.12[*]	−0.09[*]
Mean	134.96	−5.74	0.64	1612.56	46.71	0.69
Std. Dev.	189.45	2.98	0.48	1090.88	14.32	0.46
Minimum	0	−13.67	0	200	0	0
Maximum	783	4.07	1	4800	78	1

[*] $p < 0.05$

7	8	9	10	11	12	13	14	15
1.00								
0.15*	1.00							
−0.08*	0.40*	1.00						
−0.36*	0.15*	0.13*	1.00					
−0.08*	0.13*	−0.04	0.48*	1.00				
−0.05	−0.01	−0.01	−0.14*	0.08*	1.00			
−0.00	−0.04	−0.17*	0.09*	0.15*	0.12*	1.00		
0.04	−0.14*	−0.19*	0.04	0.07*	0.01	0.13*	1.00	
0.05	0.31*	0.41*	−0.08*	−0.04	0.00	−0.07*	−0.06	1.00
0.13	0.45	0.14	3.31	1.07e+07	150.77	1.64	0.32	90.16
0.34	0.50	0.34	1.27	1.35e+07	342.47	7.04	0.10	128.02
0	0	0	0.00	903773	0.79	0.02	0.11	0
1	1	1	6.04	3.80e+07	2129.38	46.27	0.77	594

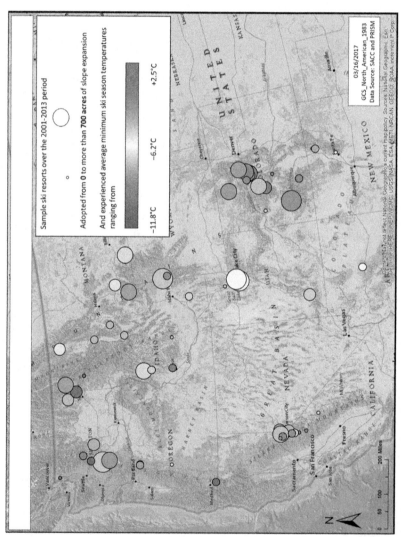

Figure 6.1 Slope expansion adoption and temperature conditions for sample of Western U.S. ski resorts, 2001–2013.

Table 6.2. *Fixed-effects regression results for the relationship between protective adaptation and nature adversity intensity*

	Model 1 (DV: Slope expansion)	Model 2 (DV: Slope expansion)
Control variables		
Age	16.13	15.12
	(15.46)	(15.38)
Sustainability program	2.20	2.04
	(10.75)	(10.69)
Size	0.38***	0.38***
	(0.05)	(0.04)
Public land	−19.70	−20.18
	(21.12)	(21.00)
Private land	60.63	62.83
	(86.61)	(86.13)
Subsidiary	26.09	24.18
	(16.61)	(16.53)
Public company	−18.55	−21.80
	(20.02)	(19.94)
State environmentalism	−11.54	−10.34
	(10.18)	(10.13)
State population	-4.02×10^{-5}***	-3.60×10^{-5}***
	(9.02×10^{-6})	(9.08×10^{-6})
County population density	−1.05***	−0.97***
	(0.17)	(0.17)
Snowpack	1.15	1.10
	(0.78)	(0.77)
Ecological uncertainty (snowpack variability)	224.06***	224.41***
	(63.18)	(62.83)
Predictor Independent Variables		
Nature adversity intensity (ski season daily minimum temperature) average, $t-4$)	1.24	−24.16*
	(5.31)	(9.80)
Nature adversity intensity *squared* $(t-4)$		−1.87**
		(0.61)
Intercept	−822.39	−895.60
	(873.05)	(868.50)
F-test	20.93***	20.70***

Table 6.2. (*cont.*)

	Model 1 (DV: Slope expansion)	Model 2 (DV: Slope expansion)
Adjusted within-$R^{2(b)}$	0.40	0.41
N	850	850

Notes: [a]Standard errors clustered by firm and indicated in parentheses; $^{+}p < 0.10$, $^{*}p < 0.05$, $^{**}p < 0.01$, $^{***}p < 0.001$. [b]Adjusted within-R^2 is reported to be more conservative in assessing model fit, since that traditional adjusted-R^2 considers the contribution of the fixed effects dummies to quantify the fit of the model (traditional adjusted-R^2 are 0.83 for Model 1, and 0.84 for Model 2).

Table 6.3. *Test of an inverted U-shaped relationship between protective adaptation and nature adversity intensity*

Estimated turning point	–6.45
95% confidence interval for turning point – Fieller method[a]	(–13.67, 4.07)
Slope test – lower bound (slope)	27.03**
Slope test – upper bound (slope)	–39.41**
Overall test of presence of an inverted U-shape (*t*-value)	2.73**

$^{+}p < 0.10$, $^{*}p < 0.05$, $^{**}p < 0.01$, $^{***}p < 0.001$
[a] The Fieller method corrects for finite sample and non-normality biases (Haans, Pieters, & He, 2016).

adversity intensity measure in Model 2 was negative and significant ($\beta = -1.87$, $p < 0.01$) (see Table 6.2). Second, we also confirmed a positive and significant (27.03, $p < 0.01$) slope at the low end of the nature adversity intensity measure and a negative and significant (–39.41, $p < 0.01$) slope at the high end for Model 2 (see Table 6.3). Third, we confirmed that Model 2's turning point, equal to –6.45 °C, is within the observed range (–13.57 to 4.07 °C) for our nature adversity intensity measure (see Table 6.3).[8,9] At its turning point, Model 2 predicted an annual slope expansion of 168.32 acres.

[8] The reported turning point is calculated using unrounded coefficients by Stata, and so it may differ slightly from the number that would be calculated using the rounded coefficients reported in Table 6.2.

[9] As an additional test, following Haans et al. (2016), we also reestimated Model 2 with the addition of a cubic term for the nature adversity intensity measure to verify if the relationship was S-shaped instead of an inverted U-shaped. This alternative cubic term model did not provide a better fit than Model 2.

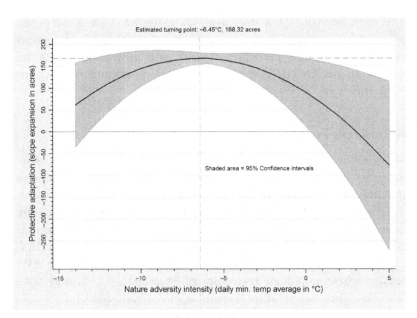

Figure 6.2 Inverted U-shaped relationship between protective adaptation and nature adversity intensity.

The findings from our curvilinear model make it difficult to interpret the marginal effects of the regression coefficients. Thus, we include a figure to illustrate how Model 2's predicted protective adaptation changes as nature adversity intensity increases (see Figure 6.2). This figure indicates that annual protective adaptation grows as nature adversity intensity increases from around –13 to the –6.45 °C turning point, where it plateaus at 168.32 acres. For these temperatures below the turning point (left side of the curve), a 1 °C rise generates an average protective adaptation increase of about 15.53 acres. In contrast, as temperatures warm above the turning point to about 5 °C, the average rate of protective adaptation declined to approximately –21.17 acres/°C.

> For temperatures below the –6.45 °C turning point, a 1 °C rise generates an average protective adaptation increase of about 15.53 acres. In contrast, as temperatures warm above the turning point, the average rate of protective adaptation declined to approximately –21.17 acres/°C.

Jointly, these results indicate that firms facing medium levels of nature adversity intensity are linked to greater levels of protective adaptation compared to firms experiencing lower and higher levels. That is, protective adaptation first increases with nature adversity intensity at a decreasing rate to reach an apex point, after which it decreases at an increasing rate. Overall, these tests suggest that nature adversity intensity and protective adaptation follow an inverted U-shaped relationship, providing support for Hypothesis 1.

Robustness Tests

We conducted additional regression analyses using alternative nature adversity intensity measures to verify the robustness of our findings in Model 2. The results of these tests are shown in Table 6.4, Models 3–12. As indicated in the Methods section, our alternative nature adversity intensity measures included the average ski season temperature, the number of days during a ski season where average temperatures exceeded −5, −2, and 0°C, and the number of days during a ski season where minimum temperatures exceeded −5, −2, and 0°C. We chose these temperature thresholds so our robustness tests would reflect a range of favorability conditions for snowfall. That is, −5°C can be considered a conservative threshold for snowfall with high humidity conditions, −2°C a standard favorability threshold for snowfall with average humidity conditions, and 0°C can be considered a higher-end threshold, necessitating low humidity conditions. We also used the Lind and Mehlum (2010) multitest approach outlined by Haans, Pieters, and He (2016) to verify the inverted U-shaped relationship in our robustness tests.

The inverted U-shaped relationship between nature adversity intensity and protective adaptation suggested by the results of Model 2 was corroborated for the following measures of nature adversity intensity lagged four years: average ski season temperature (Model 3), number of days with average temperatures above −5°C (Model 4), number of days with average temperatures above −2°C (Model 5), and number of days with minimum temperatures above −5°C (Model 6). For Model 5 these robustness test findings indicate that protective adaptation increases commensurately as the number of days in the ski season with average temperatures rises above −2°C from around 10 to 100 days (that is about 5–47 percent of the ski season). Then, it plateaus around the turning point, which is at 107.6 days (about 51 percent of ski season days). Subsequently, protective adaptation drops off progressively as the number of days in the ski season with average temperatures

Table 6.4. Robustness tests for an inverted U-shaped relationship between protective adaptation and alternative nature adversity intensity measures (lagged 4 and 5 years)

	Alternative nature adversity intensity measures (all measures lagged 4 years)						Alternative nature adversity intensity measures (all measures lagged 5 years)				
	Avg. ski season temp. (°C)	Days with avg. temp. above −5°C	Days with avg. temp. above −2°C	Days with min. temp. above −5°C	Avg. min. ski season temp. (°C)	Avg. ski season temp. (°C)	Days with avg. temp. above 0°C	Days with min. temp. above −5°C	Days with min. temp. above −2°C	Days with min. temp. above 0°C
	Model 3	Model 4	Model 5	Model 6	Model 7	Model 8	Model 9	Model 10	Model 11	Model 12
Unsquared term (coefficient, std. error)	−5.82 (6.10)	3.40* (1.49)	1.98+ (1.05)	1.29+ (0.74)	−21.76* (9.75)	−0.30 (5.93)	1.92* (0.89)	1.92** (0.72)	1.26+ (0.67)	1.63+ (0.86)
Squared term (coefficient, std. error)	−2.10* (0.93)	−0.01* (4.94×10⁻³)	−0.01* (4.06×10⁻³)	−0.01* (3.33×10⁻³)	−1.87** (0.61)	−2.03* (0.90)	−0.01* (4.09×10⁻³)	−0.01** (3.26×10⁻³)	−0.01* (4.28×10⁻³)	−0.02* (8.69×10⁻³)
Estimated turning point	−1.39	150.63	107.60	85.93	−5.82	−0.07	108.60	107.79	59.15	45.66
95% confidence interval for turning point – Fieller method	(−7.47, 8.04)	(64, 213)	(33, 209)	(12, 207)	(−13.67, 4.07)	(−7.47, 8.04)	(15, 201)	(12, 207)	(0, 180)	(0, 158)

Table 6.4. (*cont.*)

	Alternative nature adversity intensity measures (all measures lagged 4 years)					Alternative nature adversity intensity measures (all measures lagged 5 years)				
Slope test – lower bound (slope)	25.49*	1.96*	1.37*	1.11*	29.37**	30.04*	1.66*	1.70**	1.26*	1.63*
Slope test –upper bound (slope)	−39.53*	−1.41*	−1.86**	−1.81**	−36.98**	−32.95*	−1.63*	−1.76**	−2.57**	−4.01*
Overall test of presence of an inverted U-shape (*t*-value)	1.84*	1.89*	1.72*	1.65*	2.61**	1.95*	1.91*	2.36**	1.87*	1.89*

Standard errors clustered by firm: $^{+}p < 0.10$, $^{*}p < 0.05$, $^{**}p < 0.01$, $^{***}p < 0.001$

above –2 °C increases from around 125 to 210 (corresponding to about 59–100 percent of ski season days) (see Table 6.4). Model 2 findings were also corroborated when the original nature adversity intensity measure was lagged five years (Model 7) and when the following alternative measures were lagged five years: average ski season temperature (Model 8), number of days with average temperatures above 0 °C (Model 9), and number of days with minimum temperatures above –5 °C (Model 10), –2 °C (Model 11), and 0 °C (Model 12). Overall, these alternative models indicate support for Hypothesis 1.

As an additional robustness test, we used an alternative measure of protective adaptation (our dependent variable): *acres of added artificial snowmaking capacity*. Snowmaking constitutes a different approach to protective adaptation than slope expansion. While slope expansion buffers ski resorts by providing access to terrain with longer-lasting natural snow cover, the strategy behind snowmaking is to supplement or substitute natural snowfall with artificial snow (Scott & McBoyle, 2007; Tashman & Rivera, 2016). As compared with slope expansion, added snowmaking capacity also represents a more flexible investment with more clearly defined feasibility limits. We tested multiple models for snowmaking using all of the measures for nature adversity intensity outlined above. We found an inverted U-shaped relationship between snowmaking capacity and the following measures of nature adversity intensity lagged four years (see Table 6.5): daily minimum temperature average for the ski season (Model 13), and number of days with minimum temperatures above –5 °C (Model 14), and –2 °C (Model 15). Findings were also corroborated when these alternative measures were lagged five years (see Models 16–18). We should note that some of our robustness models in Table 6.5 (Models 13–15 and 18) using snowmaking as an alternative measure of protective adaptation only marginally corroborate our main findings. We suspect that this is because while our measure captures the extent to which ski resorts adopt added snowmaking capacity (e.g. equipment), it does not capture whether ski resorts actually use that capacity in a given ski season, which is more difficult to obtain. However, taken together, these additional tests, presented in Tables 6.4 and 6.5, are mostly consistent with Model 2's findings, thus providing robust support for Hypothesis 1.

Table 6.5. Robustness tests for the inverted U-shaped relationship using an alternative measure of protective adaptation: snowmaking capacity (lagged 4 and 5 years)

	Alternative nature adversity intensity Measures (all measures lagged 4 years)			Alternative nature adversity intensity Measures (all measures lagged 5 years)		
	Avg. min. ski season temp. (°C)	Days with min. temp. above −5°C	Days with min. temp. above −2°C	Avg. min. ski season temp. (°C)	Days with min. temp. above −5°C	Days with min. temp. above −2°C
	Model 13	Model 14	Model 15	Model 16	Model 17	Model 18
Unsquared term (coefficient, std. error)	−9.00+	0.59	0.45	−9.18+	0.76*	0.44
	(4.78)	(0.36)	(0.35)	(4.75)	(0.35)	(0.33)
Squared term (coefficient, std. error)	−0.58*	$-2.98 \times 10^{-3+}$	$-4.21 \times 10^{-3*}$	−0.68*	$-3.35 \times 10^{-3*}$	$-3.70 \times 10^{-3+}$
	(0.30)	(1.62×10^{-3})	(2.12×10^{-3})	(0.30)	(1.59×10^{-3})	(2.09×10^{-3})
Estimated turning point	−7.71	99.38	53.54	−6.75	113.97	60.03
95% confidence interval for turning point – Fieller method	(−13.67, 4.07)	(12, 207)	(0, 180)	(−13.67, 4.07)	(12, 207)	(0, 180)
Slope test – lower bound (slope)	6.96+	0.52+	0.45+	9.42*	0.68*	0.44+
Slope test – upper bound (slope)	−13.75*	−0.64+	−1.06*	−14.72*	−0.62*	−0.89*
Overall test of presence of an inverted U-shape (t-value)	1.44+	1.60+	1.30+	1.95*	1.72*	1.35+

Standard errors clustered by firm: + $p < 0.10$, * $p < 0.05$, ** $p < 0.01$, *** $p < 0.001$

As an additional robustness test, we used an alternative measure of protective adaptation (our dependent variable): *Acres of added artificial snowmaking capacity.*

Additionally, given that velocity or pace of change represents yet another dimension of nature adversity intensity, we created several velocity measures to perform extra robustness tests:

(a) Change in average minimum ski season temperature over the previous 2 years (Model 19)
(b) Average minimum ski season temperature over the previous 10 years (Model 20)
(c) Average change in minimum ski season temperature over the previous 10 years (Model 21)
(d) Average minimum ski season temperature over the previous 5 years (Model 22)
(e) Average change in minimum ski season temperature over the previous 5 years (Model 23)

We reestimated our main model (Model 2) to include these velocity measures as a control, and our findings remained robust (see Table 6.6, Models 19–23). The inverted U-shaped relationship held, and the velocity control was statistically insignificant at these multiple specifications.

Overall, our robustness tests provide strong support for our finding that nature adversity intensity and protective adaptation follow an inverted U-shaped relationship.

Moderating Effect Tests of Firm-Level and Institutional-Level Factors

Following the approach in Haans, Pieters, and He (2016), we were able to confirm the significance of the coefficient for the interaction term consisting of the square term of the nature adversity intensity measure and the following moderators (see Models 24–27 in Table 6.7): firm age ($\beta = 0.10$, $p < 0.01$, Model 24, regulatory environment stringency ($\beta = 2.92$, $p < 0.05$, Model 25), slack resources ($\beta = 3.47 \times 10^{-3}$, $p < 0.05$, Model 26), and public company ($\beta = -1.68$, $p < 0.05$, Model 27). These results suggest that firm age (see Figure 6.3), stringency of the regulatory environment (see Figure 6.4), and presence of slack resources (see Figure 6.5) induce a flattening of the inverted

Table 6.6. *Robustness tests for Model 2, including velocity measures as a control*

	Control variables: Alternative measures of velocity of nature adversity				
	Model 19	Model 20	Model 21	Model 22	Model 23
Nature adversity intensity un-squared term	−24.06[*]	−24.55[*]	−23.86[*]	−23.24[*]	−24.16[*]
(coefficient, std. error)	(9.81)	(9.83)	(9.81)	(10.04)	(9.81)
Nature adversity intensity squared term	−1.89[**]	−1.86[**]	−1.83[**]	−1.87[**]	−1.87[**]
(coefficient, std. error)	(0.61)	(0.61)	(0.61)	(0.61)	(0.61)
Estimated turning point	−6.36	−6.59	−6.49	−6.22	−6.45
95% confidence interval for turning point – Fieller method	(−13.67, 4.07)	(−13.67, 4.07)	(−13.67, 4.07)	(−13.67, 4.07)	(−13.67, 4.07)
Slope test – lower bound (slope)	27.68[**]	26.37[**]	26.39[**]	27.84[**]	27.01[**]
Slope test – upper bound (slope)	−39.47[**]	−39.72[**]	−38.82[**]	−38.46[**]	−39.39[**]
Overall test of presence of an inverted U-shape (t-value)	2.77[**]	2.64[**]	2.65[**]	2.67[**]	2.72[**]

Notes:

1. Standard errors clustered by firm; [+] $p < 0.10$, [*] $p < 0.05$, [**] $p < 0.01$, [***] $p < 0.001$

2. Velocity control variables:

Model 19: Change in average minimum ski season temperature over the previous 2 years

Model 20: Average minimum ski season temperature over the previous 10 years

Model 21: Average change in minimum ski season temperature over the previous 10 years

Model 22: Average minimum ski season temperature over the previous 5 years

Model 23: Average change in minimum ski season temperature over the previous 5 years

Table 6.7. *Fixed-effects regression results for moderators to the relationship between slope expansion and nature adversity intensity*

	Model 24 Slope expansion	Model 25 Slope expansion	Model 26 Slope expansion	Model 27 Slope expansion
Predictor variables				
Average minimum ski season temperature (lagged 4 years)	−44.20* (28.54)	−51.44** (16.31)	−49.45** (17.91)	−19.34+ (10.28)
Average minimum ski season temperature *squared* (lagged 4 years)	−6.15** (1.98)	−4.14*** (1.16)	−4.18*** (1.15)	−1.21+ (0.69)
Moderating variables				
Age	23.26 (15.09)	15.73 (15.21)	18.28 (15.17)	14.23 (15.17)
Age × average minimum ski season temperature (lagged 4 years)	0.47 (0.52)			
Age × average minimum ski season temperature *squared* (lagged 4 years)	0.10** (0.04)			
Public land	−18.85 (20.75)	71.17 (57.41)	−17.59 (20.94)	−14.52 (20.93)
Public land × average minimum ski season temperature (lagged 4 years)		34.23+ (18.38)		
Public land × average minimum ski season temperature *squared* (lagged 4 years)		2.92* (1.32)		
Season pass price	0.05* (0.02)	0.06** (0.02)	0.08+ (0.09)	

121

Table 6.7. (*cont.*)

	Model 24 Slope expansion	Model 25 Slope expansion	Model 26 Slope expansion	Model 27 Slope expansion
Season pass price × average minimum ski season temperature (lagged 4 years)			0.04^+ (0.02)	
Season pass price × average minimum ski season temperature *squared* (lagged 4 years)			$3.47 \times 10^{-3*}$ (1.47×10^{-3})	
Public company	-52.90^{**} (20.34)	-41.75^* (20.22)	-38.14^+ (20.10)	12.80 (38.17)
Public company × average minimum ski season temperature (lagged 4 years)				-7.46 (9.34)
Public company × average minimum ski season temperature *squared* (lagged 4 years)				-1.68^* (0.77)
Control variables				
Sustainability program	-16.90 (10.80)	-11.92 (10.93)	-15.29 (10.91)	-11.31 (10.90)
Size	0.36^{***} (0.04)	0.38^{***} (0.04)	0.37^{***} (0.04)	0.37^{***} (0.04)
Private land	30.51 (81.16)	50.05 (89.61)	12.84 (82.07)	21.99 (81.90)
Conglomerate	39.51^* (16.26)	39.00^* (16.69)	29.14^+ (16.60)	36.12^* (16.50)

Ownership change	−1.50	8.74	5.85	10.52
	(9.89)	(9.86)	(9.75)	(9.82)
State environmentalism	−0.72	−1.46	0.13	−1.11
	(11.00)	(11.16)	(11.13)	(11.10)
State population	-2.30×10^{-5}*	-2.77×10^{-5}**	-2.86×10^{-5}**	-3.04×10^{-5}***
	(9.45×10^{-6})	(9.53×10^{-6})	(9.65×10^{-6})	(9.52×10^{-6})
County population density	-0.75***	-0.88***	-0.87***	-0.93***
	(0.19)	(0.18)	(0.18)	(0.19)
Snowpack	1.34^{+}	1.22	1.28^{+}	1.13
	(0.75)	(0.76)	(0.75)	(0.75)
Ecological uncertainty	229.92***	246.75***	242.63***	255.75***
	(61.77)	(62.48)	(62.25)	(62.59)
Intercept	-1539.99^{+}	−1214.81	−1291.66	−1010.56
	(835.45)	(856.87)	(854.75)	(856.08)
F-test	18.95***	17.94***	18.23***	18.22***
R^2	2.20×10^{-3}	0.02	0.01	0.02
N	749	749	749	749

Standard errors clustered by firm and indicated in parentheses; $^{+}p < 0.10$, $^{*}p < 0.05$, $^{**}p < 0.01$, $^{***}p < 0.001$

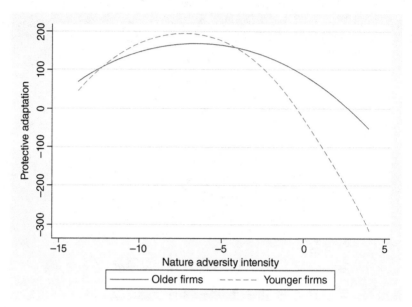

Figure 6.3 Moderating effect of firm age on the inverted U-shaped relationship between nature adversity intensity and protective adaptation.

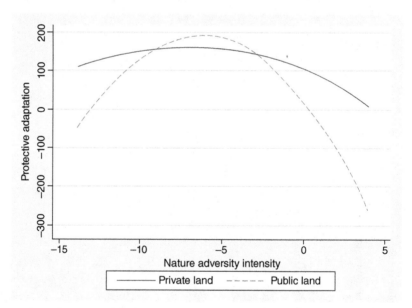

Figure 6.4 Moderating effect of regulatory environment stringency on the inverted U-shaped relationship between nature adversity intensity and protective adaptation.

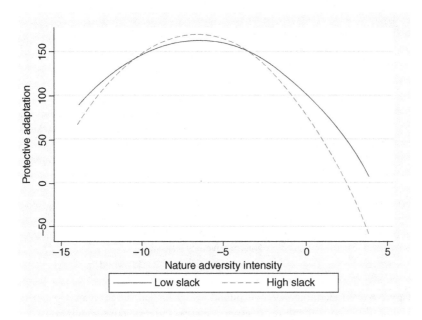

Figure 6.5 Moderating effect of presence of slack resources on the inverted U-shaped relationship between nature adversity intensity and protective adaptation.

U-shaped curve providing support for Hypotheses 2, 3, and 4, respectively. Additionally, a ski resort's status as a public company (see Figure 6.6) induces a steepening of the inverted U-shaped curve, providing support for Hypothesis 5.

> Firm age, the stringency of the regulatory environment, and presence of slack resources induce a flattening of the inverted U-shaped relationship between nature adversity intensity and protective adaptation, while ski resort status as a public company induces a steepening of this inverted U-shaped relationship.

Robustness analysis for moderating effects. We conducted additional regression analyses to verify the robustness of our moderation findings. We re-estimated the initial moderating models (Models 24–27 on Table 6.7) using our alternative measure of protective adaptation: acres of added snowmaking capacity. Findings were corroborated for two of the moderators (see Table 6.8): stringency of the regulatory environment (Model 28) and presence of slack resources

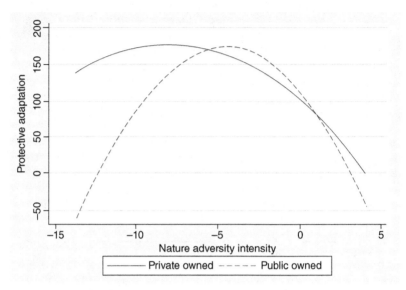

Figure 6.6 Moderating effect of public ownership on the inverted U-shaped relationship between nature adversity intensity and protective adaptation.

(Model 29). Findings were not corroborated for firm age or status as a public company. To further verify the validity of our measure of slack resources, we reestimated Model 26 using two alternative measures of the presence of slack resources. We used a ski resort's posted day lift ticket price: both the weekday lift ticket price and the weekend and/or holiday lift ticket price. These additional models (not shown) corroborated the findings from Model 26.

Discussion and Conclusions

Multiple strategic management literatures prominently highlight the importance of the external environment for firm strategy, but attention is generally limited to the economic, competitive, political, and institutional contexts, overlooking adverse conditions stemming from the natural environment. Our analysis here examined the effect of nature adversity intensity on firms' tendency to adopt protective adaptation measures that seek to preserve core organizational activities. This research area is increasingly critical for managers and public policymakers as the detrimental slow-onset effects of climate change become more pronounced and prevalent (Bansal et al., 2017; IPCC, 2014). Considering the way in which adaptation may be affected by nature adversity intensity

Table 6.8. *Moderating effects robustness test. Fixed-effects regression results for moderators to the relationship between snowmaking and nature adversity intensity*

	Model 28 Snowmaking	Model 29 Snowmaking
Predictor variables		
Average minimum ski season temperature (lagged 4 years)	−32.74*** (8.37)	−24.59** (9.36)
Average minimum ski season temperature *squared* (lagged 4 years)	−2.86*** (0.59)	−1.68** (0.60)
Moderating variables		
Public land	80.63** (29.44)	14.04 (10.94)
Public land *Average minimum ski season temperature (lagged 4 years)	29.17** (9.43)	
Public land *Average minimum ski season temperature *squared* (lagged 4 years)	2.93*** (0.68)	
Season pass price	−0.03** (0.01)	0.04 (0.04)
Season pass price *Average minimum ski season temperature (lagged 4 years)		0.02+ (0.01)
Season pass price *Average minimum ski season temperature *squared* (lagged 4 years)		$1.56 \times 10^{-3*}$ (7.69×10^{-4})
Control variables		
Sustainability program	2.12 (5.60)	1.28 (5.70)
Age	−3.53 (7.80)	−3.44 (7.92)
Size	−0.01 (0.02)	−0.02 (0.02)
Private land	63.12 (45.95)	13.93 (42.89)
Conglomerate	1.92 (8.56)	−0.45 (8.67)
Public company	39.02*** (10.36)	40.85*** (10.51)

Table 6.8. (*cont.*)

	Model 28 Snowmaking	Model 29 Snowmaking
Ownership change	2.31	0.80[*]
	(5.06)	(5.10)
State environmentalism	−9.69[+]	−8.35
	(5.72)	(5.81)
State population	$2.22e^{-06}$	$2.73e^{-06}$
	$(4.89e^{-06})$	$(5.04e^{-06})$
County population density	−0.10	−0.11
	(0.09)	(0.10)
Snowpack	−0.79[*]	−0.79
	(0.39)	(0.39)
Ecological uncertainty	51.81	49.90
	(32.04)	(32.53)
Intercept	264.43	280.36
	(439.44)	(446.68)
F-test	10.88[***]	9.89[***]
R^2	0.01	0.01
N	749	749

Standard errors clustered by firm and indicated in parentheses; $^{+}p < 0.10$, $^{*}p < 0.05$, $^{**}p < 0.01$, $^{***}p < 0.001$

also contributes to the debate between broad diverging views of organizational adaptation that respectively suggest that environmental adversity tends to be either positively or negatively related to adaptation (Astley & Van de Ven, 1983; Levinthal, 1991).

> The strategic management literature prominently highlights the importance of the external environment for firm strategy, but attention to economic, competitive, political, and institutional contexts is limited, overlooking adverse conditions stemming from the natural environment.

> Yet, paying attention to nature adversity conditions is increasingly critical for business managers and public policymakers as the detrimental slow-onset effects of climate change become more pronounced and prevalent around the world.

Our findings add to this debate by indicating that, initially, protective adaptation increases at lower than medium levels of nature adversity intensity at a declining rate to reach a turning point. Then, above medium levels of nature adversity intensity, protective adaptation decreases at a rising rate. In other words, firms tend to exhibit lower degrees of protective adaptation at both lower and upper range levels of nature adversity intensity while displaying greater levels of protective adaptation at medium levels, yielding an inverted U-shaped relationship.

We posit that mechanisms from both traditionally diverging organizational adaptation perspectives are necessary to explain the full extent and shape of the relationship between nature adversity intensity and firm protective adaptation (DesJardine et al., 2017; Gunderson & Holling, 2002). We propose that a counterbalancing combination of internal organizational inertial forces, organizational resilience resources and capabilities, and biophysical stressor barriers explain the curvilinear variation in firms' adaptation responses to nature adversity intensity. First, at lower than medium levels of nature adversity intensity, organizational inertial forces constrain organization willingness to adapt, despite the low and slowly growing costs of protective adaptation. Second, at medium levels of nature adversity intensity, the interplay between natural adversity signals and constraints, internal organizational inertial forces, and business resilience capabilities induces a firm to be more willing and able to implement greater protective adaptation. Third, at severe levels, growing natural forces eventually impose limits beyond which protective adaptation becomes unviable. Accordingly, we suggest an inverted U-shaped relationship between nature adversity intensity and protective adaptation such that firms facing lower or higher than medium levels of nature adversity intensity tend to adopt lower levels of protective adaptation. This interplay of underlying mechanisms causes the initial positive link between nature adversity intensity and adaptation to reach an apex point, after which it turns negative, yielding an inverted U-shaped relationship in which adaptation is highest at intermediate levels of nature adversity intensity.

Our findings indicate that firms tend to exhibit lower degrees of protective adaptation at both lower and upper range levels of nature adversity intensity while displaying greater levels of protective adaptation at medium levels, yielding an inverted U-shaped relationship.

We propose that a counterbalancing combination of internal organizational inertial forces, organizational resilience resources and capabilities, and biophysical stressor barriers taken together explain the curvilinear variation in firms' adaptation responses to nature adversity intensity.

The findings in this chapter add to the emerging literature examining firm adaptation to other slow-onset chronic dimensions of nature adversity in industries highly vulnerable to climate change such as the ski industry (Hoffmann et al., 2009; Linnenluecke & Griffiths, 2010; Pinkse & Gasbarro, 2019; Tashman & Rivera, 2016; Winn et al., 2011). For instance, in examining how ski resorts respond to uncertainty in the form of snowpack depth fluctuations, Tashman and Rivera (2016) find that greater snowpack variability from the long-term average has a significant positive association with the adoption of snowmaking and a marginally significant positive one with the adoption of slope expansion. This may be because snowpack variability alone may not impose strong physical constraints on firm adaptation. Snowpack variations might be detrimental or beneficial, respectively, for below or above average snowpack levels. To address this uncertainty, firms can thus focus on adaptive practices that confer more flexibility in the availability of this resource, such as snowmaking (Tashman & Rivera, 2016).

Our analysis in this chapter advances this earlier research by showing that, controlling for snowpack uncertainty, the level of nature adversity intensity in the form of adverse temperature conditions may act as a key limiting factor in firms' ability to pursue protective adaptation. While rising temperatures may at first drive the uptake of protective adaptation practices, like slope expansion, such practices may become increasingly unviable as warming temperatures exert stiffer adaptation constraints. For managers and policy makers, these findings highlight the importance of identifying specific physical and biological limits to adaptation strategies for particular businesses activities. Adaptation, as we stressed first in the front of the book, is not a panacea for coping with nature adversity linked to climate change. Adaptation is just a complement to climate change mitigation. Mitigation is, of course, the safer and more effective approach for dealing with the negative effects of climate change. This principle cannot be emphasized and reiterated enough.

The moderating effect of firm-level and institutional-level factors. The findings that the slopes of the inverted U-shaped relationship between nature adversity intensity and protective adaptation are flatter in older firms and in firms operating in more stringent regulatory environments are interesting in that these factors seem to be inducing firms to face simultaneous challenges of nonadaptation and maladaptation. Because of stronger internal inertial forces, older firms may at first be reluctant to adapt, even as increasing nature adversity intensity levels may require them to do so. Similarly, firms in more stringent regulatory environments may face initial barriers in their ability to implement preferred protective adaptation even as their need to do so increases with low to medium nature adversity intensity levels. However, because of the same inertial forces, older firms may be maladapting by persisting with protective adaptation that may no longer be effective once nature adversity intensity levels move from medium to high. Similarly, firms in more stringent regulatory environments may be locked into ineffective protective adaptation at these nature adversity intensity levels due to previously committed and high upfront investments.

> The slopes of the inverted U-shaped relationship between nature adversity intensity and protective adaptation are flatter in older firms, in firms operating in more stringent regulatory environments, and/or in firms with more slack resources.

> Because of stronger internal inertial forces, older firms may at first be reluctant to adapt when facing moderate levels of nature adversity intensity and then persist with protective adaptation that may no longer be effective for dealing with severe nature adversity intensity. For firms with more slack resources, a flattened inverted U-shaped relationship may be indicative that firms with more slack resources may not be using protective adaptation as their primary adaptation strategy.

> Conversely, our finding that the slopes of the inverted U-shaped relationship between nature adversity intensity and protective adaptation are steeper for publicly owned firms may be indicative of the fact that shareholders may pressure firms into taking a more short-term view of adaptation.

Our finding that the slopes of the inverted U-shaped relationship between nature adversity intensity and protective adaptation are flatter in firms with more slack resources is interesting for separate reasons. Here, such a flattening may be indicative that firms with more slack resources may not be using protective adaptation as their primary adaptation strategy. Indeed, protective adaption may be part of a portfolio of adaptation practices that may include diversification away from the core affected business. Because of the added buffer afforded by slack resources, these firms can more slowly ramp up and ramp down protective adaptation as needed according to the level of nature adversity intensity being experienced.

Finally, the finding that the slopes of the inverted U-shaped relationship between nature adversity intensity and protective adaptation are steeper for firms that are publicly owned may suggest that shareholders pressure firms into taking a more short-term view of adaptation (Bansal & DesJardine, 2014). Firms may thus be induced to more rapidly ramp up and ramp down protective adaptation in a way that aligns more with short-run adaptive gains. Whether this is ultimately beneficial for longer-term resilience remains to be seen. Taken together, our findings provide some preliminary insights into the types of contingencies that may affect firm adaptive responses to nature adversity intensity, warranting further exploration.

Limitations and Future Research

Our analysis in this chapter has several limitations, with implications for future research. First, although our sample includes larger ski resorts covering approximately 85 percent of the skiable acres in the Western U.S., it excludes the smallest Western U.S. ski areas. Future research could explore the particular challenges that smaller ski areas face.

Second, we do not directly test the combination of latent countervailing mechanisms that affect the inverted U-shaped relationship between nature adversity intensity and firm protective adaptation. Haans et al. (2016) point out that this is typical when theorizing and testing this type of curvilinear relationship. Future research could address this gap by conducting in-depth individual or group level case studies and surveys of managers. Doing so would enable researchers to test each of the inertial forces and decision-making mechanisms thought to underlie the inverted U-shaped relationship identified in this chapter.

Finally, our analysis focuses on nature adversity intensity. While we do account for other unfavorable dimensions of nature adversity (e.g. uncertainty and pace of change) as controls in our regression models and robustness tests, there may be others that we have not considered. Future research could further theorize on and empirically test for a fuller range of nature adversity dimensions and how these may differentially shape firm adaptation. The way in which firms adopt and implement protective adaptation in response to nature adversity intensity is also likely to be contingent on additional firm-level and institutional environment-level factors. Future research could also consider how these dimensions and other factors may moderate firm adaptation, thereby enabling a more multifaceted look at the relationship between nature adversity intensity and organizational adaptation.

7 | *MNC Disregard of Natural Disasters and the Role of Host Country Context*

And if the subways flood and the bridges break, will you lay yourself down and dig your grave? Or will you rail against your dying day...?

The Lumineers, Sleep on the Floor, 2016

In this chapter we return to the research questions conceptually discussed in Chapter 4:

(1) How do natural disasters, compared to other calamity hazards, shape multinational corporations' (MNCs') foreign subsidiary investment?[1]
(2) Is MNC subsidiary-level investment more likely to decrease in response to the natural disaster subtypes that result in the highest number of fatalities?
(3) Do stronger institutional environments and better country governance positively moderate the relationship between exogenous disasters and subsidiary-level investment?

To examine these questions, we describe and discuss an empirical study that tested hypotheses developed as propositions in Chapter 3 (see Figure 7.1 for an illustration of the conceptual model developed in Chapter 3):

> **Hypothesis 1:** In response to major disasters, MNC investment at the subsidiary level varies depending upon the disaster type. MNC subsidiary-level investment is more likely to decrease in response to

---

This chapter is a modified and updated (with new data analysis and regression models for natural disaster subtypes) version of Oh and Oetzel (2011), reproduced with permission of the journal publisher.

[1] Throughout the paper we use the terms "MNC subsidiary-level investment" and "investment at the subsidiary level" to refer to the presence of MNCs' subsidiaries in a particular host country. The change in subsidiary-level investment is the MNC's response to disaster(s) and reflects an increase or decrease in the number of subsidiaries in a host country.

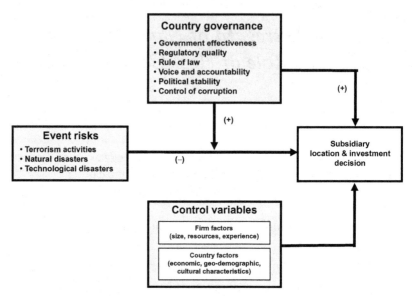

Figure 7.1 Country governance as a moderator of the relationship between disasters and subsidiary location and investment decisions.

technological disasters and terrorist attacks than in response to natural disasters.

Hypothesis 2: Natural disaster types that show a pattern of significantly deadlier consequences, year after year, become hard to ignore and underestimate as one-time historical anomalies. MNC subsidiary-level investment is more likely to decrease in response to the natural disasters showing higher levels of fatalities.

Hypothesis 3: Governance quality in the host country will moderate the relationship between disasters and subsidiary-level investment in such a way that major disasters are less likely to lead to subsidiary disinvestment.

We test our hypotheses using a dynamic panel negative binomial regression model with industry and year fixed effects. The panel dataset includes 31,285 observations from 71 European Fortune Global 500 MNCs and their subsidiaries operating across 101 countries during the period 2001–2006. Our findings indicate that MNC foreign subsidiary investment is likely to decrease ~~(disinvestment)~~ in response to severe terrorist attacks or technological disasters but not in response to natural disasters, except for the case of windstorms and their surges, which are the deadliest weather-related natural disasters. For natural disasters, the likelihood of MNC subsidiary-level disinvestment was directly proportional to a host country's democratic freedoms and inversely proportional to the host country's regulatory enforcement quality. Additionally, we found that in the case of terrorist attacks, MNC subsidiary-level disinvestment was less likely when the host country government was considered more effective. Thus, while the findings suggest a significant and negative relationship exists between terrorist activity and subsidiary location and investment, high-quality governance reduces the likelihood that firms will disinvest after a major terrorist attack. We did not find a similar relationship between governance and technological disasters. Indeed, greater voice and accountability in the host country was associated with disinvestment at the subsidiary level.

> **Our findings indicate that MNC foreign subsidiary disinvestment is likely to decrease in response to terrorist attacks or technological disasters *but not natural disasters*, except for the case of windstorms and their surges, the deadliest weather related natural disasters.**

> **For natural disasters, the likelihood of MNC subsidiary-level disinvestment was direct proportional to a host country's democratic freedoms and inversely proportional to the host country's regulatory enforcement quality.**

Methodology

Data Source and Sample

We drew our sample from the 227 European firms listed as Fortune Global 500 firms (where size is measured in terms of revenue) during any year between 2001 and 2006. We used the annual reports of each of these 227 large European firms to hand collect the subsidiary locations for 128 firms.[2] On average, these 128 MNCs had 28 subsidiaries in their home country and 58 subsidiaries across 17 foreign countries. After excluding the purely domestic firms, we merged four datasets: the location of subsidiary data, the natural and technological disaster data, the terrorism activity data, and a set of control variables. We were able to obtain data for only 71 of the European MNCs, however, due to

---

[2] The list of firms is available upon request.

limitations on firm-level information.[3] Thus, to test our hypotheses we used a final sample of 31,285 observations for the locations of 71 large European MNCs and their wholly owned subsidiaries operating across 101 countries during the period 2001–2006. Appendix 7.1 presents the list of 101 host countries across different geographic regions. The 71 European MNCs originate from twelve different European countries: Belgium, Finland, France, Germany, Italy, the Netherlands, Norway, Russia, Spain, Sweden, Switzerland, and the United Kingdom. We included only the wholly owned subsidiaries because many firms did not report partially owned subsidiaries.

Dependent Variable

To measure **MNC investment at the subsidiary level**, we used the number of a firm's subsidiaries in a country (NUMSUB) for the dependent variable. Thus, changes in investment are measured in terms of the increase or decrease in the number of a firm's subsidiaries in a given host country. This measure captures substantial changes in a firm's resource commitment in a particular host country. For several reasons, we believe that the NUMSUB is a better measure than a simple binary measure of the existence of subsidiaries in a country, which is used in most of the entry and survival research. First, the binary measure treats all entering countries with the same magnitude of strategic importance, while the NUMSUB can scale the strategic importance of the countries. Second, we are interested in the firms' perceived level of exogenous risk, which is reflected in the NUMSUB but not in a simple binary measure. A firm may not entirely exit a country in the face of a major disaster; rather, it might reduce its level of investments or operations according to its perceived level of risk.[4]

---

[3] The average revenue and profit of these 227 MNCs totaled 36 billion USD and 16 billion USD, respectively, while those of the 71 MNCs were 33 billion USD and 14 billion USD, respectively.

[4] One may argue that NUMSUB is an imperfect indicator representing the real value of investments in each country. The count variable is a widely used dependent variable in strategy research (e.g. Almeida & Phene, 2004; Arregle, Beamish, & Hébert, 2009; Baum, Calabrese, & Silverman, 2000). We compared the number of subsidiaries to the sales and assets of those subsidiaries in Europe, which is only available at the micro level for subsidiary investments. The sample firms have about 71 percent of their subsidiaries within Europe since 72 percent of their sales and 74 percent of assets are within Europe. Thus, NUMSUB is a good proxy for the real value of investments in each country. Moreover, it is possible that disasters affect not only the level of MNC investment in a host

Explanatory Variables

We used three sets of explanatory variables in our study: (1) **the severity of generic disasters**; (2) **the subtypes of natural disasters**; and (3) **the characteristics of country governance**. The specific generic types of disaster included natural disasters, technological disasters, and terrorist activities. Natural disasters were also divided into nine subtypes in order to test Hypothesis 2: earthquakes, volcanic eruptions, wave/surge,[5] extreme temperatures, floods, windstorms, droughts, wildfires, and landslides (the analysis also controls for subcategories of technological disasters: industrial accidents, transportation accidents, and miscellaneous accidents). For natural and technological disasters, we used the Emergency Events Database (EM-DAT, 2008) provided by the Center for Research on the Epidemiology of Disaster at the Catholic University of Louvain in Belgium.[6]

From this database, we also collected information on the **severity of each individual subtype of natural disaster** (weather-related disasters, such as floods, storms, surges, slides, droughts, extreme temperatures, and wildfires; and geological disasters such as earthquakes and volcano eruptions).

For **terrorist activities**, we used the International Terrorism Activity Database (ITERATE) presented by Mickolus et al. (2008). The ITERATE is widely used in political science and economics to study terrorist activities. To assess country governance, we included the Worldwide Governance Indicators (WGI) published by the World Bank (2008b). The WGI includes government effectiveness, voice and accountability (i.e. democratic freedoms), political stability, control of corruption, regulatory quality, and rule of law. Each of these governance indicators is measured based on the combined views of a large number of business, citizen, and expert survey respondents in industrial and developing countries.

---

    country but also its geographic focus. As a robustness check, we tested our model with the ratio of a firm's subsidiaries in a country over total firm subsidiaries as a dependent variable. We discuss the results of these and other robustness checks at the end of the Results section.

[5] Surge' is an atypical rise of water from the ocean that is pushed toward the shore by the force of storms winds. Source: www.nhc.noaa.gov/surge/.

[6] The database covers nine types of natural disasters: drought, earthquake, extreme temperature, flood, landslide, volcanic eruption, wave/surge, wildfire, and windstorm; and three types of technological accidents (disasters): industrial, transportation, and miscellaneous.

We operationalized the severities of the disasters (i.e. natural disasters and their subtypes, technological disasters, and terrorist attacks) using the number of people killed as this is a common measure in research on disasters (Eisensee & Strömberg, 2007; Strömberg, 2007; Van der Vink et al., 2007). The average number of individuals killed in terrorist activities was 4 per year per country, while the averages of individuals killed in natural disasters and technological disasters were 757 and 73 per year per country, respectively. We used a logarithm transformation of one plus the number killed, that is, ln(1+number of killed). We also tried other methods such as replacing ln(0) with −1, −0.5, or −0.1 after the transformation; the results were consistent.

Appendix 7.2 shows the top 25 countries most affected by each disaster. Bangladesh, India, Indonesia, Pakistan, Philippines, Russia, and the United States ranked high for all three disaster types, while other countries ranked high in one or two disaster types. The types of disaster are not rare occurrences. Among the 101 host countries in this study, about 60 percent, 96 percent, and 80 percent of countries experienced terrorist activities, natural disasters, and technological disasters, respectively, between 2001 and 2006. All countries, except Mauritius, were affected by at least one disaster and 50 countries were affected by all three types of disaster during the observation period. Thus, disasters are not rare or skewed phenomena limited to specific countries or regions.

> Natural disasters are not rare occurrences. Among the 101 host countries in this study, about 96 percent experienced natural disasters compared to 80 percent and 60 percent of countries experiencing technological disasters and terrorist activities, respectively, between 2001 and 2006.
>
> Moreover, the average number of individuals killed in natural disasters – 757 deaths per year per country – was many orders of magnitude greater than for other types of disaster. The average number of individuals killed in terrorist activities, in contrast, was 4 per year per country, and for industrial accidents, 73 per year per country.

Table 7.1 provides the definitions for the measures of each of the six governance indicators in our study: government effectiveness, regulatory quality, rule of law, voice and accountability, political stability, and control of corruption. These composite measures, scored between −2.5 to +2.5, were developed by Kaufmann, Kraay, and Zoido-Lobaton, in 1999, and most recently updated, in 2008, by Kaufmann, Kraay, and Mastruzzi. The higher the score received for an

Table 7.1. *Definitions, sources, and summary statistics for variables*

Variable	Definition	Data source
Dependent variables		
Subsidiaries	The number of an MNC's subsidiaries in a host country	Annual reports
Explanatory variables		
Terrorist activities	Log of (1 + number killed by terrorist activities)	ITERATE
Natural disasters	Log of (1 + number killed by natural disasters)	EM-DAT
Technological disasters	Log of (1 + number killed by technological disasters)	EM-DAT
Government effectiveness	Score measure of the quality of public service and its independence, policy formulation and implementation, and credibility of government policies	WGI
Regulatory quality	Score measure of the ability of the government to formulate and implement sound policies and regulations	WGI
Rule of law	Score measure of the quality of contract enforcement, property rights, the police, and the courts	WGI
Voice and accountability (i.e. democratic freedoms)	Score measure of freedom of the press and speech, freedom of association and freedom of political participation and the right to vote	WGI
Political stability	Score measure of the ability of the government to destabilize violence and terrorism	WGI
Control of corruption	Score measure of the extent to which public power is exercised for private gain	WGI
Control variables		
Country size	Log of real GDP in 2000 US dollars	WGI
Population	Log of population	WDI
Openness to trade	Percentage rate of imports to GDP	WDI

Table 7.1. (*cont.*)

Variable	Definition	Data source
Openness to FDI	Percentage rate of inward FDI to GDP	WDI
Adjacency	If two countries share a common border, common border = 1, otherwise = 0	CIA *World Factbook*
Language	If two countries share the same main language, common language = 1, otherwise = 0	CIA *World Factbook*
Colonial relationship	If two countries were involved in a colonial relationship with each other, colonial relationship = 1, otherwise = 0	CIA *World Factbook*
Physical distance	Log of distance between trading partners	Fratianni and Oh (2009)
Land size	Log of land size (km²)	WDI
Institutional closeness	If two countries belong to the European Union in the year of the observation, institutional closeness = 1, otherwise = 0	Fratianni and Oh (2009)
Literacy rate	Percentage rate of adult literacy	WDI
Unemployment rate	Percentage rate of unemployment	WDI
Firm size	Log of sales	Compustat Global; Annual reports
International experience	Percentage rate of foreign to total sales	Annual reports
R&D capability	R&D expenditures over total sales	Compustat Global; Annual reports
Marketing capability	Selling, general, and administrative expenditures over total sales	Compustat Global; Annual reports
Financial slack	Current assets over current liability	Compustat Global; Annual reports

Notes: Zero values in the "number of people killed" by terrorist activities, natural disasters, and technological disasters were replaced with –1 after the logarithm transformation.

indicator, the higher the quality of the institutional environment for that indicator. We draw readers' attention to Kaufmann et al. (2008) for more information about these six indicators.

To control for possible endogeneity problems, we used one-year lagged explanatory variables for both the disasters and the governance indicators. It was important to do so since, although unlikely, reverse causality could exist; that is, number of foreign subsidiaries may affect number of people killed in those disasters as well as country governance. The potential for endogeneity problems is reduced, however, by using lagged variables. In addition, we tested Heckman's (1976) two-stage self-selection model and several other methods to check the robustness of our finding.

Control Variables

We used country-level, industry-level, and firm-level control variables. Country-level controls included measures for geo-demographic, economic, and cultural characteristics collected from various sources, including the World Development Indicators database produced by the World Bank (2008a) and the Central Intelligence Agency's (CIA) *World Factbook* (2008). The data for the firm resource characteristics were collected from Compustat Global (2008) by Standard & Poor's and supplemented with annual reports of sample firms. Table 7.1 presents the data sources and definitions of each of our variables.

At the country level, we included the geo-demographic characteristics (country size, population, land size, and literacy rate), economic characteristics (unemployment rate, openness to trade, and openness to foreign investment), geographic closeness (adjacency and physical distance), cultural closeness (language and colonial relationship), and institutional closeness (European Union). These (host) country-level variables were consistent with the cultural, administrative, geographic, and economic distances underlined by Ghemawat (2007).

We used industry fixed effects to control for unobserved industry characteristics. At the firm level we included firm size, international experience, R&D capability, marketing capability, and financial slack resources. We expected these firm resources would increase incentives to overcome the liability of foreignness. One-year lagged control variables were also used to reduce the endogeneity problem. The summary descriptive statistics and correlation matrix for the variables are presented in Table 7.2. We note that pairwise correlations between

Table 7.2. *Descriptive statistics and correlation matrix*

	Mean (S.D.)	1.	2.	3.	4.
1. Subsidiaries	0.545 (2.761)				
2. Terrorist activities	0.300 (0.918)	0.001			
3. Natural disasters	2.180 (2.411)	0.079	0.225		
4. Technological disasters	1.990 (2.259)	0.047	0.261	0.534	
5. Government effectiveness	0.375 (0.954)	0.175	–0.126	–0.198	–0.311
6. Regulatory quality	0.391 (0.838)	0.157	–0.157	–0.247	–0.383
7. Rule of Law	0.234 (0.956)	0.163	–0.134	–0.230	–0.333
8. Voice and accountability	0.321 (0.859)	0.143	–0.196	–0.218	–0.385
9. Political stability	0.069 (0.880)	0.100	–0.357	–0.313	–0.439
10. Control of corruption	0.261 (1.045)	0.168	–0.141	–0.242	–0.350
11. Firm size	9.790 (0.910)	0.016	0.002	–0.002	–0.003
12. International experience	57.106 (30.554)	0.059	0.003	0.004	0.004
13. R&D capability	0.025 (0.050)	0.025	0.001	0.003	0.002
14. Marketing capability	0.106 (0.126)	0.060	0.000	0.003	0.002
15. Financial slack resources	1.486 (2.490)	0.007	–0.004	–0.001	–0.002

Notes: Number of observations is 31,285. Correlations greater than | ± 0.015 | are significant at the 0.05 level. Values in dimmed lettering represent the variables that do not enter the model at the same time. In the interest of space, we do not report country-level control variables (these are available upon request). When we exclude 0 values, the correlation between natural and technological disasters is 0.4.

5.	6.	7.	8.	9.	10.	11.	12.	13.	14.
0.955									
0.965	0.929								
0.845	0.864	0.836							
0.801	0.794	0.826	0.773						
0.967	0.930	0.972	0.823	0.801					
0.002	0.001	0.002	0.002	−0.003	0.002				
−0.002	−0.001	−0.003	−0.003	0.001	−0.002	0.214			
−0.001	−0.001	−0.001	−0.001	0.000	−0.001	0.022	0.474		
−0.001	−0.001	−0.002	−0.001	0.001	−0.001	−0.061	0.313	0.397	
0.000	−0.001	0.001	0.001	−0.004	0.000	−0.204	−0.043	0.028	0.190

the six governance indicators are very high. For this reason we do not include those indicators in our model at the same time.[7]

Model

Our approach is unique in that we use subsidiary-level location and investment decisions regarding both disasters and country governance in our econometric models. Our empirical model can be represented as:

$$\text{NUMSUB}_{ijt} = \alpha_0 + \sum_{l=1}^{3} \alpha_l \, \text{DISASTERS}_{jt} + \sum_{l=4}^{9} \alpha_l \, \text{GOVERN}_{jt}$$

$$+ \sum_{l=1}^{18} \delta_l \left(\text{DISASTERS}_{jt} \times \text{GOVERN}_{jt} \right)$$

$$+ \sum_{l=1}^{12} \gamma_l \, \text{COUNTRY}_{jt} + \gamma_{13} \text{INDUSTRY}_k$$

$$+ \sum_{l=14}^{18} \gamma_l \, \text{FIRM}_{it} + \gamma_{19} \text{YEAR}_t + \varepsilon_{ijkt},$$

where NUMSUB is the number of subsidiaries in a country; DISASTERS is a vector of natural disasters, technological disasters, and terrorist activities; GOVERN is a vector of the six components comprising the measure of host country governance; COUNTRY is a vector of the country-level control variables; INDUSTRY is an industry fixed effect; FIRM is a vector of the firm-level control variables; YEAR is a year fixed effect and ε_{ijkt} is an idiosyncratic error term. Subscripts i, j, k, and t represent firm, country, industry, and year, respectively.

We also included the interaction terms (δ) between the three types of disasters (DISASTERS) and the six governance variables (GOVERN) to test the moderating relationships suggested by Hypothesis 3 (see beginning of this chapter). These moderating effects, theorized in Chapter 4, constitute a key aspect of our study: namely, that each of the governance variables moderates the relationship between disaster and subsidiary strategic response.

---

[7] In the interest of space, we did not report the descriptive statistics and correlations for the country-level control variables. These are available upon request.

Since our dependent variable is a count variable with all positive integer values, a Poisson model is usually suggested for estimating our model. However, our initial analysis revealed that the variance (2.76) of our dependent variable is greater than the mean value (0.54; see Table 7.2) – a symptom of overdispersion due to unobserved heterogeneity. For this reason, we estimated our model using negative binomial regression, which accounts for greater than Poisson variation, thus correcting for problems related to unobserved heterogeneity (e.g. Almeida & Phene, 2004; Arregle et al., 2009).[8]

Results

Table 7.3 presents the results of the negative binomial regression model. We used White's (1980) heteroskedasticity-robust standard error clustered by company method to reduce the possible presence of heteroskedasticity. In the first column, we included only the control variables. The degree of overdispersion is positive and significant, indicating that the negative binomial regression model is more appropriate than a Poisson regression model. In regard to the firm-level control variables, each of the control variables showed the expected results except for R&D capability. Better firm resources (size, marketing capability, and financial slack resources) and more international experience lead MNCs to locate more subsidiaries in foreign countries. With regard to the country-level control variables, most variables showed the expected signs across the eight specifications. Overall, a country's economic size, geographic closeness, and institutional

---

[8] As a diagnostic procedure for our sample and variables, we estimated our model with ordinary least squares (OLS) regression and replaced the dependent variable (NUMSUB) with the log of (1+number of subsidiaries). Average value inflation factors (VIF) are between 4.67 and 5.04, and the highest individual VIF is about 8, except year and industry dummy variables for all eight specifications in Table 7.3. These VIF values are less than 10 and are not considered to be the symptom of multicollinearity. To identify the possible influence of outliers, we obtained information about leverage and influence. We found that two company outliers existed in the sample: Swiss Life, a Swiss MNC, and Edison SpA, an Italian MNC. We tested our model without these two companies and could not find any statistical differences in the results. Overall, the results from the OLS regression model are broadly consistent with our findings in Tables 7.3 and 7.4. We do not report the OLS regression results here, but they are available upon request.

Table 7.3. *Disasters, country governance, and subsidiary investment of MNCs: negative binomial regression model*

Dependent variable: number of a firm's foreign subsidiaries in a host country

	Base model (a)	Disasters (b)	Government effectiveness (1)	Regulatory quality (2)
Explanatory variables				
Terrorist activities		−0.1317***	−0.1248***	−0.1197***
		(0.0220)	(0.0219)	(0.0221)
Natural disasters		0.0105	0.0122	0.0096
		(0.0149)	(0.0146)	(0.0147)
Technological disasters		−0.0439*	−0.0308†	−0.0148
		(0.0182)	(0.0178)	(0.0176)
Country governance			0.4278***	0.6616***
			(0.0805)	(0.1005)
Control variables				
Firm size	0.1991***	0.2016***	0.2054***	0.2047***
	(0.0513)	(0.0510)	(0.0509)	(0.0514)
International experience	0.0075***	0.0078***	0.0079***	0.0082***
	(0.0012)	(0.0012)	(0.0012)	(0.0012)
R&D capability	−4.6915***	−4.7926***	−4.4229***	−4.5645***
	(1.0857)	(1.0619)	(1.0104)	(1.0325)
Marketing capability	0.8629***	0.8900***	0.8556***	0.9551***
	(0.2498)	(0.2488)	(0.2509)	(0.2552)
Financial slack resources	0.0200*	0.0211*	0.0207*	0.0201*
	(0.0094)	(0.0094)	(0.0095)	(0.0098)
Country size	0.6759***	0.6636***	0.3987***	0.3456***
	(0.0246)	(0.0251)	(0.0591)	(0.0553)
Population	−0.0408	0.0300	0.2891***	0.3516***
	(0.0284)	(0.0435)	(0.0668)	(0.0654)
Openness to trade	0.0087***	0.0081***	0.0054***	0.0050***
	(0.0012)	(0.0012)	(0.0011)	(0.0011)
Openness to FDI	0.0034***	0.0039***	0.0041***	0.0041***
	(0.0006)	(0.0007)	(0.0007)	(0.0006)

Country governance			
Rule of law (3)	Voice and accountability (4)	Political stability (5)	Control of corruption (6)
−0.1288***	−0.1139***	−0.0800***	−0.1276***
(0.0220)	(0.0224)	(0.0231)	(0.0218)
0.0131	0.0022	0.0142	0.0175
(0.0146)	(0.0142)	(0.0145)	(0.0145)
−0.0314†	−0.0073	−0.0273	−0.0253
(0.0184)	(0.0174)	(0.0181)	(0.0180)
0.2504**	0.6172***	0.3376***	0.3673***
(0.0812)	(0.0752)	(0.0704)	(0.0661)
0.2054***	0.2135***	0.2021***	0.2044***
(0.0510)	(0.0530)	(0.0510)	(0.0505)
0.0078***	0.0079***	0.0080***	0.0080***
(0.0012)	(0.0012)	(0.0011)	(0.0012)
−4.5612***	−4.6102***	−4.6973***	−4.5175***
(1.0144)	(0.9825)	(1.0345)	(1.0205)
0.8771***	1.0243***	0.8797***	0.8646***
(0.2492)	(0.2503)	(0.2497)	(0.2502)
0.0211*	0.0188*	0.0214*	0.0207*
(0.0094)	(0.0096)	(0.0094)	(0.0095)
0.5135***	0.4013***	0.5572***	0.4001***
(0.0589)	(0.0430)	(0.0366)	(0.0568)
0.1764**	0.3554***	0.1692**	0.2944***
(0.0655)	(0.0609)	(0.0544)	(0.0649)
0.0073***	0.0108***	0.0062***	0.0066***
(0.0011)	(0.0013)	(0.0012)	(0.0011)
0.0040***	0.0043***	0.0040***	0.0042***
(0.0007)	(0.0007)	(0.0007)	(0.0007)

Table 7.3. (*cont.*)

	Base model (a)	Disasters (b)	Government effectiveness (1)	Regulatory quality (2)
Adjacency	0.6667***	0.6692***	0.6941***	0.7313***
	(0.0949)	(0.0957)	(0.0961)	(0.0980)
Language	0.1775*	0.1731*	0.1199	0.1305
	(0.0879)	(0.0879)	(0.0902)	(0.0927)
Colonial relationship	−0.0085	0.0144	0.0419	0.0201
	(0.0981)	(0.0979)	(0.0977)	(0.1015)
Geographic distance	−0.1675***	−0.1651***	−0.1527***	−0.1728***
	(0.0323)	(0.0324)	(0.0318)	(0.0315)
Land size	0.1170***	0.1058***	0.0801***	0.0914***
	(0.0223)	(0.0220)	(0.0212)	(0.0212)
Institutional closeness	0.3625***	0.3561***	0.2866***	0.2071**
	(0.0648)	(0.0639)	(0.0633)	(0.0661)
Literacy rate	0.0039	0.0027	0.0077*	0.0061†
	(0.0037)	(0.0035)	(0.0032)	(0.0033)
Unemployment rate	−0.0015	0.0006	0.0063	0.0073†
	(0.0044)	(0.0044)	(0.0043)	(0.0042)
Log of the estimate of degree of overdispersion	1.2910*** (0.0416)	1.2829*** (0.0406)	1.2656*** (0.0400)	1.2494*** (0.0402)
Log-likelihood	−19,407	−19,372	−19,325	−19,280
Akaike information criterion	38,890	38,825	38,735	38,645
LR-test of estimation fit, χ^2		From (a) 48.65***	From (b) 28.26***	From (b) 43.34***

Notes: N = 31,285. † if $p < 0.10$, * if $p < 0.05$, ** if $p < 0.01$, *** if $p < 0.001$.
Two-tailed test. Constant, industry-fixed and year-fixed effects are estimated but not reported here. Heteroskedasticity robust standard errors are in the parentheses.
LR-test: likelihood ratio test.

Country governance			
Rule of law (3)	Voice and accountability (4)	Political stability (5)	Control of corruption (6)
0.6857***	0.7123***	0.6876***	0.6766***
(0.0964)	(0.0982)	(0.0964)	(0.0954)
0.1428	0.1054	0.1575†	0.1330
(0.0902)	(0.0928)	(0.0889)	(0.0889)
0.0290	0.0995	0.0531	0.0278
(0.0976)	(0.1016)	(0.0977)	(0.0975)
−0.1506***	−0.1422***	−0.1304***	−0.1701***
(0.0323)	(0.0316)	(0.0329)	(0.0317)
0.0996***	0.0867***	0.0745***	0.0884***
(0.0216)	(0.0212)	(0.0221)	(0.0212)
0.3242***	0.2021**	0.3282***	0.2826***
(0.0631)	(0.0643)	(0.0638)	(0.0634)
0.0064†	0.0050	0.0033	0.0096**
(0.0033)	(0.0031)	(0.0033)	(0.0033)
0.0054	−0.0018	0.0087*	0.0056
(0.0044)	(0.0046)	(0.0044)	(0.0043)
1.2782***	1.2574***	1.2791***	1.2653***
(0.0399)	(0.0385)	(0.0395)	(0.0396)
−19,353	−19,256	−19,336	−19,324
38,790	38,596	38,756	38,733
From (b)	From (b)	From (b)	From (b)
9.50**	67.36***	23.03***	30.83***

closeness positively determined an MNC's subsidiary location decision. In particular, both openness to trade and openness to FDI showed positive signs. Both variables implied that trade and FDI by European countries have a complementarity nature instead of a substitutability nature (Nearly, 2007).

The results in Table 7.3 also indicate that overall higher quality governance in the host country is positively associated with subsidiary-level investment. As shown in Table 7.3, we tested the effect of six individual governance by adding, one by one, to our regression analysis (see columns 1–6). All six governance indicators are positively related to location decision of MNCs. The LR test statistics that compare the estimation in each column with column 2 (Model b) confirms that adding governance indicators enhances the model's fit.

Disasters and Subsidiary-Level Investment (Hypothesis 1)

In the second column of Table 7.3 are the results for each of the three disaster models. The last row of the second column reports the likelihood ratio (LR) test statistics of estimation fit for the inclusion of three disaster variables. It shows the statistical significance at a $p < 0.001$ confidence level, indicating that the three disasters should be included in the European MNC location choice regression. The Akaike information criterion (Akaike, 1974), which provides information for choosing a better model fit, concludes the same results (i.e. a lower value is better). Results in column (b) offer support for Hypothesis 1, that regardless of the severity of the disaster, foreign subsidiary investment is more likely to decrease in response to technological disasters and terrorist attacks than in response to natural disasters. Indeed, there is no significant relationship between natural disasters and the number of a firm's foreign subsidiaries in the host country. We discuss this finding in more detail in the Discussion and Conclusions section of this chapter. The results of the control variables were the same as those found in the first column.

> Our findings indicated support for Hypothesis 1, that regardless of the severity of the disaster, foreign subsidiary investment is more likely to decrease in response to technological disasters and terrorist attacks than in response to natural disasters.
>
> Indeed, there is no significant relationship between natural disasters and the number of a firm's foreign subsidiaries in the host country.

Natural Disaster Subtype and MNC Subsidiary Investment (Hypothesis 2)

We disaggregated natural disasters into nine subtypes in order to test Hypothesis 2, which proposed that MNC subsidiary-level investment will be more likely to decrease in response to the natural disasters showing the highest levels of fatalities (see Table 7.4).[9] Our analysis of the direct effect of each natural disaster subtype also allowed us to identify possible aggregation bias. Consistent with our initial aggregate findings (see Table 7.3), our disaggregated analysis indicates that for five out seven subtypes of weather-related natural disasters – extreme temperature, flood, drought, wildfire, and landslide – there is no significant direct relationship between natural disasters and number of MNC foreign subsidiaries in the host country.

The exception to this trend involves windstorms and storm surges, whose significant negative direct effects indicate higher subsidiary disinvestment linked to greater severity of the deadliest subtypes of natural disasters. These findings provide support for Hypothesis 2. That is, catastrophic natural disaster types that show a pattern of significantly deadlier consequences, year after year, become harder to ignore and to underestimate as one-time historical anomalies.

Compared to other types natural disaster subtypes, windstorms and their related storm surges have been the deadliest weather-related disasters during the last few decades (Wahlstrom & Guha-Sapir, 2016). Earthquakes, as a subtype of geological disasters, also appear to show a negative and significant relationship with the number of foreign subsidiaries.[10]

MNC subsidiary disinvestment does not appear to be significantly related with weather-related natural disaster severity, except for windstorms and their surges, the deadliest weather-related natural disasters.

---

[9] The nine subtypes of natural disasters are earthquake, volcano, wave/surge, extreme temperature, flood, windstorm, drought, wildfire, and landslide (the analysis also includes subcategories of technological disasters: industrial accident, transportation accident, and miscellaneous accident).

[10] Earthquakes are the most unpredictable natural disasters, since they are not weather-related disasters linked to climate change, so we do not discuss them in our analysis.

Table 7.4. *Natural disaster subtype and MNC subsidiary investment*

Dependent variable: number of firm's foreign subsidiaries in a host country

		Country governance					
		Government effectiveness (1)	Regulatory quality (2)	Rule of law (3)	Voice and accountability (4)	Political stability (5)	Control of corruption (6)
	Natural disasters						
1.	Earthquake	-0.0699**	-0.0671**	-0.0732**	-0.0798***	-0.0697†	-0.0518†
	Country governance	0.4546***	0.6864***	0.2809***	0.7012***	0.4011***	0.3788***
	Governance × earthquake	0.0496	0.0463	-0.0026	-0.1145***	-0.0087	0.046
2.	Volcano	-0.1559	-0.1096	-0.1114	-0.3638	0.047	-0.0031
	Country governance	0.4491***	0.6800***	0.2694***	0.6993***	0.3830***	0.3757***
	Governance × volcano	0.0798†	0.0810*	0.0394	-0.0897***	0.0390*	0.0862**
3.	Storm surge	-0.0593**	-0.0476*	-0.0539*	-0.0864***	-0.0343	-0.0469*
	Country governance	0.4575***	0.6810***	0.2764***	0.7157***	0.3818***	0.3780***
	Governance × wave / surge	0.0724†	0.0771*	0.0329	-0.0899***	0.0352*	0.0803**
4.	Extreme temperature	0.0077	0.0023	0.0036	-0.0092	0.0035	0.0111
	Country governance	0.4502***	0.6798***	0.2697***	0.7000***	0.3831***	0.3792***
	Governance × extreme temperature	0.0844*	0.0830*	0.0412	-0.0872***	0.0386*	0.0865**

		(1)	(2)	(3)	(4)	(5)	(6)
5.	Flood	−0.0084	−0.0032	−0.0045	−0.0092	−0.0051	0.0051
	Country governance	0.4478***	0.6794***	0.2680***	0.6970***	0.3830***	0.3770***
	Governance × flood	0.0817†	0.0821*	0.041	−0.0893***	0.0378*	0.0871**
6.	Windstorm	−0.0610**	−0.0494*	−0.0527**	−0.0499*	−0.0601**	−0.0525**
	Country governance	0.4634***	0.6805***	0.2762***	0.7023***	0.3961***	0.3798***
	Governance × windstorm	0.1042*	0.0894*	0.0512†	−0.0930***	0.0422*	0.0931**
7.	Drought	0.1246	0.0932	0.1205	0.1132	0.1642	0.1423
	Country governance	0.4472***	0.6767***	0.2681***	0.6975***	0.3822***	0.3746***
	Governance × drought	0.0862*	0.0853*	0.041	−0.0905***	0.0434*	0.0905***
8.	Wildfires	−0.0205	−0.0444	−0.0218	−0.0303	−0.0074	−0.0169
	Country governance	0.4497***	0.6843***	0.2706***	0.6997***	0.3831***	0.3760***
	Governance × wildfires	0.0839*	0.0845*	0.0423	−0.0875***	0.0385*	0.0870**
9.	Landslides	−0.0396	−0.0331	−0.0367	−0.0225	−0.0091	−0.0334
	Country governance	0.4464***	0.6777***	0.2646***	0.6925***	0.3806***	0.3755***
	Governance × land slides	0.0699	0.0698†	0.0299	−0.0907***	0.0364*	0.0747**
	Technological disasters						
10.	Industrial accident	−0.0700**	−0.0375	−0.0580*	−0.0319	−0.0688**	−0.0547*
	Country governance	0.4731***	0.6784***	0.2846***	0.6908***	0.4055***	0.3872***
	Governance × industrial accident	0.0758†	0.0655†	0.0279	−0.1030***	0.0309†	0.0702*
11.	Transportation accident	−0.0523**	−0.0440	−0.0555**	−0.0336*	−0.0411*	−0.0443*
	Country governance	0.4226***	0.6549***	0.2383***	0.6744***	0.3567***	0.3507***
	Governance × transportation accident	0.0717†	0.0752*	0.031	−0.0890***	0.0336*	0.0768**

Table 7.4. (*cont.*)

| | Country governance | | | | | |
	Government effectiveness (1)	Regulatory quality (2)	Rule of law (3)	Voice and accountability (4)	Political stability (5)	Control of corruption (6)
12. Miscellaneous accident	-0.0095	0.013	-0.0062	0.006	-0.0109	-0.0054
Country governance	0.4487***	0.6848***	0.2685***	0.6993***	0.3844***	0.3757***
Governance × miscellaneous accident	0.0825†	0.0852*	0.0411	-0.0868***	0.0374*	0.0856**

Notes: We estimated all control variables but do not report them here. † if $p < 0.10$, * if $p < 0.05$; ** if $p < 0.01$; *** if $p < 0.001$. We do not report standard error, in the interest of space. One subtype of disasters is included in each model at a time. This table also reports the findings of additional regression models examining the moderating effect of country governance characteristics on each disaster subtype. See also notes in Table 7.3.

Moderating Effects of Country Governance Characteristics (Hypothesis 3)

In Hypothesis 3 we suggest that governance quality in the host country may moderate the relationship between disasters and subsidiary-level investment in such a way that major disasters will be less likely to lead to subsidiary disinvestment. To test this hypothesis, we included the interaction terms between our generic categories of disasters (i.e. natural, technological, and terrorist attacks) and the six governance indicators (see Table 7.5). All control variables showed consistent results with those found in Table 7.3. The last row of each column in Table 7.5 reports the LR test result that compares the model fit of the interaction model with the corresponding noninteraction model in Table 7.3 (Models 1–6). The statistics show that adding the interaction terms significantly improves the model fit.

The importance of different quality governance indicators as moderators does vary based on the generic type of disaster. For instance, the coefficient was positive and significant in the case of terrorist attacks. Yet, with respect to natural disasters, Hypothesis 3 was not supported. We found that only regulatory quality was significantly associated with a lower likelihood of subsidiary-level disinvestment after natural disasters (see Model 2 in Table 7.5).

Regulatory quality was significantly associated with a lower likelihood of subsidiary-level disinvestment after natural disasters.

For technological disasters, it does not appear that higher quality governance lowers the likelihood of subsidiary-level disinvestment post major disaster. In fact, the interaction between voice and accountability and technological disasters was significant and negative indicating that in countries where voice and accountability are higher, subsidiary-level disinvestment is significantly more likely post disaster. Thus, for technological disasters, Hypothesis 3 was also not supported.

Marginal analysis for moderating effects of country governance. As the negative binomial model is nonlinear, we further analyzed the moderating effect of country governance on the relationship between disasters and subsidiary-level investment. The marginal effect of the number of killed in terrorist activities on subsidiary-level investment is less negative for four of the country governance indicators: government effectiveness, rule of law, political stability, and control of corruption (see Figure 7.2).

Table 7.5. *Effects of interaction between disasters and country governance: negative binomial regression model*

Dependent variable: number of a firm's foreign subsidiaries in a host country

	Country governance					
	Government effectiveness (1)	Regulatory quality (2)	Rule of law (3)	Voice and accountability (4)	Political stability (5)	Control of corruption (6)
Explanatory variables						
Terrorist activities	-0.1632***	-0.1422***	-0.1455***	-0.1281***	-0.0457†	-0.1365***
	(0.0275)	(0.0265)	(0.0243)	(0.0246)	(0.0246)	(0.0241)
Natural disasters	0.0071	-0.0125	0.0146	-0.0023	0.0141	0.0126
	(0.0197)	(0.0204)	(0.0182)	(0.0181)	(0.0148)	(0.0173)
Technological disasters	-0.0231	0.0073	-0.0249	0.0173	-0.0267	-0.0207
	(0.0232)	(0.0247)	(0.0222)	(0.0231)	(0.0199)	(0.0213)
Country governance	0.3989***	0.6196***	0.2386**	0.7152***	0.2789***	0.3184***
	(0.0740)	(0.0966)	(0.0785)	(0.0805)	(0.0738)	(0.0612)
Interaction terms						
Country governance × terrorist activities	0.0909***	0.0709**	0.0716**	0.0616*	0.0694*	0.0577**
	(0.0255)	(0.0275)	(0.0237)	(0.0254)	(0.0338)	(0.0206)
Country governance × natural disasters	0.0109	0.0351*	0.0012	0.0060	0.0062	0.0135
	(0.0139)	(0.0164)	(0.0138)	(0.0143)	(0.0141)	(0.0121)
Country governance × technological disasters	-0.0009	-0.0218	-0.0060	-0.0404*	0.0010	0.0078
	(0.0148)	(0.0184)	(0.0146)	(0.0165)	(0.0179)	(0.0129)

Control variables

	(1)	(2)	(3)	(4)	(5)	(6)
Firm size	0.2029***	0.2041***	0.2027***	0.2117***	0.2008***	0.2016***
	(0.0509)	(0.0513)	(0.0508)	(0.0524)	(0.0511)	(0.0506)
International experience	0.0078***	0.0081***	0.0077***	0.0079***	0.0079***	0.0079***
	(0.0012)	(0.0012)	(0.0012)	(0.0012)	(0.0011)	(0.0012)
R&D capability	−4.4223***	−4.5226***	−4.5947***	−4.6143***	−4.7322***	−4.5123***
	(0.9896)	(1.0074)	(1.0069)	(0.9759)	(1.0276)	(1.0012)
Marketing capability	0.8959***	0.9815***	0.9065***	1.0123***	0.9059***	0.9117***
	(0.2500)	(0.2542)	(0.2481)	(0.2491)	(0.2486)	(0.2496)
Financial slack resources	0.0205*	0.0205*	0.0207*	0.01833†	0.0213*	0.0208*
	(0.0096)	(0.0098)	(0.0094)	(0.0094)	(0.0095)	(0.0097)
Country size	0.3825***	0.3343***	0.5103***	0.4040***	0.5599***	0.3831***
	(0.0607)	(0.0554)	(0.0588)	(0.0439)	(0.0364)	(0.0580)
Population	0.2976***	0.3594***	0.1705**	0.3401***	0.1613**	0.3053***
	(0.0684)	(0.0665)	(0.0656)	(0.0612)	(0.0540)	(0.0665)
Openness to trade	0.0057***	0.0053***	0.0076***	0.0112***	0.0064***	0.0070***
	(0.0011)	(0.0011)	(0.0012)	(0.0013)	(0.0012)	(0.0011)
Openness to FDI	0.0041***	0.0041***	0.0040***	0.0041***	0.0040***	0.0042***
	(0.0007)	(0.0006)	(0.0007)	(0.0006)	(0.0007)	(0.0007)
Adjacency	0.7116***	0.7463***	0.7014***	0.7308***	0.6978***	0.6955***
	(0.0967)	(0.0984)	(0.0964)	(0.0980)	(0.0967)	(0.0960)
Language	0.1238	0.1256	0.1427	0.0843	0.1575†	0.1388
	(0.0906)	(0.0926)	(0.0904)	(0.0929)	(0.0895)	(0.0894)
Colonial relationship	0.0414	0.0253	0.0307	0.1175	0.0576	0.0244
	(0.0989)	(0.1018)	(0.0984)	(0.1007)	(0.0984)	(0.0989)
Geographic distance	−0.1513***	−0.1686***	−0.1515***	−0.1308***	−0.1310***	−0.1656***
	(0.0317)	(0.0314)	(0.0323)	(0.0320)	(0.0330)	(0.0316)

Table 7.5. (*cont.*)

| | Country governance | | | | | |
	Government effectiveness (1)	Regulatory quality (2)	Rule of law (3)	Voice and accountability (4)	Political stability (5)	Control of corruption (6)
Land size	0.0825***	0.0904***	0.1043***	0.0875***	0.0750***	0.0913***
	(0.0209)	(0.0208)	(0.0214)	(0.0211)	(0.0221)	(0.0209)
Institutional closeness	0.2891***	0.2132**	0.3273***	0.1871**	0.3318***	0.2896***
	(0.0629)	(0.0658)	(0.0630)	(0.0639)	(0.0641)	(0.0632)
Literacy rate	0.0081*	0.0066*	0.0068*	0.0041	0.0034	0.0102**
	(0.0032)	(0.0032)	(0.0033)	(0.0029)	(0.0034)	(0.0032)
Unemployment rate	0.0053	0.0056	0.0051	0.0013	0.0076†	0.0034
	(0.0044)	(0.0044)	(0.0045)	(0.0046)	(0.0044)	(0.0045)
Log of the estimate of degree of overdispersion	1.2597***	1.2429***	1.2744***	1.2533***	1.2753***	1.2593***
	(0.0393)	(0.0394)	(0.0397)	(0.0381)	(0.0393)	(0.0390)
Log-likelihood	−19,313	−19,267	−19,345	−19,244	−19,330	−19,312
Akaike information criterion	38,715	38,623	38,780	38,579	38,750	38,715
LR test of estimation fit, χ^2 (From the same model of Table 7.3)	25.44***	27.51***	16.00**	23.30***	12.48**	24.25***

Note: See Notes in Table 7.3. † if $p < 0.10$, * if $p < 0.05$, ** if $p < 0.01$, *** if $p < 0.001$. LR test: likelihood ratio test.

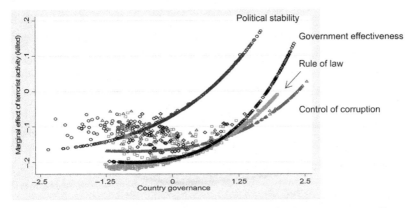

Figure 7.2 Marginal effects of terrorism, political stability, government effectiveness, rule of law, and corruption.

This suggests that the likelihood of MNC subsidiary disinvestment after a terrorist attack decreases as the quality of the host country governance increases; particularly the quality of the legal system and greater political stability. The marginal effect of terrorist activity ranges from around −0.2 when the country has the lowest scores in the four indicators, to around 0 when the country has the highest scores in rule of law and control of corruption, to 0.2 when the country has the highest governance scores in governance effectiveness and political stability.[11]

The marginal effect of natural disasters on subsidiary-level investment is positive and increases with regulatory quality, as shown in Figure 7.3, suggesting that as MNC subsidiaries gain confidence in a country's regulatory ability, they are more likely to invest in the aftermath of natural disasters. Comparatively, the marginal effect of terrorist activity on subsidiary-level investment does not change significantly as regulatory quality increases (see Figure 7.3).

Figures 7.4 show that the marginal effect of terrorist activity is negative and has a U-shaped relationship with voice and accountability. This figure also shows that the marginal effect of technological disasters on subsidiary-level investment changes from positive to negative with voice and accountability. Host countries with high voice and

[11] Our measure of the severity of event risks is number of people killed in the event. The numerical value of the marginal effect is likely much bigger when we consider the number of people killed per year in each event.

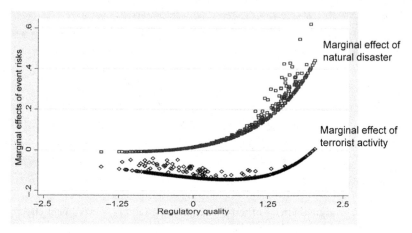

Figure 7.3 Marginal effects of terrorism, natural disaster, and regulatory quality.

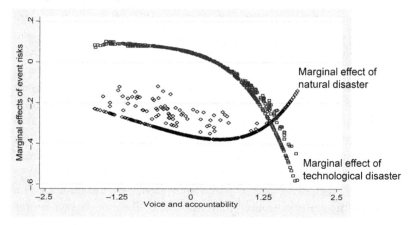

Figure 7.4 Marginal effects of terrorism, technological disaster, and voice and accountability.

accountability appear to be linked with higher MNC disinvestment when countries suffer technological disasters.

Natural Disaster Subtypes and the Moderating Effect of Country Governance on Various Dimensions on MNC Investment

We also estimated additional regression models to examine the moderating effect of country governance characteristics for different subtypes of natural disasters on MNC investment (see interaction coefficients on Table 7.4). Consistent with Hypothesis 3, regulatory quality, political stability, and/or corruption control show a consistent, positive moderating effect on the relationship between weather related disasters and subsidiary-level investment (see columns 2, 5, and 6 in Table 7.4). That is, in general the likelihood of MNC subsidiary disinvestment after weather-related disasters decreases as regulatory quality, political stability, and/or corruption control in a host country increase.

It is important to note that contrary to what we predicted in Hypothesis 3, voice and accountability, our proxy for democratic freedoms and rights, shows a negative moderating effect on the relationship between natural disasters and MNC subsidiary-level investment across all subtypes of natural disaster (see column 4 on Table 7.4). In other words, the likelihood of MNC subsidiary disinvestment across all subtypes of natural disaster increases as democratic freedoms and rights in a host country governance improve.

> The likelihood of MNC subsidiary disinvestment after weather-related disasters decreases as regulatory quality, political stability, and/or corruption control in a host country governance increase.

> Contrary to Hypothesis 3, the tendency of MNC subsidiary disinvestment across all subtypes of natural disaster increases as democratic freedoms and rights in a host country are higher.

Robustness Checks

There may exist a self-selection issue in our sample; this is because a firm is likely to set up subsidiaries in countries having lower disaster risks and better governance quality. Heckman's selection model (Heckman, 1976; Zajac & Westphal, 1996) can be implemented in a negative binomial regression model for addressing self-selection issues (McCarthy & Casey, 2008).[12] The estimation procedure is as follows: (1) we predict the probability of entering a country using a probit

---

[12] We used a non-two-stage model for our main results (1) as a parsimony principle since the results are very close, and (2) as a limitation of Heckman's two-stage model for count data and nonlinear models (Greene, 2001). In addition, we used a fixed-effects estimator by including individual firm fixed effects (or individual firm random effects), industry-fixed, and year-fixed effects. The fixed-effects estimators control both unobservable attributes and an unbalanced panel problem. We also tested our model by adding a dummy for entry in $t-1$ rather than the two-stage model. Both methods generate similar results.

model at the first stage; (2) we construct an inverse Mills ratio in order to predict the hazard of selection; and (3) we include the hazard into our negative binomial regression model at the second stage. The results of our explanatory variables and control variables are consistent with those in Table 7.5.[13]

Second, we used the ratio of the number of MNC subsidiaries in a country over the total number of MNC subsidiaries globally as a dependent variable by using an OLS regression model. Third, we used two other measures of the severity of disasters: number of incidents and duration of events. And fourth, instead of country governance indicators of WGI, we used the subcomponents of the International Country Risk Guide data by Political Risk Services (2008): government stability for government effectiveness; bureaucracy quality for regulatory quality; law and order for rule of law; democratic accountability for voice and accountability; internal and external conflict for political stability; corruption for control of corruption. Sixth, we tested our model with a larger sample by excluding some firm-level variables from the model. Overall, the robustness checks yielded results consistent with those in Tables 7.3 and 7.5.

Discussion and Conclusions

The purpose of this chapter was: (1) to empirically investigate how natural disasters, compared to other deadly hazards, shape MNCs' foreign subsidiary investments; (2) to evaluate the effect of different subtypes of natural disaster on MNC foreign subsidiary investment; and (3) to evaluate how host country governance characteristics moderate the relationship between disasters and subsidiary-level location and investment.

An important initial contribution of our study is the finding that MNC foreign subsidiary investment varies substantially depending upon the type of disaster involved. More severe terrorist attacks and technological disasters decrease MNC foreign subsidiary investment.

---

[13] A small difference is that the direct effect of rule of law turns out to be insignificant, but it is marginally significant at a 0.07 level of a one-tailed test. The direct effect of terrorist activity, which was marginally significant in Table 7.5, is insignificant, but still negative. Thus, the literature generally finds no differences between a selection model and a negative binomial regression model in count data (e.g. Baum et al., 2000).

Alternatively, natural disaster severity does not appear to affect MNC foreign subsidiary investment.

These findings challenge the commonly accepted wisdom that managers employ a risk calculus where the firm's response would be in proportion to the loss of life and the duration and severity of the disaster. In Chapter 4, we argued that, contrary to this "common wisdom," managers tend to ignore natural disasters and pay more attention to other types disasters that are perceived to be more "controllable" and to some degree more preventable, such as terrorist attacks and technological disasters (Slovic et al., 2000). To be sure, as we mentioned earlier for our period of analysis, **the average number of individuals killed in natural disasters – 757 deaths per year per country – was, respectively, about 190 times and 10 times greater than the number of fatalities for terrorist attacks and technological disasters.**

This may be because compared with natural disasters the fear and anxiety associated with terrorist attacks and industrial accidents leads to biases that exaggerate their perceived risks, leading firms to disinvest or take other dramatic steps, regardless of the actual threat to the firm or its investments.

> Our findings challenge the commonly accepted wisdom that managers employ a risk calculus where the firm's response would be in proportion to the loss of life and the duration and severity of the disaster.

> The average number of individuals killed in natural disasters – 757 deaths per year per country – was, respectively, about 190 times and 10 times greater than the number of fatalities for terrorist attacks and technological disasters. Yet, we only found that more severe terrorist attacks and technological disasters significantly decrease MNC foreign subsidiary investment. Alternatively, natural disaster severity does not appear to affect MNC foreign subsidiary investment.

> Compared to natural disasters, the fear and anxiety associated with terrorist attacks and industrial accidents generates large biases that exaggerate their risks, leading firms to disinvest regardless of the actual threat. One exception to this finding concerns windstorms and storm surges, which do appear to increase the likelihood of divestment.

Our analysis of the differential effects of natural disaster subtypes indicates that windstorms and storm surges are the exception to this trend. Windstorm and storm surge severity does appear to be linked to significantly higher MNC foreign subsidiary disinvestment. For all

other subtypes of weather-related natural disasters – extreme temperatures, floods, droughts, wildfires, and landslides – there is no significant
relationship between natural disasters and number of MNC foreign
subsidiaries in the host country. We argued in Chapter 4 that natural
hazards that that show a pattern of the highest deadly consequences,
year after year, become hard to ignore or to dismiss as one-time
historical anomalies or uncontrollable "acts of God." Compared to
other natural disasters subtypes, windstorms and their related storm
surges have been the deadliest weather-related disasters over the last
few decades (Wahlstrom & Guha-Sapir, 2016). As we discussed in the
introduction of our book (Chapter 1), climate change trends are now
known to have contributed to exacerbate the severity of windstorms
over the last few decades (IPCC, 2017).

> **Despite the typical tendency to dismiss natural disasters as uncontrol-
> lable "acts of God," catastrophic natural hazards, like windstorms,
> which show an annual pattern of the deadliest consequences, become
> hard to ignore and underestimate as one-time historical anomalies.**

Our findings also contribute to research and practice by assessing
how country governance characteristics moderate disasters' direct
effects on MNC foreign subsidiary investments. By focusing exclusively on the direct effects of disasters on subsidiary-level investment,
managers might overestimate or underestimate the risk that major
disasters pose. As a result, managers may mistakenly discontinue
(or continue) their businesses and lose a competitive position in the
market. An additional important general contribution of our study is
the finding that host country governance matters in different ways
depending upon the type of risk involved. More specifically, we find
that it is not wholly accurate to say that good governance is important
to business investment in the aftermath of disasters. When considering
our three generic disaster categories (i.e. natural, technological, and
terrorist attacks), it appears that governance quality dimensions decrease
the tendency of MNC disinvestment in the aftermath of terrorist attacks.
Similarly, when considering natural disaster subtypes, we found that
the likelihood of MNC subsidiary disinvestment after weather-related
disasters decreases as regulatory quality, political stability, and/or
corruption control in a host country governance increase.

A very interesting and counterintuitive finding (contrary to what we
predicted in Hypothesis 3) from our analysis indicates that in countries

where voice and accountability are higher, MNC subsidiary disinvestment is significantly more likely after technological disasters. Our analysis of individual natural disaster subtypes also indicates that higher voice and accountability (i.e. democratic freedoms) exacerbates the tendency of MNC subsidiary disinvestment in the aftermath of specific of natural disaster subtypes.

At first glance this appears to be a puzzling finding; the more citizens enjoy democratic freedoms that allow them to be involved in their government, to express themselves, and to be able to hold their governments accountable, the more likely MNCs are to reduce investments after technological disasters and certain types of natural disasters. Public protest in the aftermath of technological disasters – although often vital for addressing systemic problems and alleviating a disaster – can be destabilizing to governments during an emergency. Public protest may spread concerns about a government's ability to address these types of disasters and raise the possibility that more technological accidents may be forthcoming. China's responses to some recent technological and industrial crises may illustrate these concerns. After reports of lead in toys (2008), baby milk products tainted with melamine (2007), and an explosion at a state-owned chemical factory in Jilin City (2005), the Chinese government tried to suppress publicity surrounding the events in an effort to limit public protest.

Alternatively, we argued in Chapter 3 that higher disinvestment after technological disasters, and the most severe natural disaster subtypes, occurring in countries with higher levels of voice and accountability, may indicate that higher democratic freedoms allow civil society groups to more prominently highlight the negative consequences of technological and natural disasters. These enhanced freedoms and rights also allow civil society groups to pressure a government to punish those responsible and to enact better disaster preparedness policies and regulations. This is because *free speech traditions* make it easier for populations to publicly and in a timely fashion convey concerns and demands to business managers, the media, and government officials about the consequences of problematic business practices that enhance the vulnerability to disasters (Rivera, Oetzel, de Leon, & Starik, 2010). Additionally, *freedom of association* facilitates the organization of advocacy groups and coalitions that are better able to debate, promote, and politically mobilize to sustain demands for disaster prevention and response (Rivera & Oh, 2013). *Freedom of political participation and the right to vote* also play a role in promoting adequate disaster prevention and recovery regulations because groups advocating for them can support the election of like-minded politicians. Although these explanations are promising, clearly more empirical research is needed to determine exactly how the voice and accountability of citizens affects MNC responses to technological disasters and why it might lead to greater subsidiary-level disinvestment.

> Higher MNC subsidiary disinvestment after natural disasters in countries with greater democratic freedoms indicates that these freedoms and rights may allow civil society groups to more prominently highlight the negative consequences of these disasters and pressure government to punish those responsible and enact better disaster preparedness policies.

Another finding that merits further discussion concerns the fact that regulatory quality was associated with a lower likelihood of subsidiary-level disinvestment after natural disasters (as a generic group). As we discussed in Chapter 4, regulatory quality is related to the degree of devastation post natural disaster. The inability of governments to formulate and enforce sound regulations was considered a key factor in the loss of many lives and a significant portion of the property damage after the earthquakes in Turkey, in 1999, and China, in 2008. In both cases, it was alleged that the Turkish and Chinese governments did not effectively impose regulatory controls on the construction of schools, offices, and other structures (Kinzer, 2001; Transparency International, 2008). On the other hand, in response to Hurricanes Katrina and Rita, the U.S. Department of Commerce supported and organized seminars and trade missions that promoted foreign investment and tightly monitored the recovery in the Gulf Coast (U.S. Department of Commerce, 2007). Companies may strategically transform natural catastrophic disasters from risks to opportunities in countries whose higher regulatory quality provides effective implementation of post disaster recovery and preparedness plans, doing so in a way that leads to more favorable business investment environments. Depending upon the context in which disasters occur, entrepreneurial opportunities can be created if recovery plans are effective (Gopal, 2009).

Overall, our findings have important implications for business. Given the increasing frequency and severity of weather-related disasters,

MNCs that disregard these disasters do so at their peril. Additionally, firms that overreact to disasters that are perceived to be more controllable, and to some degree preventable (such as terrorist attacks and technological accidents), and disinvest in response, may be forgoing valuable business opportunities. Effectively reacting to risk is a central concern in strategic management. If an MNC develops a competency around risk assessment and management, then it may be able to more unbiasedly evaluate the competitive benefits of foreign subsidiary investment or disinvestment in the aftermath of disasters (Li & Tong, 2007).

Understanding how country governance can mitigate or exacerbate the effect of major disasters on subsidiaries can help managers better calculate investment risk when formulating their location strategy. Prior research has shown that firms' experiences and capabilities around risk management can improve strategy formulation and firm performance (Delios & Henisz, 2003). Thus, a firm may be able to develop a competitive advantage in its location strategy and response to risk. For instance, managers will be better able to analyze a host country's ability to rebound from a natural disaster ex post and thus determine whether disinvestment is an appropriate strategic response.

For policy makers, our findings demonstrate that even though governments cannot always prevent disasters, they can minimize their impact and reduce the likelihood that foreign firms will disinvest by enhancing their capabilities for addressing them. While scholars have long noted that country-level disasters do not necessarily result in financial loss or firm failure, the literature in this area does not yet fully explain when and under what conditions these disasters are likely to threaten an MNC's subsidiary-level investment. For instance, if one examines only the direct effects of major disasters on subsidiary-level investment, one will conclude that terrorist attacks and technological disasters have a negative impact. This approach (viz., only looking at direct effects) would lead managers to overestimate such risk and thus dissuade them from investing in countries that face greater risks but have the capacity to address those risks. Similarly, those MNCs that have subsidiaries on the ground when a disaster occurs may unnecessarily disinvest rather than step back and analyze how the country will address the crisis and whether or not the government has the capabilities necessary to effectively do so.

Our study may explain, at least partially, why scholars have found that similar disasters often produce widely differing casualty numbers, property losses, and economic disruptions in different countries (Davis & Seitz, 1982; Kasperson & Pijawka, 1985). For policy makers and government officials, these findings suggest that host country governments can reduce the economic damage and loss of life associated with a disaster through effective governance, better regulatory quality, more effective rule of law, greater political stability, greater public voice, and more efficient control of corruption in the policy process. Through the same mechanisms, governments may also reduce the likelihood that MNCs will disinvest after a major disaster.

Limitations. One limitation of the empirical analysis in this chapter is that we studied only large firms. Entrepreneurial firms are likely to have different decision-making rules and processes against disasters due to the differences in risk-taking behaviors and organizational responsiveness. According to Lumpkin and Dess (1996), risk-taking, proactiveness, and competitive aggressiveness are three dimensions among five in entrepreneurial orientation that determine the performance of entrepreneurial ventures. Firm-level factors may also moderate the disaster subsidiary-level response relationship. Greening and Johnson (1996) found that firms' communication-processing capabilities reduced their vulnerability to recurring crises. Similarly, other firm-level characteristics such as subsidiary experience and firm size are likely to moderate the disaster – subsidiary-level response relationship. Other research methodologies may assist in answering the research questions examined here. Survey methods, for instance, may enable researchers to obtain information on small and medium-sized firms not generally available.

In terms of future directions, a next step is to determine which firm-level factors and subsidiary characteristics may reduce (or enhance) the risk that major disasters pose to firms' investment activities and survival. It is also important to understand how managers perceive different disasters, how disasters disrupt different business functions, which strategies and tactics are most appropriate for mitigating the impact of disasters, and whether firms can gain a competitive advantage in managing disaster risk.

Appendix 7.1. *List of countries included in this study*

Western Europe	North America	Sub-Saharan Africa	Australia & Pacific Islands
Austria	Canada	Botswana	Australia
Belgium	Mexico	Cameroon	New Zealand
Denmark	United States	Ghana	Papua New Guinea
Finland		Madagascar	
France	**Central America**	Malawi	**Central & South Asia**
Germany	Bahamas	Mali	Bangladesh
Greece	Barbados	Mauritius	Cambodia
Ireland	Costa Rica	South Africa	India
Italy	Dominican Rep.	Tanzania	Indonesia
Latvia	El Salvador	Uganda	Kazakhstan
Luxembourg	Grenada	Yemen, Rep.	Malaysia
Netherlands	Guatemala	Zambia	Nepal
Norway	Guyana		Pakistan
Portugal	Honduras	**Middle East**	Philippines
Spain	Jamaica	**& North Africa**	Singapore
Sweden	Nicaragua	Armenia	Sri Lanka
Switzerland	Panama	Cyprus	Thailand
United Kingdom	Trinidad & Tobago	Egypt	Vietnam
		Georgia	
Eastern Europe	**South America**	Iran	**Eastern Asia**
Albania	Argentina	Israel	China
Bulgaria	Bolivia	Jordan	Hong Kong
Croatia	Brazil	Kuwait	Japan
Czech Republic	Chile	Morocco	Republic of Korea
Estonia	Colombia	Syria	
Hungary	Ecuador	Tunisia	
Macedonia	Paraguay	Turkey	
Poland	Peru		
Romania	Uruguay		
Russia	Venezuela		
Slovak Republic			
Slovenia			
Ukraine			

Note: 101 countries.

Appendix 7.2. *Top 25 countries affected by natural disasters, technological disasters and terrorism activities during 2001–2006*

Rank	Natural disasters Country name	Number of killed per year	Technological disasters Country name	Number of killed per year	Terrorism activities Country name	Number of killed per year
1	Indonesia	25,222.6	China	1,588.6	Russia	94.7
2	Pakistan	10,816.3	India	750.0	Indonesia	36.7
3	India	7,436.0	Bangladesh	554.6	Israel	36.6
4	Iran	4,069.1	Indonesia	476.4	United States	35.9
5	France	2,997.7	Egypt	388.1	Spain	27.4
6	Italy	2,886.9	Iran	339.0	Philippines	15.4
7	Spain	2,174.7	Russia	256.7	Pakistan	14.1
8	Germany	1,351.4	Pakistan	202.1	Egypt	10.3
9	Thailand	1,323.1	Peru	186.7	India	9.1
10	China	1,150.5	Philippines	164.3	Colombia	6.6
11	Philippines	1,011.1	Turkey	144.0	Sri Lanka	6.3
12	Bangladesh	470.4	Brazil	143.1	Thailand	5.6
13	United States	468.3	United States	136.9	Turkey	5.1
14	Portugal	397.0	Tanzania	130.9	United Kingdom	4.4
15	Vietnam	333.9	South Africa	124.6	Bangladesh	3.9
16	Belgium	303.4	Uganda	114.1	Yemen	3.9
17	Netherlands	281.3	Nepal	111.0	Morocco	3.3
18	Russia	269.7	Rep. of Korea	94.4	Tunisia	2.7
19	Guatemala	253.1	Ukraine	81.3	Uganda	2.6
20	Nepal	214.3	Morocco	78.6	Jordan	2.3
21	El Salvador	183.4	Ghana	77.7	Peru	1.4
22	Switzerland	152.3	Mexico	68.6	Syria	1.3
23	Colombia	126.6	Colombia	67.6	Armenia	1.3
24	Croatia	119.4	Paraguay	61.0	Kuwait	1.1
25	Ukraine	117.4	Vietnam	59.0	Venezuela	1.0

Note: The numbers are an average of the number of people killed by each event risk during 2000–2006.

Source: Emergency Events Database (EM-DAT) for natural and technological disasters; International Terrorism Activity Database for terrorism activities.

8 | *MNC Disaster Experience and Foreign Subsidiary Investment*

In this chapter, we empirically examine the research questions conceptually discussed in Chapter 5:

(1) Are MNCs able to gain experiential advantages from managing during natural disasters – including disasters with both low and high impacts – that enable them to enter and expand into other countries experiencing similar risks?
(2) How do MNC experiences with natural disasters compare to those associated with terrorist attacks and technological disasters?

To answer these questions, we test the following hypotheses developed as propositions in Chapter 5:

Hypothesis 1: Firm experience with natural disaster risk moderates the negative relationship between natural disaster risk and firm entry and expansion in such a way that firms with greater levels of experience operating in countries with natural disaster risk are more likely to enter and expand into other countries experiencing similar disasters.

Hypothesis 2: Firm experience with high-impact natural disasters will moderate the negative relationship between natural disaster severity and firm entry and expansion in such a way that firms with greater levels of experience with high-impact natural disasters will be more likely to enter and expand into other countries experiencing the same type of high-impact natural disaster than firms with experience with low-impact impact natural disasters.

Hypothesis 3: Compared to experience with low-impact terrorist attacks and industrial disasters, experience with low-impact natural disasters is less likely to show a positive moderating effect on the relationship between disaster severity and entry and expansion.

This chapter is a modified and updated version (with new data analysis and regression models for natural disaster subtypes) of Oetzel and Oh (2016), reproduced with permission of the journal publisher.

We find that experience with high-impact natural disasters (as well as terrorist attacks, and technological disasters) can be leveraged in expansions within an existing host country but not for initial entry into other countries experiencing similar high-impact disasters. This finding is particularly interesting when considered against prior research on experience in managing high-risk political hazards. In that research, scholars found that experience operating in countries with high-risk political hazards (defined as those with greater policy uncertainty) (Delios & Henisz, 2003) was positively related to higher entry rates into other high-risk countries (Delios & Henisz, 2003; Holburn & Zelner, 2010).

We also find that experience with low-impact **natural disasters does not appear to reduce the negative effect of** disaster severity on expansion (or entry). Yet, experience with low-impact terrorist attacks and technological disasters does **show a significant** positive moderating effect on the relationship between disaster severity and expansion. A notable exception to the lack of significant moderating effects on MNC entry models is the case of floods. Experience with high-impact floods does show a positive and significant moderating effect on the negative link between disaster severity and MNC entry. As we discussed in Chapter 4, natural disasters that show a pattern of the highest deadly consequences, year after year, become hard to ignore or to dismiss as one-time historical anomalies or uncontrollable "acts of God."

> Experience with *high-impact natural disasters* can be leveraged in expansions within an existing host country *but not for initial entry* into other countries experiencing similar high-impact disasters. Experience with low-impact natural disasters does not appear to reduce the negative effect of natural disaster severity on expansion (or entry).

A notable exception on our entry model analysis: *Experience with high-impact floods* does show a positive and significant moderating effect on the negative link between disaster severity and MNC entry.

Methodology

Data Source and Sample

We used a panel dataset with 57,500 observations from 106 European Global Fortune 500 MNCs and their subsidiaries operating across 109 countries during a seven-year period, 2001–2007. The unit of our analysis is per firm-country dyad per year. It is important to highlight that this updated dataset includes almost twice as many observations as the one used for our analysis in Chapter 7 (it also expands the period of observation an additional year to 2007). Also, the methodology in this chapter – although similar to one used in Chapter 7 – involves important differences in detail. Hence, for the sake of clarity, we chose to repeat some of the description about data, models, and variables for these two chapters.

The subsidiary information was hand-collected from each company's annual report. We included only the wholly owned subsidiaries because many firms did not report partially owned subsidiaries or the ownership information for these subsidiaries. Initially our sample of subsidiaries was taken from the 265 large European firms listed as Global Fortune 500 firms during any year between 2001 and 2007. From this group, we were able to hand-collect 152 firms' subsidiary locations from each firm's annual reports. On average, these 152 European MNCs have 29 subsidiaries in their home country and 58 subsidiaries across 18 foreign countries.

The discontinuous disasters include natural and technological disasters and terrorist attacks. For natural and technological disasters, we used the Emergency Events Database (EM-DAT 2009) provided by the Center for Research on the Epidemiology of Disaster at the Catholic University of Louvain, in Belgium. The first category, natural disasters, includes nine subtypes of disasters: droughts, earthquakes, extreme temperatures, floods, landslides, volcanic eruptions, waves/surges, wildfires, and windstorms. Technological disasters, the second category, include three subtypes of disasters: industrial accidents, transportation accidents, and miscellaneous accidents. For terrorism attacks, we used the International Terrorism Activity Database (ITERATE) assembled by Mickolus et al. (2008). The ITERATE is well-known for its use in political science and economics studies on terrorism activities.

The next step was to collect data on firm, country, and dyadic (home-host country) factors determining MNC entry and expansion. These factors were used as control variables. The sources for firm factors included Compustat Global by Standard & Poor's, OSIRIS by Bureau van Dijk, and the annual reports of sample firms. The country factors included measures for geo-demographic and economic characteristics that were mainly collected from the World Development Indicators database, produced by the World Bank. To measure the quality of country governance, we included the Worldwide Governance

Indicators presented by the World Bank. We also controlled for political constraints by using the political constraints index (POLCONIII) by Henisz (2002). The dyadic factors are geographic, institutional, and cultural closeness between home and host countries, which were collected from the U.S. Central Intelligence Agency's World Factbook and various other sources.

After removing the purely domestic firms and nonpublic firms from the sample, we merged all datasets discussed above. Due to the limitation of firm-level information and lagged information, we were able to obtain data on 106 of the European MNCs. Thus, the final sample includes 57,500 observations on the subsidiaries of 106 European MNCs operating across 109 host countries between 2001 and 2007. The home countries of 106 European MNCs include 18 European countries: Austria, Belgium, Denmark, Finland, France, Germany, Ireland, Italy, Luxembourg, Netherlands, Norway, Portugal, Russia, Spain, Sweden, Switzerland, Turkey, and the United Kingdom.[1] To ensure the final sample would be representative of the larger sample of European MNCs, we compared revenue, profits, number of foreign subsidiaries, and number of foreign countries of the 265 MNCs in the initial sample with the 106 MNCs in our final sample. We found no statistical differences between the initial and final samples.

Measures

Dependent variable. To measure MNC entry and expansion in a host country at the subsidiary level we have two dependent variables: one for an entry model and the other for an expansion model. **Entry is a binary dependent variable** (0/1), which is equal to one when a firm enters a country for the first time and zero before first entry. **The number of a firm's subsidiaries (NSUB),** our dependent variable, which is a positive integer, is a count variable for the expansion model. This measure captures substantial changes in a firm's resource commitments in a host country. The count variable is a widely used dependent variable in management research (e.g. Baum, Calabrese, & Silverman, 2000; Miller & Parkhe, 1998; Oh & Oetzel, 2011; Wadhwa & Kotha, 2006). When we compared the number of firm subsidiaries in Europe to their sales and assets there, we found the sample firms to have about

---

[1] The list of firms and host countries is available upon request.

74 percent of their subsidiaries, 70 percent of their sales, and 72 percent of their assets within the European region. Thus, we argue that NSUB is a good dependent variable for the real value of commitments in each country.

Independent variables. We used two sets of independent variables in our study: type and severity of generic disaster categories (i.e. natural, technological, and terrorist) and firm experience with a specific type of disaster. **The first independent variable was disaster severity.** We operationalized disaster severities using three types of variables: number of incidents, number of people killed, and duration of disaster. We tested each of the variables but report only on the results from the number of people killed because the results are consistent across the three types and because it is a common measure in research on disasters (Eisensee & Strömberg, 2007; Godschalk, Beatley, Berke, Brower, & Kaiser, 1998; Strömberg, 2007). The mean number of individuals killed in natural disasters was 654, and in technological disasters, 72 per year per country. The mean number of individuals killed in terrorism activities was 3 per year per country. We took a logarithmic transformation of one plus the number killed, that is, $\ln(1+\text{number killed})$. We also tested a normalized measure of disaster severity (number of people killed divided by national population) as a robustness check to reduce the skewness in the raw data. The disasters are neither rare nor skewed phenomena limited to specific countries or regions. Among the 110 host countries in this study, about 95 percent, 55 percent, and 80 percent of countries experienced natural disasters, terrorism activities, and technological disasters respectively, between 2001 and 2007 (see Appendix A for additional information). Except for Mauritius, all countries experienced more than one disaster, and 50 countries experienced all three types of disasters during the sample period.

> The mean number of individuals killed in natural disasters and technological disasters, respectively, was 654 and 72 per year per country. The mean number of individuals killed in terrorism activities was 3 per year per country.

> Among the 110 host countries in this study, about 95 percent experienced natural disaster (55 percent experienced terrorism activities, and 80 percent technological disasters) between 2001 and 2007.

Experience in disasters is our second independent variable. It accounts for MNC experience with specific disasters (i.e. natural disasters, technological disasters, and terrorist attacks). To measure disaster-specific experience we count the number of subsidiaries in countries that are affected by each type of disaster in which an MNC operated in the prior year. **We also divided the disaster-specific experience into experience in high-impact disasters and experience in low-impact disasters.** We measured experience in high-impact (low-impact) disasters by counting the number of subsidiaries in countries affected by disasters that killed more people (less people) on average than other disasters of the same type. As a robustness check, we used the 10 percent-tail of the distribution in each disaster type as a break point for high-impact and low-impact disasters. We took a log transformation to operationalize the variables of the three disaster experiences. We expect that even if a subsidiary was not directly affected by a disaster, the subsidiary would likely gain indirect experience from other available sources such as partners, suppliers, government and nongovernment agencies, and mass media.

Control variables. We controlled for firm-, country-, and dyadic-level variables. Researchers have identified several firm- and country-level factors associated with MNC entry, expansion, or survival (e.g. Delios & Henisz, 2000; Holburn & Zelner, 2010; Mata & Portugal, 2002). At the firm-level we included international diversification, firm size, financial slack resources, research and development (R&D), and marketing capabilities (Delios & Beamish, 2001). Prior research has shown that international diversification is positively associated with foreign entry and expansion. International diversification experience enables firms to overcome difficulties in entry and expansion, owing to their previous experience in foreign countries. International diversification allows a firm to gain scale or scope economies and accumulate valuable international experience for additional expansion (Hitt, Hoskisson & Kim, 1997; Wan & Hoskisson, 2003). To measure a firm's international diversification, we used an entropy measure of diversification (e.g. Errunza & Senbet, 1984; Hitt et al., 1997) based on the number of subsidiaries in Europe, North America, Asia Pacific, Latin America, and Africa. Firm size is measured using the log of the number of employees. We also tested the log of sales and the log of assets, and the results were consistent. Financial slack resources was measured by current assets divided by current liabilities; R&D capability was measured by R&D expenditures divided by sales; marketing capability was measured by selling, general, and administrative expenditures divided by sales; and managerial efficiency was measured by Tobin's q. We expected these firm resources to be positively related to firm entry and expansion into a host market. We used industry-fixed effects to control for unobserved industry characteristics.

At the country-level we included five geo-demographic characteristics, three economic characteristics, a measure of country governance quality, and a measure of political constraints. The five geo-demographic characteristics were country size (log of real gross domestic product [GDP]), population (log of population), economy growth (GDP growth), land size (log of square kilometers), and literacy rate (adult literacy rate, %). The three economic characteristics were unemployment rate (%), openness to trade (imports divided by GDP), and openness to FDI (FDI inflows divided by GDP). Our country governance quality measure was an average of six indicators (government effectiveness, voice and accountability, political stability, control of corruption, regulatory quality, and rule of law). Higher scores indicate higher governance quality and lower continuous institutional risk in a host country. The measure of political constraints was feasibility of policy change, with higher scores indicating fewer policy risks in a host country. To control for unobserved country characteristics such as disaster potential and other types of entry and expansion barriers we used country-fixed effects.

At the dyadic-level (home-host countries), we controlled for geographic closeness, cultural closeness, and institutional closeness. Two variables for geographic closeness are adjacency (a dummy for sharing common national borders) and physical distance (log of distance between home and host countries in miles). Two variables for cultural closeness are common language (a dummy for the fact that a common official language is spoken) and colonial relationship (a dummy for a post Second World War colonial relationship). A variable for institutional closeness is membership in the European Union (a dummy). The closeness provided by each of these variables lowers the costs of managerial coordination, control, and monitoring (e.g. Vachani, 1991). These country-level and dyadic-level variables are close to the cultural, administrative, geographic, and economic distances emphasized in Ghemawat (2007). All of the control variables at the firm-, country-, and dyadic-levels are conventional measures used in the literature. In addition, we included year-fixed effects to control for the effects of macro-economic policy and sociological trends such as economic liberalization and its effects on culture and information.

Model

Given that our dependent variables are binary (0/1) for an entry model and a count variable for an expansion model, we used an unconditional logit regression model for the entry model (Holburn & Zelner, 2010) and an unconditional negative binomial regression model for the expansion model. We tested both conditional and unconditional estimators of the fixed-effects logit and negative binomial models. Differences between the two estimators were minor.[2] For the expansion model, the negative binomial regression was appropriate given the overdispersion deriving from unobserved heterogeneity in our count dependent variable (standard deviation, i.e. 12.3, of our dependent variable was larger than its mean, i.e. 4.7; see Table 8.1; McFayden & Cannella, 2004; Oh & Oetzel, 2011). The probability of entry into a given country and the probability of expanding in the country are functions of the set of firm, country, and dyadic characteristics discussed above.

In our expansion model, self-selection issues may pose a limitation since a firm having extensive experience is likely to set up subsidiaries in countries having lower (or higher) disaster risks. For these reasons, we implemented Heckman's selection model (Heckman, 1979) in the negative binomial regression models (e.g. McCarthy & Casey, 2008). We will discuss several other methods used to check the robustness of our finding in the results section.

For an entry model we used the logit regression model:

$$P_{i,j,t}\left(y_{i,j,t} = 1; X\right) = f(1) = \frac{\exp\left(X_{i,j,t}\beta\right)}{1 + \exp\left(X_{i,j,t}\beta\right)}, \tag{1}$$

where $y_{i,j,t}$ is the entry (0/1) of firm i in country j at year t; $X_{i,j,t}$ is a vector of independent and control variables; and β is the vector of coefficients to be estimated by the modeling.

For an expansion model, at the first stage we use a probit regression model to predict the probability of presence in a country. At the second stage we estimate the negative binomial regression model by including an inverse Mills ratio to predict the hazard of selection, which was

---

[2] The only noticeable change was that the interaction between natural disaster and experience in low-impact disaster gained statistical significance; this was negative, providing findings quite consistent with other types of disasters.

constructed in the first stage. All variables except the interaction variables we used in the second stage were included in the first stage. In the second stage, we used the negative binomial regression model, which is:

$$P(z_{i,j,t} > 0; X) = \ln\left\{1 - \exp\left[-\exp\left(X_{i,j,t}\beta\right)\right]\right\} + y_{i,j,t}\left\{\ln\left[\frac{\exp\left(X_{i,j,t}\beta\right)}{1 + \exp\left(X_{i,j,t}\beta\right)}\right]\right\}$$

$$- \ln\left[\frac{1 + \exp\left(X_{i,j,t}\beta\right)}{\alpha}\right] + \ln\Gamma\left(y_{i,j,t} + \frac{1}{\alpha}\right) - \ln\Gamma\left(y_{i,j,t} + 1\right) - \ln\Gamma\left(\frac{1}{\alpha}\right)$$

$$- \ln\left\{1 - \left(\left[1 + \exp\left(X_{i,j,t}\beta\right)\right]\right)^{-1/\alpha}\right\}, \tag{2}$$

where $z_{i,j,t}$ is the number of subsidiaries (NSUB), Γ is a gamma function, and α is an overdispersion parameter. We estimate Equations (1) and (2) including year-, industry-, and host country-fixed effects.

Although the two-stage self-selection model efficiently reduced the potential for endogeneity and self-selection issues, we also used one-year lagged variables for both independent and control variables to control for potential endogeneity problems. It was important to do so since it is possible for reverse causality to exist; that is, the entry or expansion of foreign subsidiaries may affect variables such as international diversification, country size (GDP), country governance, political constraints, and openness to FDI.

In the entry model, we excluded the firm-country-year data points from the sample after a given firm had entered a given host country. In the expansion model, we excluded the firm-country-year data points from the sample before a given firm entered a host country. Observation numbers recorded were 47,711 for the entry model and 10,518 for the expansion model (729 entry point observations are included for both the entry and expansion models).

Results

Descriptive statistics and the correlation matrix for the variables, including interaction variables, are shown in Table 8.1. In this table we do not show the division of entry sample or the expansion sample by the total sample, due to space limitations. The descriptive statistics and correlation matrix for each sample is available upon request. We used mean-centered variables for the interaction variables. The correlations between the three disaster-experience variables (experience in natural disasters, experience in technological disasters, experience in

Table 8.1. *Mean, standard deviations, and correlation of variables[a]*

	Mean	S.D.	1.	2.	3.
1. Number of subsidiaries	0.630	3.110			
2. Killed in terrorist attacks (KTA)	0.288	0.893	−0.001		
3. Killed in natural disasters (KND)	2.215	2.449	0.080	0.227	
4. Killed in technological disasters (KTD)	2.095	2.300	0.037	0.269	0.524
5. Experience in terrorist attacks (ETA)	2.998	1.258	0.156	0.023	0.019
6. ETA × KTA	0.026	1.162	0.002	0.078	0.015
7. Experience in natural disasters (END)	3.709	1.169	0.195	0.005	0.005
8. END × KND	0.016	2.875	0.095	0.008	0.021
9. Experience in technical disasters (ETD)	3.312	1.384	0.182	0.005	−0.010
10. ETD × KTD	−0.003	3.193	0.053	0.010	0.011
11. Experience in high-impact TA (EHTA)	1.070	1.164	0.139	−0.015	−0.002
12. Experience in low-impact TA (ELTA)	3.843	1.125	0.204	0.007	−0.002
13. EHTA × KTA	−0.016	1.033	0.040	−0.030	−0.001
14. ELTA × KTA	0.007	0.964	−0.004	0.031	0.003
15. Experience in high-impact ND (EHND)	1.391	1.483	0.156	−0.008	0.031
16. Experience in low-impact ND (ELND)	3.762	1.083	0.197	−0.004	−0.018
17. EHND × KND	0.116	3.808	0.119	−0.012	0.105
18. ELND × KND	−0.046	2.683	0.069	0.001	−0.025
19. Experience in high-impact TD (EHTD)	2.194	1.426	0.175	−0.001	0.016
20. Experience in low-impact TD (ELTD)	3.653	1.063	0.202	−0.002	−0.008
21. EHTD × KTD	0.003	3.285	0.064	−0.005	0.025
22. ELTD × KTD	−0.005	2.445	0.046	0.000	−0.002
23. International experience	1.019	0.384	0.103	−0.001	−0.002
24. Firm size	9.740	1.138	0.037	−0.008	−0.005
25. Financial slack resources	0.967	0.770	0.032	0.007	0.002
26. R&D capability	0.020	0.047	0.020	0.000	−0.002
27. Marketing capability	0.418	0.428	−0.019	−0.019	−0.007
28. Managerial efficiency	0.434	0.213	−0.005	−0.001	0.000
29. Country size (log)	24.477	1.987	0.251	0.174	0.405
30. Population (log)	16.356	1.646	0.141	0.276	0.648
31. Economy growth	1.043	0.038	−0.052	0.059	0.026
32. Openness to trade	45.159	25.894	−0.052	−0.176	−0.299
33. Openness to FDI	6.994	35.450	0.008	−0.047	−0.089
34. Land size (log)	12.149	2.101	0.086	0.188	0.416
35. Literacy rate	86.945	15.918	0.108	−0.099	−0.153
36. Unemployment rate	9.406	6.664	−0.056	−0.003	−0.128
37. Adjacency country governance	0.226	0.902	0.167	−0.172	−0.242
38 Political constraints	0.359	0.193	0.076	−0.097	−0.047
39. Geographic distance	7.855	0.934	−0.129	0.070	0.176
40. Adjacency	0.033	0.178	0.170	−0.033	0.003
41. Common language	0.169	0.375	0.013	0.026	−0.082
42. Colonial relationship	0.135	0.342	−0.021	0.025	−0.079
43. Institutional closeness	0.160	0.366	0.140	−0.098	−0.101

4.	5.	6.	7.	8.	9.	10.	11.	12.	13.	14.
0.004										
0.012	0.014									
−0.002	0.699	0.017								
0.012	0.020	0.159	0.018							
−0.002	0.634	0.011	0.885	0.022						
0.020	0.025	0.174	0.030	0.449	0.036					
−0.011	0.472	0.012	0.537	0.008	0.476	0.015				
0.000	0.651	0.014	0.859	0.023	0.851	0.031	0.341			
0.003	0.012	0.512	0.009	0.125	0.019	0.145	−0.002	0.025		
0.003	0.016	0.711	−0.010	0.191	−0.017	0.222	0.025	−0.019	0.447	
−0.010	0.477	0.015	0.597	0.027	0.496	0.016	0.361	0.584	0.016	−0.005
0.002	0.646	0.009	0.838	0.016	0.827	0.031	0.525	0.881	0.017	−0.007
0.012	0.035	0.103	0.026	0.604	0.020	0.242	0.012	0.026	0.091	0.121
−0.003	0.004	0.144	0.016	0.823	0.025	0.425	0.014	0.021	0.127	0.200
0.000	0.702	0.015	0.770	0.023	0.772	0.028	0.473	0.726	0.019	−0.006
−0.002	0.604	0.013	0.826	0.017	0.762	0.029	0.477	0.904	0.015	−0.005
0.039	0.026	0.197	0.027	0.398	0.028	0.773	0.014	0.026	0.143	0.195
0.005	0.024	0.172	0.029	0.424	0.029	0.762	0.018	0.033	0.146	0.247
0.000	0.382	0.008	0.490	0.013	0.544	0.021	0.343	0.525	0.011	−0.003
−0.002	0.078	0.008	0.150	0.004	0.156	0.007	0.015	0.194	0.001	0.001
0.000	0.097	0.001	0.118	0.002	0.132	0.005	0.132	0.100	0.002	−0.002
−0.003	0.053	−0.002	0.030	−0.001	0.046	0.002	0.062	0.030	−0.005	−0.003
−0.002	−0.134	−0.016	−0.145	−0.007	−0.184	−0.007	−0.071	−0.186	−0.010	−0.008
0.000	−0.118	−0.006	−0.064	−0.007	−0.056	−0.003	−0.031	−0.061	0.000	−0.011
0.329	−0.009	0.001	0.000	0.010	−0.004	0.005	0.000	0.001	0.012	0.005
0.687	−0.001	0.014	0.002	0.009	0.001	0.013	0.001	0.003	0.001	0.006
0.060	−0.052	0.005	−0.013	0.001	−0.014	0.001	0.006	0.002	0.009	−0.001
−0.416	−0.019	−0.001	−0.006	−0.006	−0.006	−0.004	0.004	−0.003	−0.011	−0.002
−0.094	0.004	−0.006	−0.003	0.002	−0.002	0.003	−0.004	−0.005	0.004	0.000
0.504	0.002	0.010	0.002	0.005	0.002	0.010	0.000	0.002	−0.002	0.004
−0.322	−0.004	−0.012	−0.001	−0.007	−0.003	−0.007	0.000	−0.002	0.006	0.000
−0.083	0.003	0.002	0.001	−0.004	0.000	−0.007	0.000	0.001	0.000	−0.002
−0.397	−0.001	−0.020	−0.002	−0.001	−0.002	−0.007	−0.004	−0.002	0.014	−0.003
−0.229	0.010	−0.005	−0.006	−0.004	0.001	0.004	−0.010	−0.005	0.005	−0.002
0.203	−0.015	0.010	−0.027	−0.004	−0.021	−0.004	−0.009	−0.033	−0.014	−0.003
−0.041	0.036	−0.004	0.049	0.041	0.047	0.015	0.018	0.042	−0.002	−0.004
−0.015	−0.135	−0.029	−0.187	0.046	−0.187	0.009	−0.082	−0.190	−0.021	−0.037
−0.004	−0.114	−0.015	−0.178	0.067	−0.174	0.018	−0.076	−0.203	−0.008	−0.021
−0.160	−0.048	−0.008	−0.024	0.004	−0.027	0.001	−0.009	−0.021	0.007	0.006

	15.	16.	17.	18.	19.	20.
16. Experience in low-impact ND (ELND)	0.355					
17. EHND × KND	0.066	−0.002				
18. ELND × KND	−0.002	0.036	0.321			
19. Experience in high-impact TD (EHTD)	0.603	0.690	0.025	0.021		
20. Experience in low-impact TD (ELTD)	0.544	0.885	0.021	0.019	0.548	
21. EHTD × KTD	0.017	0.026	0.302	0.357	0.037	0.019
22. ELTD × KTD	0.020	0.031	0.271	0.454	0.020	0.036
23. International diversification	0.386	0.492	0.015	0.019	0.571	0.478
24. Firm size	0.184	0.119	0.007	0.001	0.097	0.182
25. Financial slack resources	0.139	0.110	0.002	0.004	0.151	0.092
26. R&D capability	0.096	0.019	0.004	−0.002	0.058	0.028
27. Marketing capability	−0.038	−0.170	−0.016	−0.005	−0.159	−0.140
28. Managerial efficiency	0.008	−0.056	−0.009	−0.003	−0.018	−0.071
29. Country size (log)	0.009	0.001	0.057	−0.011	−0.004	0.003
30. Population (log)	0.004	0.003	0.008	0.005	0.001	0.003
31. Economy growth	0.025	0.013	−0.012	0.007	−0.044	0.027
32. Openness to trade	0.009	0.002	0.004	−0.002	−0.010	0.005
33. Openness to FDI	−0.015	−0.003	0.029	−0.007	0.004	−0.010
34. Land size (log)	0.001	0.002	−0.012	0.008	0.001	0.002
35. Literacy rate	0.002	−0.001	0.028	−0.008	−0.002	−0.001
36. Unemployment rate	0.003	0.000	−0.019	0.003	0.001	0.001
37. Adjacency	−0.004	−0.002	0.059	−0.019	0.001	−0.005
38 Country governance	−0.022	−0.006	0.004	−0.007	0.005	−0.014
39. Political constraints	−0.017	−0.026	−0.092	0.035	−0.013	−0.035
40. Common language	0.029	0.033	0.092	−0.004	0.036	0.032
41. Colonial relationship	−0.131	−0.164	0.024	0.037	−0.155	−0.165
42. Geographic distance	−0.132	−0.174	0.030	0.067	−0.145	−0.183
43. Institutional closeness	−0.009	−0.015	0.079	−0.028	−0.049	0.002

	31.	32.	33.	34.
32. Openness to trade	0.050			
33. Openness to FDI	−0.019	0.337		
34. Land size (log)	0.072	−0.603	−0.225	
35. Literacy rate	−0.030	0.171	0.078	−0.183
36. Unemployment rate	0.074	−0.074	−0.086	0.014
37. Adjacency	−0.148	0.238	0.166	−0.311
38 Country governance	−0.093	0.019	0.076	−0.091
39. Political constraints	0.024	−0.168	−0.220	0.240
40. Common language	−0.061	0.047	0.125	−0.051
41. Colonial relationship	−0.068	0.043	0.051	−0.060
42. Geographic distance	−0.018	0.050	−0.038	−0.053
43. Institutional closeness	−0.096	0.137	0.190	−0.183

Notes: [a] N = 57,500. Values in dimmed lettering represent the variables that do not enter the model at the same time.

Correlations above |R| = 0.0082 are significant at $p < 0.5$; correlations above |R| = 0.0106 are significant at $p < 0.01$.

21.	22.	23.	24.	25.	26.	27.	28.	29.	30.
0.550									
0.023	0.016								
0.005	0.004	0.276							
0.006	0.004	0.188	−0.248						
0.002	0.000	0.204	0.032	0.221					
−0.006	−0.008	−0.126	0.066	0.102	−0.012				
−0.001	−0.002	−0.032	−0.117	0.539	0.041	0.279			
0.017	−0.003	−0.003	0.004	−0.001	0.001	0.006	0.002		
0.029	0.000	0.000	0.001	−0.001	−0.002	0.001	0.000	0.672	
−0.008	0.007	−0.003	0.030	−0.016	0.003	0.041	−0.001	−0.026	0.106
−0.018	0.000	−0.001	0.008	−0.003	0.004	0.014	0.003	−0.341	−0.508
−0.002	0.004	0.001	−0.009	0.004	0.001	−0.010	−0.001	−0.069	−0.225
0.022	0.001	0.000	0.001	−0.001	−0.001	0.002	−0.001	0.451	0.755
−0.008	−0.004	−0.002	−0.001	0.001	0.003	0.003	0.001	0.353	−0.216
−0.009	0.001	0.000	0.000	0.001	0.001	0.001	0.000	−0.218	−0.166
−0.007	−0.006	−0.002	−0.004	0.003	0.004	−0.003	0.002	0.413	−0.292
0.001	−0.014	−0.003	−0.013	0.005	0.000	−0.013	0.002	0.207	−0.121
0.006	−0.004	−0.023	−0.021	0.002	−0.009	0.005	0.019	−0.172	0.158
0.013	0.011	0.012	0.019	−0.001	−0.011	−0.023	−0.021	0.168	0.002
0.011	0.008	−0.059	−0.056	−0.038	0.034	0.109	0.034	−0.048	−0.064
0.012	0.020	−0.055	−0.052	−0.034	0.047	0.137	0.039	−0.086	−0.061
0.018	−0.010	−0.008	0.019	−0.014	0.008	0.050	0.003	0.281	−0.099

35.	36.	37.	38.	39.	40.	41.	42.
0.098							
0.559	−0.172						
0.334	0.059	0.461					
−0.299	−0.050	−0.417	−0.247				
0.123	−0.060	0.223	0.139	−0.392			
−0.092	−0.068	0.064	−0.076	0.065	0.177		
−0.103	−0.060	0.000	−0.096	0.130	0.020	0.686	
0.304	−0.126	0.526	0.297	−0.580	0.263	−0.070	−0.096

terrorist attacks, and experience in high-/low-impact disasters) are high, but these variables do not enter into our model at the same time. In Table 8.1 we used dimmed lettering to identify the variables that do not enter the model at the same time. The correlation matrix does not show any symptoms of multicollinearity. As a diagnostic procedure for our sample and variables, the average variance inflation factors are less than 3 for the entry model and less than 4 for the expansion model. Thus, multicollinearity is not considered a statistical issue in our analysis.

Hypotheses Tests

Table 8.2 reports the results of the entry and expansion models. In Models 1 and 2 in Table 8.2, we estimated our base models. We included the international diversification and country governance variables and control variables since the literature frequently shows that international diversification and governance quality increase the likelihood of entry and expansion into foreign countries. In Models 3–8 in Table 8.2, we included three disasters, experience with disasters, and interaction terms (interaction for disasters and experience in disasters) to test Hypothesis 1. We controlled for the interaction between disasters and international diversification because overall international diversification experience might provide valuable information about disaster risks in a foreign country. We also controlled for the interaction between disasters and country governance because a country equipped with higher governance quality might efficiently recover from disasters more quickly and effectively. Akaike information criterion (AIC) and likelihood ratio tests also show that adding new variables improves the model specifications from the base model.

In Models 3–8 in Table 8.2, natural disasters and technological disasters are negative and marginally significant ($p < 0.10$) in the entry model and negative and significant ($p < 0.001$) for the expansion model. Terrorist attacks are negative and significant only for the expansion ($p < 0.001$) models. These results indicate that generic disaster categories are negatively associated with firm expansion (but not entry).

The interactions between natural disasters (and technological disasters and terrorist attacks) and experience in such disasters are positive and significant ($p < 0.001$) only for the expansion model, providing partial support for Hypothesis 1. In general, the direct effects of natural disaster severity are negative and significant on MNC expansion. Natural disaster severity does not appear to show a significant effect on MNC entry. Similarly, experience in a natural disaster appears to show a positive and significant moderating effect on MNC expansion decisions but not their entry decisions. It is also important to note that the interaction between disasters and international diversification is positive and significant for both entry and expansion models, except for terrorist attacks in the entry model. The interaction between disasters and country governance is positive and significant only for the expansion model in cases of terrorist attacks and technological disasters.

Natural Disaster Severity Does Not Appear to Show a Significant Effect on MNC Entry

Table 8.3 shows the results for Hypotheses 2 and 3. Hypothesis 2, which predicts that firms with experience in high-impact natural disasters are more likely to enter and expand in foreign countries that are experiencing the same types of disasters than firms with experience in low-impact disasters, was supported only for the expansion model. The interaction effect between natural disasters and experience in high-impact natural disasters is positive and significant ($p < 0.001$) for the expansion models but not for the entry models. This provides partial support for Hypothesis 2 in the case of MNC expansion decisions.

> Experience with high-impact natural disasters can be leveraged in MNC subsidiary expansions in an existing host country *but not for initial entry* into other countries experiencing similar high-impact disasters.

> Experience in low-impact natural disasters does not appear to ameliorate the negative effect of natural disaster severity on MNC expansion and/or entry. Yet, experience with low-impact terrorist attacks and technological disasters can be leveraged in MNC subsidiary expansions in an existing host country experiencing similar low-impact disasters.

Hypothesis 3 suggested that compared to experience with low-impact terrorist attacks and industrial disasters, experience with low-impact natural disasters is less likely to show a positive moderating effect on the relationship between disaster severity and entry and expansion. The interaction effects between the three categories of disasters and experience in low-impact disasters is positive and significant in the expansion model for terrorist attacks ($p < 0.001$) and

Table 8.2. *Subsidiary entry and expansion: disaster, experience, and disaster-specific experience*[a]

Model	Base model		Terrorist attacks	
Variable	Entry (1)	Expansion (2)	Entry (3)	Expansion (4)
Independent variables				
Disasters			−0.1130	−0.0973***
			(0.0935)	(0.0155)
Experience in disasters[b]			0.2489***	0.4803***
			(0.0478)	(0.0364)
Interaction				
Disasters ×			0.0235	0.0503***
Experience in disasters[b]			(0.0563)	(0.0119)
Control variables				
International	2.0427***	0.0846	1.8733***	0.2406
diversification	(0.1783)	(0.2634)	(0.1830)	(0.1866)
Disasters ×			0.2273	0.1091*
International			(0.2329)	(0.0450)
diversification				
Country governance	0.5240	0.0416	0.4850	0.1061
	(0.5410)	(0.1386)	(0.5453)	(0.1316)
Disasters ×			0.0408	0.0225*
country governance			(0.0864)	(0.0107)
Firm size	0.2509***	0.1387**	0.2235***	0.0736†
	(0.0604)	(0.0469)	(0.0610)	(0.0377)
Financial slack resources	−0.0643	0.0177	−0.0912	−0.0146
	(0.0910)	(0.0180)	(0.0900)	(0.0160)
R&D capability	−8.6645***	−6.2771***	−7.6718***	−4.9825***
	(2.0908)	(0.7615)	(2.0550)	(0.5867)
Marketing capability	−0.5782***	−0.1108†	−0.5077***	−0.2148***
	(0.1219)	(0.0605)	(0.1242)	(0.0543)
Managerial efficiency	0.1463	−0.8708***	0.4993	0.2871
	(0.3259)	(0.2127)	(0.3183)	(0.2216)
Country size	3.3880***	−0.5245*	3.2787**	−0.2463
	(1.0363)	(0.2400)	(1.0463)	(0.2672)
Population	−6.0853*	0.0126	−5.9638*	−0.5805
	(2.8156)	(0.7213)	(2.8030)	(0.7123)
Economy growth	−2.5510	0.5072	−2.3565	−1.2663*
	(2.0783)	(0.6812)	(2.0869)	(0.6071)

Natural disasters		Technological disasters	
Entry (5)	Expansion (6)	Entry (7)	Expansion (8)
−0.0530†	−0.0428***	−0.0646†	−0.0737***
(0.0312)	(0.0104)	(0.0347)	(0.0140)
0.4827***	0.6373***	0.4508***	0.6029***
(0.0487)	(0.0427)	(0.0454)	(0.0379)
−0.0157	0.0239***	−0.0012	0.0280***
(0.0153)	(0.0063)	(0.0159)	(0.0078)
1.5096***	−0.0090	1.5612***	−0.0098
(0.1870)	(0.1532)	(0.1837)	(0.1543)
0.2892***	0.0749**	0.3151***	0.1056**
(0.0650)	(0.0262)	(0.0680)	(0.0362)
0.4499	0.1372	0.4369	0.1163
(0.5486)	(0.1356)	(0.5467)	(0.1244)
0.0073	0.0048	0.0470	0.0148*
(0.0274)	(0.0052)	(0.0340)	(0.0061)
0.1873**	−0.0145	0.1733**	−0.0172
(0.0603)	(0.0339)	(0.0600)	(0.0338)
−0.0684	−0.0109	−0.0538	0.0228
(0.0889)	(0.0157)	(0.0900)	(0.0155)
−6.3184**	−3.4620***	−6.0899**	−3.3429***
(2.0526)	(0.5256)	(2.0687)	(0.5282)
−0.4201***	−0.1082*	−0.3855**	−0.0944*
(0.1252)	(0.0484)	(0.1260)	(0.0478)
0.3594	0.2177	0.4381	0.3466†
(0.3167)	(0.1962)	(0.3167)	(0.1955)
3.4992***	−0.3159	3.3074**	−0.2650
(1.0575)	(0.2302)	(1.0509)	(0.2346)
−6.2460*	0.0798	−6.3116*	−0.2389
(2.8355)	(0.6829)	(2.8370)	(0.6795)
−2.4344	−1.1194†	−2.4727	−1.1650*
(2.0930)	(0.5855)	(2.0898)	(0.5759)

Table 8.2. (*cont.*)

Openness to trade	0.0010	0.0022	0.0011	0.0049*
	(0.0120)	(0.0022)	(0.0120)	(0.0022)
Openness to FDI	0.0010	0.0015*	0.0008	0.0016*
	(0.0019)	(0.0007)	(0.0019)	(0.0006)
Land size	14.8174	−1.9502	13.8801	−0.0878
	(24.6139)	(4.0650)	(24.2380)	(4.3059)
Literacy rate	0.0943	0.0230	0.0988	0.0201
	(0.0749)	(0.0192)	(0.0753)	(0.0187)
Unemployment rate	−0.0126	−0.0157	−0.0154	−0.0105
	(0.0413)	(0.0110)	(0.0413)	(0.0108)
Political constraints	−0.7184	0.1805	−0.7131	0.2220
	(0.5460)	(0.1529)	(0.5546)	(0.1510)
Adjacency	0.6841**	0.0212	0.6057*	0.0825
	(0.2472)	(0.1485)	(0.2484)	(0.1311)
Common language	−0.4216*	0.1115	−0.3610†	0.2401**
	(0.2058)	(0.1009)	(0.2057)	(0.0915)
Colonial relationship	0.5467**	−0.0018	0.5949**	0.1501
	(0.2080)	(0.1108)	(0.2039)	(0.1004)
Geographic distance	−0.5980***	−0.2641**	−0.6184***	−0.3262***
	(0.1689)	(0.0989)	(0.1601)	(0.0889)
Institutional closeness	0.2112	0.1401†	0.1988	0.1921*
	(0.1935)	(0.0817)	(0.1900)	(0.0760)
Self-selection bias		−0.0293		0.5118**
(lambda)		(0.2204)		(0.1594)
Log of degree of		−0.7798***		−1.0006***
overdispersion		(0.0619)		(0.0657)
Log-likelihood	−3,036.90	−2,2202.44	−3,015.55	−2,1490.94
AIC	6,357.81	4,4696.89	6,327.10	4,3281.88
LR-test against base model			42.71***	1,423.01***

Notes: [a] N = 47,711 for entry and 10,518 for expansion. † if $p < 0.10$, * if $p < 0.05$, ** if $p < 0.01$, *** if $p < 0.001$, two-tailed test. The expansion model is the second stage of Heckman's two-stage selection model. Constant, industry-fixed, country-fixed, and year-fixed effects are estimated but not reported here. AIC represents Akaike information criterion.

[b] As detailed in the section on the measurement of our independent variables, experience with disasters is always disaster-specific (experience with terrorist attacks is used in the terrorism model (columns 3 and 4), experience with natural disasters is used with the natural disasters model (columns 5 and 6), and experience with technological disasters in the technological disaster model (columns 7 and 8).

0.0010	0.0031	0.0009	0.0029
(0.0122)	(0.0022)	(0.0121)	(0.0023)
0.0006	0.0014*	0.0001	0.0014*
(0.0019)	(0.0006)	(0.0018)	(0.0006)
13.9965	2.5311	15.5228	2.7934
(24.6837)	(4.0828)	(24.7473)	(4.0182)
0.0959	0.0042	0.0963	0.0134
(0.0768)	(0.0186)	(0.0757)	(0.0182)
−0.0165	−0.014	−0.0201	−0.0152
(0.0421)	(0.0102)	(0.0417)	(0.0103)
−0.7070	0.2705*	−0.6107	0.3502*
(0.5559)	(0.1334)	(0.5661)	(0.1380)
0.5336*	−0.057	0.4997*	−0.0533
(0.2494)	(0.1169)	(0.2487)	(0.1176)
−0.3170	0.2513**	−0.3002	0.2510**
(0.2074)	(0.0859)	(0.2059)	(0.0864)
0.7122***	0.2405*	0.7049***	0.2299*
(0.2015)	(0.0966)	(0.2005)	(0.0962)
−0.6373***	−0.3237***	−0.6650***	−0.3454***
(0.1532)	(0.0832)	(0.1506)	(0.0836)
0.1848	0.2209**	0.1693	0.1916**
(0.1863)	(0.0722)	(0.1852)	(0.0728)
	0.3095*		0.3185*
	(0.1355)		(0.1361)
	−1.1634***		−1.1603***
	(0.0710)		(0.0710)
−2,970.92	−2,0974.38	−2,967.95	−2,0969.08
6,237.84	4,2248.75	6,229.90	4,2238.16
131.97***	2,456.14***	137.90***	2,466.72***

Table 8.3. *Experience in high-impact and low-impact disasters: role of experience*[a]

Model	Terrorist attacks		Natural disasters		Technological disasters	
Variable	Entry (1)	Expansion (2)	Entry (3)	Expansion (4)	Entry (5)	Expansion (6)
Independent variables						
Disasters	-0.1097	-0.1025***	-0.0552†	-0.0378***	-0.0676*	-0.0550***
	(0.0930)	(0.0171)	(0.0305)	(0.0104)	(0.0342)	(0.0128)
Experience in high-impact disasters	0.1178*	0.0800***	0.2516***	0.1010***	0.1528**	0.2162***
	(0.0464)	(0.0150)	(0.0416)	(0.0189)	(0.0484)	(0.0242)
Experience in low-impact disasters	0.4166***	0.6637***	0.2666***	0.5756***	0.3346***	0.4837***
	(0.0536)	(0.0372)	(0.0567)	(0.0378)	(0.0622)	(0.0366)
Interactions						
Disasters × experience in high-impact disasters	0.0186	0.1106***	0.0031	0.0231***	0.0069	0.0412***
	(0.0434)	(0.0149)	(0.0106)	(0.0033)	(0.0165)	(0.0077)
Disasters × experience in low-impact disasters	0.0187	-0.0726***	-0.0286	-0.0098	-0.0019	-0.0238**
	(0.0657)	(0.0123)	(0.0177)	(0.0065)	(0.0206)	(0.0091)
Control variables						
International diversification	1.5147***	-0.0053	1.4066***	-0.1260	1.4554***	-0.1596
	(0.1899)	(0.1352)	(0.1852)	(0.1379)	(0.1979)	(0.1348)
Disasters × international diversification	0.2089	0.0721†	0.2932***	0.0474†	0.2985***	0.0479
	(0.2329)	(0.0434)	(0.0647)	(0.0257)	(0.0703)	(0.0365)
Country governance	0.5007	0.0463	0.5051	0.1756	0.4652	0.044
	(0.5472)	(0.1260)	(0.5502)	(0.1301)	(0.5462)	(0.1315)
Disasters × country governance	0.0334	-0.0144	0.0044	-0.0014	0.0443	0.0120†
	(0.0845)	(0.0110)	(0.0272)	(0.0054)	(0.0342)	(0.0063)

	(1)	(2)	(3)	(4)	(5)	(6)
Firm size	0.1948**	−0.0046	0.1955**	0.0131	0.2058***	0.0052
	(0.0611)	(0.0329)	(0.0602)	(0.0339)	(0.0612)	(0.0329)
Financial slack resources	−0.0732	−0.0011	−0.0954	−0.0018	−0.0753	−0.0019
	(0.0898)	(0.0155)	(0.0903)	(0.0156)	(0.0894)	(0.0157)
R&D capability	−6.6200**	−3.1329***	−7.4008***	−3.3133***	−6.4138**	−3.0875***
	(2.1028)	(0.5227)	(2.1871)	(0.5253)	(2.0856)	(0.5178)
Marketing capability	−0.3829**	−0.0879†	−0.4522***	−0.0952*	−0.4208***	−0.1062*
	(0.1250)	(0.0475)	(0.1253)	(0.0483)	(0.1244)	(0.0480)
Managerial efficiency	0.2548	0.0575	0.3374	−0.0508	0.2534	0.0702
	(0.3138)	(0.1856)	(0.3130)	(0.1814)	(0.3160)	(0.1835)
Country size	3.2309**	−0.1767	3.4058**	−0.4343†	3.3883**	−0.0389
	(1.0496)	(0.2361)	(1.0640)	(0.2311)	(1.0547)	(0.2418)
Population	−5.8255*	0.1896	−6.2043*	−0.3142	−6.1217*	−0.2755
	(2.8080)	(0.6706)	(2.8202)	(0.6895)	(2.8443)	(0.6803)
Economy growth	−2.3136	−1.3726*	−2.5072	−0.9951	−2.4649	−1.1332†
	(2.0886)	(0.5777)	(2.1063)	(0.6058)	(2.1032)	(0.6027)
Openness to trade	0.0009	0.0029	0.0015	0.0018	0.0018	0.0031
	(0.0120)	(0.0022)	(0.0121)	(0.0022)	(0.0121)	(0.0022)
Openness to FDI	0.0005	0.0015**	0.0005	0.0009†	0.0002	0.0017**
	(0.0019)	(0.0006)	(0.0019)	(0.0006)	(0.0019)	(0.0006)
Land size	14.5279	2.7194	14.2241	6.8221	14.8113	1.8622
	(24.4573)	(4.0477)	(24.7769)	(4.2245)	(24.7494)	(4.0375)
Literacy rate	0.0983	0.0083	0.0963	−0.0028	0.0998	0.0246
	(0.0760)	(0.0186)	(0.0763)	(0.0187)	(0.0758)	(0.0190)
Unemployment rate	−0.0205	−0.0154	−0.0183	−0.0162	−0.0206	−0.0179†
	(0.0416)	(0.0102)	(0.0423)	(0.0105)	(0.0418)	(0.0103)

Table 8.3. (cont.)

Model	Terrorist attacks		Natural disasters		Technological disasters	
Variable	Entry (1)	Expansion (2)	Entry (3)	Expansion (4)	Entry (5)	Expansion (6)
Political constraints	-0.7184	0.1744	-0.6735	0.2170	-0.6140	0.2809*
	(0.5585)	(0.1321)	(0.5556)	(0.1406)	(0.5669)	(0.1368)
Adjacency	0.5667*	0.0114	0.6045*	-0.0223	0.6028*	0.002
	(0.2539)	(0.1146)	(0.2482)	(0.1140)	(0.2519)	(0.1144)
Common language	-0.3258	0.2377**	-0.3443†	0.2389**	-0.3352	0.2444**
	(0.2083)	(0.0849)	(0.2075)	(0.0847)	(0.2074)	(0.0847)
Colonial relationship	0.7246***	0.3273***	0.7241***	0.2681**	0.7018***	0.2890**
	(0.2031)	(0.0951)	(0.2010)	(0.0950)	(0.2018)	(0.0936)
Geographic distance	-0.6024***	-0.2957***	-0.5922***	-0.2980***	-0.6236***	-0.2856***
	(0.1643)	(0.0826)	(0.1597)	(0.0821)	(0.1584)	(0.0833)
Institutional closeness	0.2189	0.2247**	0.1947	0.2169**	0.1652	0.1799*
	(0.1885)	(0.0708)	(0.1875)	(0.0712)	(0.1883)	(0.0726)
Self-selection bias (lambda)		0.3886**		0.2624*		0.3313**
		(0.1218)		(0.1229)		(0.1246)
Log of degree of overdispersion		-1.2031***		-1.1768***		-1.1796***
		(0.0710)		(0.0716)		(0.0712)
Log-likelihood	-2,982.77	-2,0850.46	-2,973.86	-2,0932.02	-2,977.38	-2,0915.37
AIC	6,263.53	4,2006.92	6,245.73	4,2168.03	6,252.76	4,2134.74
LR-test against base model	108.27***	2,703.97***	126.08***	2,540.86***	119.05***	2,574.14***

[a] See notes in 8.2.

Figures 8.1–8.2 Interaction effects of experience in high- and low-impact disasters as a function of terrorist attacks.

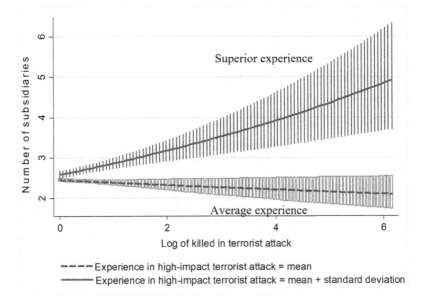

Figure 8.1 High-impact terrorist attacks.

technological disasters ($p < 0.01$), and insignificant for natural disasters. The effects are insignificant in the entry model for all three generic types of disasters. Therefore, Hypothesis 3 is supported for the expansion decision but not supported for the entry decision. We discuss the differences between the entry and expansion models in the Discussion section.

It is also noteworthy that our results indicate that the direct effect of experience in high-impact disasters, of all generic types, is weaker than the direct effect of experience in low-impact disasters. This suggests that a firm with catastrophic disaster experience is likely to be more conservative in making foreign expansion decisions. On the other hand, experiencing trivial disasters may lead a firm to generate overconfidence (or negative experience spillover, as described in Zollo & Reuer, 2010) in international expansion. However, when a foreign country has a disaster, only experience with high-impact disasters enables a firm to transform country risks into business opportunities.

Figures 8.1–8.6 depict the interaction effects of experience with high- and low-impact disasters as a function of each of the three discontinuous

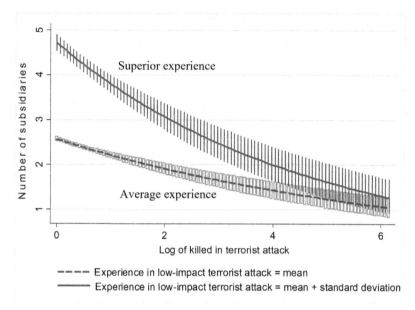

Figure 8.2 Low-impact terrorist attacks.

Figures 8.3–8.4 Interaction effects of experience in high- and low-impact disasters as a function of natural disasters.

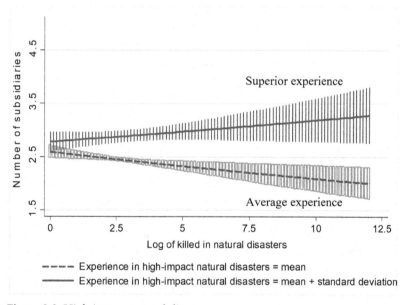

Figure 8.3 High-impact natural disasters.

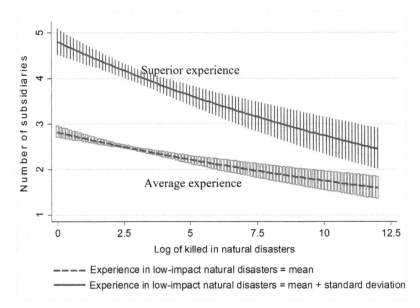

Figure 8.4 Low-impact natural disasters.

Figures 8.5–8.6 Interaction effects of experience in high- and low-impact disasters as a function of technological disasters.

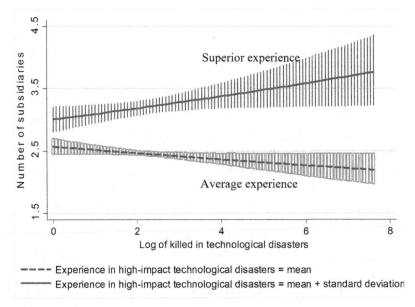

Figure 8.5 High-impact technological disasters.

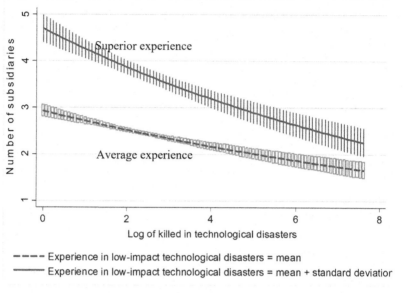

Figure 8.6 Low-impact technological disasters.

disasters in the expansion model. Due to the nonlinearity of our model, we cannot easily identify the estimated change in the dependent variable from the coefficients of the variables (Greene, 2010; Zelner, 2009). Zelner (2009). Hence, as we did in Chapter 7, we employed a simulation-based approach suggested by King, Tomz and Wittenberg (2000). In fact, Figures 8.1–8.6 depict an informative graphical interpretation for the interaction effects. One thousand simulations were used to estimate the 95 percent confidence intervals (deemed vertical lines in these figures) for the distribution of the coefficients.

Along with the 95 percent confidence intervals, the predicted number of subsidiaries associated with experience in high- and low-impact disasters at different levels of disaster severity is shown in Figures 8.1–8.6. Each graph has two predicted values: one for the mean (i.e. average experience in disasters represented by the dotted lines) and the other one for the mean plus one standard deviation (i.e. superior experience in disasters represented by the solid lines). Three interaction effects regarding high-impact disasters (see the three graphs on the left-hand side, Figures 8.1, 8.3, and 8.5) show that in countries where disasters are severe, having greater experience operating during high-impact disasters enables an MNC to use its experience to invest and expand into the country (i.e. increase its number of subsidiaries). In contrast, an MNC having only average experience in high-impact disasters may not be able to leverage its experience as a resource (i.e. it slightly reduces its number of subsidiaries). Thus, the effect of experience with high-impact disasters on the predicted number of subsidiaries is an increasing function with respect to severity of disaster.

> In countries where natural disasters are severe, the possession of superior experience in high-impact natural disasters enables the MNC to use its experience to increase the number of its subsidiaries in a country. In contrast, an MNC having only moderate levels of experience with high-impact natural disasters may not be able to leverage its experience as a resource to increase the number of subsidiaries.

As examples, firms having one standard deviation more experience in high-impact natural disasters (e.g. L'Oréal, Novartis, Royal Dutch Shell) are predicted to have 0.2 more subsidiaries in a country (such as Russia and Vietnam) that has one standard deviation above the mean killed than a country at the mean such as Argentina, Saudi Arabia, and South Africa, ceteris paribus. These cases illustrate that our results are not only statistically significant but also economically meaningful.[3] In particular, an experience-based capability can be shared within an MNC, and the economic effect of experience in high-impact disasters at the MNC-level should be significant enough to generate competitive advantages.

In comparison, the three interaction effects regarding low-impact disasters (see the three graphs on the right-hand, Figures 8.2, 8.4,

---

[3] Similarly, Danone, Lafarge, and Maersk, which have a single standard deviation more experience in high-impact terrorist attacks, are predicted to have 0.35 more subsidiaries in a country (such as Bangladesh and the U.K.) where number of persons killed is one standard deviation above the mean compared to countries like Peru, Slovenia, and Venezuela, where the statistic is equal to the mean, ceteris paribus. This increase in the number of subsidiaries is 10 percent of the mean and 5 percent of the standard deviation of the dependent variable. The magnitude of this effect is equivalent to the magnitude estimated when we reduce the geographic distance from France–Turkey to France–Sweden (which is about one-third the standard deviation of the geographic distance variable). Likewise, firms (e.g. Bertelsmann, Carrefour, Enel, and Nestlé) having one standard deviation more experience in high-impact technological disasters are predicted to have 0.25 more subsidiaries in a country (such as United States and Turkey) having one standard deviation above the mean killed compared with a country where the number killed is equal to the mean, such as Ecuador and Japan, ceteris paribus.

and 8.6) COshow that when an MNC has superior experience with low-impact disasters, it is likely to expand in countries where disaster severity is low. However, when disaster severity is high, an MNC with superior experience with low-impact disasters is not likely to expand more than other MNCs with average experience. Superior experience with low-impact disasters is always more valuable than average experience, but the effect of experience with low-impact disasters on the predicted number of subsidiaries is always a decreasing function of the severity of each disaster. Thus, experience with low-impact disasters cannot be transferred as a resource to countries in which disasters are severe. In sum, the interaction effects are theoretically important, statistically significant, and economically meaningful.

> When an MNC has superior experience with low-impact natural disasters, it is likely to expand in countries where disaster severity is low. However, when disaster severity is high the MNC with superior experience with low-impact disasters is not better than other MNCs with average experience with low-impact disasters.

Natural Disaster Subtypes and the Moderating Effect of High- and Low-Impact Experience

Besides examining generic categories of disasters – natural, technological, and terrorist events – we extended our regression analysis to examine our hypotheses for nine specific subtypes of natural disaster: earthquakes, volcano eruptions, extreme temperatures, floods, storms, droughts, wildfires, landslides, and epidemics (see Tables 8.4 and 8.5 for entry models, and Tables 8.6 and 8.7 for expansion models). As we mentioned before, weather-related disasters (e.g. floods, storms, slides, extreme temperatures, droughts, and wildfires) have attracted the most international attention because of the acute increase in their frequency and their exponential growth in fatalities and economic damage. Natural scientists increasingly agree that climate change is one of the key factors contributing toward the increased intensity, frequency, and duration of these calamitous events (IPCC, 2017; NAS, 2016).

Table 8.4 reports the results of the entry models for different subtypes of natural disasters. None of the subtypes show a significant direct impact on an MNC's entry decision (see Models 1–9 on Table 8.4). The interactions between natural disaster subtypes and experience with such disasters are also insignificant for all the different subtypes of natural

Table 8.4. *Direct effects of natural disasters by subtype on MNC subsidiary entry*

Dependent variable: Firm entry into a host country

Type of disaster Variable	Earthquake (1)	Volcano (2)	Drought (3)	Epidemic (4)	Extreme temp. (5)	Floods (6)	Mass movements (7)	Storm (8)	Wildfire (9)
Independent variables									
Disasters	0.0223	0.3014	0.0271	−0.0356	0.0021	−0.0161	0.0027	−0.0737	−0.0289
	(0.0331)	(0.4357)	(0.0963)	(0.0463)	(0.0243)	(0.0394)	(0.0491)	(0.0467)	(0.1089)
Log-likelihood	−3,080.88	−3,080.89	−3,081.07	−3,080.81	−3,081.10	−3,081.02	−3,081.11	−3,079.85	−3,081.07
AIC	6,447.77	6,447.77	6,448.14	6,447.61	6,448.21	6,448.05	6,448.21	6,445.69	6,448.14

Notes: † if $p < 0.10$, * if $p < 0.05$; ** if $p < 0.01$; *** if $p < 0.001$. See also notes in Table 8.2. We estimated all control variables but do not report them here due to the interest of space. One subtype of disaster at a time is included in each model.

Table 8.5. *The moderating effects of international experience by natural disaster subtype*

Dependent variable: Firm entry into a host country

Type of disaster Variable	Earthquake (1)	Volcano (2)	Drought (3)	Epidemic (4)	Extreme temp. (5)	Floods (6)	Mass movements (7)	Storm (8)	Wildfire (9)
Independent variables									
Disasters	-0.0103	0.0390	-0.0109	-0.0588	-0.0259	-0.0080	-0.0399	-0.0772	0.0416
	(0.0386)	(0.4768)	(0.1320)	(0.0567)	(0.0278)	(0.0469)	(0.0602)	(0.0539)	(0.1313)
Experience in disasters	0.1811***	0.1991***	0.2356***	0.2460***	0.2858***	0.2949***	0.1466**	0.2554***	0.2620***
	(0.0426)	(0.0558)	(0.0457)	(0.0482)	(0.0444)	(0.0478)	(0.0462)	(0.0493)	(0.0418)
Interaction									
Disasters × experience in disasters	-0.0020	0.3029	-0.2002+	-0.0189	-0.0122	0.0090	0.0602+	-0.0189	-0.1378+
	(0.0228)	(0.3724)	(0.1145)	(0.0380)	(0.0173)	(0.0225)	(0.0335)	(0.0275)	(0.0762)
Log-likelihood	-2,405.04	-2,407.47	-2,399.04	-2,399.62	-2,393.18	-2,394.48	-2,407.32	-2,399.04	-2,393.41
AIC	5,088.08	5,092.94	5,076.07	5,077.24	5,064.37	5,066.95	5,092.64	5,076.08	5,064.82

Notes: † if $p < 0.10$, * if $p < 0.05$; ** if $p < 0.01$; *** if $p < 0.001$. See also notes in Table 8.2. We estimated all control variables but do not report them here due to the interest of space. One subtype of disaster at a time is included in each model.

Table 8.6. Direct effects of natural disasters by subtypes on MNC subsidiary expansion

Dependent variable: the number of firm's foreign subsidiaries in a host country

Type of disaster Variable	Earthquake (1)	Volcano (2)	Drought (3)	Epidemic (4)	Extreme temp. (5)	Floods (6)	Mass movements (7)	Storm (8)	Wildfire (9)
Independent variables									
Disasters	-0.0007	-0.0473	-0.0024	-0.0024	0.0016	-0.0010	-0.0071	-0.0192+	-0.0192+
	(0.0097)	(0.1416)	(0.0284)	(0.0284)	(0.0049)	(0.0097)	(0.0115)	(0.0103)	(0.0103)
Self-selection bias (lambda)	-0.0773	-0.0773	-0.0772	-0.0773	-0.0777	-0.0772	-0.0771	-0.0776	-0.0785
	(0.0830)	(0.0830)	(0.0830)	(0.0830)	(0.0830)	(0.0830)	(0.0830)	(0.0829)	(0.0830)
Log-likelihood	-22,475.23	-22475.18	-22475.2307	-22475.1996	-22475.1807	-22475.2289	-22475.0431	-22473.4821	-22474.8916
AIC	45,254.46	45254.36	45254.4614	45254.3991	45254.3615	45254.4579	45254.0861	45250.9641	45253.7831

Notes: † if $p < 0.10$, * if $p < 0.05$; ** if $p < 0.01$; *** if $p < 0.001$. See also notes in Table 8.2. We estimated all control variables but do not report them here due to the interest of space. One subtype of disaster at a time is included in each model.

Table 8.7. *The moderating effects of international experience by natural disaster subtype*

Dependent variable: the number of firm's foreign subsidiaries in a host country

Type of disaster Variable	Earthquake (1)	Volcano (2)	Drought (3)	Epidemic (4)	Extreme temp. (5)	Floods (6)	Mass movements (7)	Storm (8)	Wildfire (9)
Independent variables									
Disasters	-0.0303*	-0.2371	-0.0903*	-0.0330*	-0.0026	-0.0404***	-0.0366*	-0.0674***	-0.1052***
	(0.0143)	(0.2021)	(0.0383)	(0.0138)	(0.0054)	(0.0119)	(0.0152)	(0.0119)	(0.0246)
Experience in disasters	0.3225***	0.2430***	0.2941***	0.2677***	0.4726***	0.5003***	0.2903***	0.4588***	0.3854***
	(0.0172)	(0.0191)	(0.0171)	(0.0167)	(0.0183)	(0.0197)	(0.0173)	(0.0209)	(0.0165)
Interaction									
Disasters × experience in disasters	0.0209**	0.1089	0.0708**	0.0278***	0.0023	0.0298***	0.0286***	0.0434***	0.1246***
	(0.0069)	(0.1342)	(0.0223)	(0.0081)	(0.0032)	(0.0055)	(0.0074)	(0.0052)	(0.0136)
Control variables	Included	Included	Included	Included	Included	Included	Included	Included	Included
Self-selection bias (lambda)	0.1438+	-0.0064	-0.0349	0.0137	0.2241**	0.0951	0.0747	0.1561*	0.1277
	(0.0760)	(0.0810)	(0.0756)	(0.0739)	(0.0757)	(0.0742)	(0.0751)	(0.0769)	(0.0796)
Log-likelihood	-18,293.63	-18,508.02	-18,306.61	-18,412.26	-17,948.59	-17,924.44	-18,353.70	-17,986.48	-18,030.94
AIC	36,895.27	37,324.05	36,921.23	37,132.51	36,205.18	36,156.88	37,015.40	36,280.97	36,369.89

Notes: † if $p < 0.10$, * if $p < 0.05$; ** if $p < 0.01$; *** if $p < 0.001$. See also notes in Table 8.2. We estimated all control variables but do not report them here in the interest of space. One subtype of disaster is included in each model at a time.

disasters (see Table 8.5, Models 1–9). **These findings for entry models do not provide support for the Hypothesis 1 prediction** that MNC experience with natural disaster risk ameliorates the negative relationship between natural disaster risk and firm entry. The findings for natural disaster subtypes are consistent with those observed for the entry models grouping natural disasters into a single generic category (see Table 8.2).

Regarding MNC expansion and natural disaster subtypes, Models 1–9 in Table 8.6 also show that the severity of different subtypes of natural disasters does not appear to be directly and significantly related to MNC subsidiary expansion. Storms and wildfires (Models 8 and 9 in Table 8.6) show a marginally significant direct negative effect ($p < 0.10$). For these expansion models, the interactions between natural disaster subtypes and experience with such disasters are positive and significant for all the different subtypes of weather-related natural disasters except extreme temperatures (see Table 8.7, Models 1–9). **These findings for the expansion models provide partial support for the Hypothesis 1 prediction** that MNC experience with natural disaster risk ameliorates the negative relationship between natural disaster risk and firm expansion. These findings for natural disaster subtypes are consistent with those observed for the expansion models that group natural disasters into a single generic category (see Table 8.2).

Tables 8.8 and 8.9 show the natural disaster subtype results for experience with high- and low-impact disaster severity. **Hypothesis 2**–which predicts that firms having experience with high-impact natural disasters are more likely to enter and expand in foreign countries experiencing the same types of disasters than are firms having experience with low-impact disasters – **was supported only for the expansion model** (see Table 8.9) but not for the entry models (see Table 8.8). For the expansion models, the interaction effects between natural disasters and experience with high-impact natural disasters is positive and significant for all weather-related disaster subtypes *except droughts* (see Model 3 and Models 5–9). These findings provide partial support for Hypothesis 2 and are consistent with those observed for the expansion models grouping natural disasters into a single generic category (see Table 8.2). High-impact experience ameliorates the negative relationship between disaster severity and expansion (but not entry) for the following subtypes of weather-related natural disasters: extreme temperatures, floods, mass movements, storms, and wildfires. For MNC entry, a notable exception is the case of floods and mass movements (see Models 6 and 7,

Table 8.8. *Experience with high-impact and low-impact natural disaster sub-types and MNC subsidiary entry*

Dependent variable: Firm entry into a host country

Type of disaster Variable	Earthquake (1)	Volcano (2)	Drought (3)	Epidemic (4)	Extreme temp. (5)	Floods (6)	Mass movements (7)	Storm (8)	Wildfire (9)
Independent variables									
Disasters	0.0062	−0.0071	−0.2253	−0.0285	−0.0243	0.0020	−0.0252	−0.0708	0.0463
	(0.0389)	(0.5825)	(18.6661)	(0.0593)	(0.0299)	(0.0473)	(0.0632)	(0.0555)	(0.1294)
Experience in high-impact disasters	−0.2558*	−0.4175+	−0.8139	−0.0175	0.2838***	−0.1490**	−0.0620	−0.4279***	−0.0807+
	(0.1077)	(0.2205)	(12.7947)	(0.0736)	(0.0582)	(0.0487)	(0.0545)	(0.0593)	(0.0488)
Experience in Low-impact disasters	0.5666***	0.5444***	0.5638***	0.5404***	0.3556***	0.6703***	0.5896***	0.8532***	0.5914***
	(0.0562)	(0.0552)	(0.0557)	(0.0595)	(0.0594)	(0.0659)	(0.0633)	(0.0667)	(0.0620)
Interaction									
Disasters × experience in High-impact disasters	0.0364	1.0839	−5.7568	0.0619	−0.0008	0.0506*	0.0817*	0.0116	0.0219
	(0.0546)	(0.9518)	(331.4565)	(0.0623)	(0.0238)	(0.0213)	(0.0363)	(0.0268)	(0.0774)
Disasters × experience in Low-impact disasters	−0.0376	−0.0134	−0.1853+	−0.0657	0.0056	−0.0596*	−0.0309	−0.0143	−0.1458
	(0.0322)	(0.4905)	(0.0990)	(0.0540)	(0.0198)	(0.0298)	(0.0497)	(0.0344)	(0.1065)
Log-likelihood	−2,362.50	−2,364.02	−2,360.54	−2,360.78	−2,361.27	−2,354.93	−2,359.30	−2,325.44	−2,363.56
AIC	5,007.00	5,010.04	5,003.08	5,003.57	5,004.54	4,991.86	5,000.61	4,932.88	5,009.13

Notes: † if $p < 0.10$, * if $p < 0.05$; ** if $p < 0.01$; *** if $p < 0.001$. See also notes in Table 8.2. We estimated all control variables but do not report them here in the interest of space. One disaster subtype is included in each model at a time.

Table 8.9. *Experience with high-impact and low-impact natural disaster sub-types and MNC subsidiary expansion*

Dependent variable: Number of firm's foreign subsidiaries in a host country

Type of disaster Variable	Earthquake (1)	Volcano (2)	Drought (3)	Epidemic (4)	Extreme temp. (5)	Floods (6)	Mass movements (7)	Storm (8)	Wildfire (9)
Independent variables									
Disasters	−0.0060	−0.0164	−0.0177	−0.0166	−0.0306***	−0.0162	−0.0315*	−0.0610***	−0.0491*
	(0.0130)	(0.2862)	(0.0386)	(0.0129)	(0.0066)	(0.0115)	(0.0160)	(0.0119)	(0.0245)
Experience in high-impact disasters	−0.0060	0.0102	−0.0780*	0.0292+	0.1183***	0.0452***	0.0469***	0.0515***	0.1306***
	(0.0173)	(0.0307)	(0.0376)	(0.0154)	(0.0144)	(0.0119)	(0.0133)	(0.0140)	(0.0112)
Experience in low-impact disasters	0.6549***	0.6512***	0.6590***	0.6316***	0.5295***	0.6114***	0.6111***	0.5540***	0.5298***
	(0.0221)	(0.0223)	(0.0222)	(0.0220)	(0.0203)	(0.0217)	(0.0212)	(0.0227)	(0.0228)
Interaction									
Disasters × experience in high-impact disasters	0.0127	0.1493	0.0677	0.0262*	0.0179***	0.0337***	0.0276**	0.0635***	0.0372***
	(0.0095)	(0.2429)	(0.0703)	(0.0103)	(0.0048)	(0.0058)	(0.0096)	(0.0061)	(0.0108)
Disasters × experience in low-impact disasters	0.0005	−0.1057	0.0138	0.0013	−0.0040	−0.0301***	−0.0109	−0.0283***	0.0602***
	(0.0088)	(0.1619)	(0.0259)	(0.0101)	(0.0038)	(0.0082)	(0.0141)	(0.0072)	(0.0173)
Self-selection bias (lambda)	0.2077**	0.2013**	0.2058**	0.1889**	0.1659*	0.1952**	0.1849**	0.1237+	0.1311+
	(0.0671)	(0.0671)	(0.0668)	(0.0661)	(0.0675)	(0.0671)	(0.0657)	(0.0669)	(0.0670)
Log-likelihood	−17,673.65	−17,675.23	−17,672.75	−17,694.45	−17,722.61	−17,664.33	−17,681.98	−17,644.05	−17,664.00
AIC	35,659.30	35,662.46	35,657.50	35,700.90	35,757.22	35,640.67	35,675.96	35,600.10	35,640.00

Notes: † if $p < 0.10$, * if $p < 0.05$, ** if $p < 0.01$, *** if $p < 0.001$. See also notes in Table 8.2. We estimated all control variables but do not report them here due in the interest of space. One subtype of disaster at a time is included in each model.

Table 8.8). Experience with high-impact floods and mass movements shows a positive and significant moderating effect on the negative link between disaster severity and MNC entry ($p < 0.05$).

> High-impact experience ameliorates the negative relationship between disaster severity and expansion (but not entry) for the following sub-types of weather-related natural disasters: extreme temperatures, floods, mass movements, storms, and wildfires.

> For MNC entry, a notable exception to the trend is the case of floods. Experience with high-impact floods shows a positive and significant moderating effect on the negative link between disaster severity and MNC entry.

Regarding experience with low-impact disaster severity, in general, natural disasters subtypes do not appear to show a significant moderating effect for either entry and expansion (see Tables 8.8 and 8.9). These findings offer support for Hypothesis 3, that experience with low-impact natural disasters is less likely to show a positive moderating effect on the relationship between disaster severity and entry and expansion. Our results are consistent with those observed for the entry and expansion models that group natural disasters into a single generic category (see Table 8.2).

Robustness Checks

To check the robustness of our findings, we tested our results in multiple ways. The results from all nine of the robustness checks we performed were not appreciably different when compared with our main results found in Tables 8.2 and 8.3, and thus strengthened our findings. We do not report these results, in the interest of space, but we will provide them to interested readers upon request.

First, we used a normalized measure of severity, number of people killed divided by the total population (per million), recognizing that a heavily populated country will likely have more victims in a disaster than a less populated one. The only significant differences from our main results are seen in the expansion mode. There the interaction between natural disasters and experience with low-impact disasters turns out to be significant and negative, while the interaction between technological disasters and experience with high-impact disasters is no longer significant. These small differences do not matter because the interaction coefficients of disasters with high- and low-impact disasters are statistically different from each other for all three types of disasters. Recall that our main models in Tables 8.2 and 8.3 controlled for host country population.

Second, the effects of disasters can be limited within a city or region; thus a disaster in one city or region might not directly affect a firm in another city or region, particularly in large countries. Therefore, we excluded large host countries such as Australia, Brazil, Canada, China, India, Russia, and the United States from our sample for a robustness check. The results are strongly consistent with our main results. We prefer the results that include all the countries because the indirect effects of the disaster would prevail even in other cities and regions in large countries. Recall that our main models in Tables 8.2 and 8.3 controlled for host country land size.

Third, although disasters are largely unpredictable and exogenous, some countries are more prone to specific types of disasters. Therefore, it is possible that managers might access information about disaster risks in a host country instead of using realized disaster risks. We used a country-level natural disaster risk index presented by the United Nations Development Programme (UNDP 2004) in which UNDP calculated the average number of people killed in natural disasters by country over a 21-year period (1980–2000). We used the same logic for terrorist attacks and technological disasters. The results show that although MNCs do not expand in disaster-prone countries, their experience benefits do not moderate the effect of disaster potential on subsidiary expansion (i.e. the interaction between the disaster risk index and experience in high/low disasters is statistically insignificant). In addition, we tested two-year lagged disaster experience variables instead of one-year lagged disaster variables in our models. We found that the interactions between disasters and two-year lagged disaster experience are insignificant, while the direct effects of two-year lagged disaster experience are significant. Thus, the results imply that dynamic learning, information updating, and decision-making exist in MNC disaster risk management, which supports our theoretical arguments. In addition, the results support the notion of so-called *retrospective bias* – managers' limited capacity to remember past events (Golden, 1992).

Fourth, the damage caused by disasters in a host country might be correlated with the level of economic and social development of the country. Firms that have experience in less-developed countries might be likely to invest in less-developed countries in the future. Therefore, our results could not rule out a potential alternative explanation. To test the alternative explanation, we controlled for experience in developed and less-developed countries and their interactions with disasters in our main model. We find that experience in both developed and less-developed countries increases the likelihood of entry and expansion in a host country, but that these experiences do not significantly alter a firm's decision to enter and expand in a foreign country in the case of disasters.

In addition, we also tested other forms of international experience, such as similar income levels, similar levels of country governance quality, same colonizers in history, and common language ties. In general, the direct effects of other types of experience are positive and statistically significant, but their interaction effects are insignificant. Our key results and conclusions do not change. Thus, we extensively reduced the possibility of alternative explanations. Recall that we originally controlled both for country governance and its interaction with disasters.

Fifth, as we discussed in the Methodology section, we checked the robustness of our results using a 10 percent tail of the distribution in each disaster severity measure as a breakpoint for the high- and low-impact disasters instead of the mean of the disaster severity. The only significant differences from our main results are that: (1) in the expansion model, the interaction between natural disasters and experience in low-impact disasters turns out to be significant, and (2) the interaction between technological disasters and experience in low-impact disasters loses its statistical significance.

Sixth, unobserved firm-level heterogeneity might be correlated with other variables and generate biased results. Therefore, we controlled for unobserved heterogeneity by adding firm-fixed effects. In this robustness check, we controlled for firm-fixed, country-fixed, and year-fixed effects. The industry-fixed effects were dropped due to their multicollinearity with firm-fixed effects. The only significant difference from our main results is that in the expansion model the interaction between technological disasters and experience in low-impact disaster loses its statistical significance. This robustness check also embraces the home country effect, which is firm-specific, such as disaster experience in home country or home country cultural values.

Seventh, as we discussed in the Methodology section, we used other measures of disaster severity (i.e. the number of incidents and the duration of the events) and international diversification (i.e. number of subsidiaries) to test the robustness of our measures. These results are consistent with those found in Tables 8.2 and 8.3. The only minor difference is, when we used the number of subsidiaries for the measure of international diversification, the interaction effect between techno- logical disasters and experience with high-impact technological disas- ter is marginally significant for the entry model.

Eighth, instead of using Heckman's two-stage selection model for the expansion model, we used a hurdle model, which was developed by Mullahy (1986), to estimate the expansion model. A hurdle model is divided into two parts. The first part (presence) is a binary process generating positive integers versus zero, and the second part (expansion) is a process generating positive integers. We used a complementary log-log model for the first part (Reuer & Tong, 2005) and a negative binomial model for the second part. The hurdle model bears resem- blance to Heckman's (1979) two-stage selection model (e.g. Helpman, Melitz & Rubinstein, 2008). The results are statistically stronger in the hurdle model than in the two-stage selection model in Tables 8.2 and 8.3. In addition, for the expansion model we tested a negative binomial regression model without controlling for selection bias and our key results do not change. However, we chose to use the two-stage selec- tion model for our main results because of its popularity in the litera- ture and the statistical significance of selection bias coefficients.

Ninth, we included a lagged dependent variable in order to control for unobserved heterogeneity in each country (Wooldridge, 2002) and address the possibility of residual serial correlation (Holburn & Zelner, 2010) in the expansion model. Overall, the results are consist- ent with those in Tables 8.2 and 8.3 for our key variables. The only significant difference from the results of the expansion models in Table 8.3 is that the interaction between natural disasters and experi- ence with low-impact disasters turns out to be significant and negative. We prefer the results without the lagged dependent variable because of the possibility of downward bias in the coefficients of independent and control variables when used with fixed effects (Barkema & Schijven, 2008; Nickell, 1981).

Discussion

The purpose of this chapter was to test the proposition and arguments developed in Chapter 5 and empirically examine whether it is possible for firms to gain experience advantages from operating during seemingly unmanageable natural disasters and other catastrophes. That is, can firms gain experiential advantages associated with major natural disasters (compared to terrorist attack and technological disasters) and could these advantages enable firms to enter and expand into countries experiencing similar risks? For scholars and managers, determining how to respond to various types of risks is critical for effective strategy formulation, firm survival, and expansion. If such experiential advantages are possible and valuable, then experience operating under natural disaster risk is a potential source of competitive advantage, an advantage that is difficult to acquire since it arises from learning by doing (Barkema, Bell, & Pennings, 1996). Moreover, for managers understanding why some firms survive and even thrive after a major disaster while others go out of business may reveal a valuable source of competitive advantage. After nearly every disaster there are many anecdotal stories about firms that survive and even expand after the crisis, suggesting that some firms may develop unique capabilities or response strategies for managing risk.

Our findings indicate benefits do seem to arise from experience, specifically experience with high-impact natural disasters (and also experience with high-impact terrorist attacks and industrial disasters). Firms that had experience with high-impact natural disasters were more likely to expand into countries facing natural disasters (terrorist attacks and technological disasters also show similar results). Despite the fact that major natural disasters tend to occur irregularly and unexpectedly and have traditionally been perceived to be outside the control or purview of managers, our study suggests that managers can gain experiential advantages from addressing discontinuous risks.

Noteworthy, however, is our finding that experience with high-impact natural disasters positively moderates the negative link between natural disaster severity and expansion, but not new entry. These results are particularly interesting when considered against prior research on the value of experience managing risk. Scholars have found that firms with more extensive international experience in countries with high political hazards, defined as those with greater policy uncertainty (Delios & Henisz, 2003) have higher entry rates into other high-risk countries (Delios & Henisz, 2003; Holburn & Zelner, 2010). Our findings are closer to García-Canal and Guillén (2008), who found that greater experience operating in countries with a high degree of policy uncertainty discouraged managers from entering new markets with similar characteristics. Here, we find that experience with high-impact natural disasters (and technological disasters and terrorist attacks) can be leveraged in an MNC's existing host country, but not into new countries experiencing similar high-impact disasters.

Firms that had experience with high-impact natural disasters were more likely to expand into countries experiencing natural disasters.

This finding suggest that managers can gain experiential advantages from operating during high-impact natural disaster risks. Moreover, experience with high-impact natural disasters can be leveraged to expand in an MNC's existing host country *but not to enter* into other countries experiencing similar high-impact disasters. Disaster experience needs to be accompanied with country-specific knowledge to be valuable. Contrary to experience with host country policymaking risks, experience with natural disaster risks does not appear to be transferrable across borders.

One explanation for this finding may be that while firms do not enter new countries experiencing major disasters, they are able to identify new business opportunities, post disaster, in countries where they currently operate. In the aftermath of major natural disasters, governments often spend large sums of money in the recovery process, which acts as a short-term stimulus (Vigdor, 2008). Alternatively, it may also be that in the event of high-impact natural disasters, subsidiaries located near the event experience lower output, which in turn may spur expansion into other parts of the host country.

Since our findings show that experience with natural disasters did not lead to increased entry into new markets facing similar risks, a key contribution of our study is to indicate that disaster experience may need to be accompanied with country-specific knowledge to be valuable in the case of natural disasters. This is an important finding because it indicates that experience with certain types of risk is transferrable across borders, while experience with other types of risk must be context-specific to be valuable. Comparing our results with those of Delios and Henisz (2003), who found that experience in high-risk policy environments could be leveraged in new markets, we argue that the nature of the risk explains, at least in part, the differences in our findings.

For instance, managers can study the decision-making process of the executive or legislative chambers (whether democratic or not) in a country prior to any investment. Knowledge of decision-making systems can then be applied to many country contexts, so although one cannot necessarily know, a priori, what specific policy changes might occur, one can understand how a particular government may react (or at least the likely range of responses) based on their typical processes and on precedent. García-Canal and Guillén (2008), for example, found that although firms in regulated industries were initially attracted to operating in countries whose governments were characterized by a high degree of policy discretion (and therefore policy uncertainty), greater experience operating in such environments actually diminished the likelihood that firms would enter similar markets in the future.

A country's ability to respond to a disaster may only be known once the event occurs. If the event is infrequent or rare it will be more difficult to glean relevant information. Managers can gain knowledge about the general capacity of a country's government, but the manner in which local/regional governments, police, firefighters, and bureaucrats will respond when faced with a crisis may be knowledge obtainable only from operating in that country. Thus, an important finding of this study is that risks, and the knowledge needed to manage them, differ across risk type. For certain types of risk this knowledge can be transferred across borders, but for others the knowledge may need to be context-specific to be valuable.

A notable exception to the lack of significant moderating effects on MNC entry models is the case of floods. Experience with high-impact floods does show a positive and significant moderating effect on the negative link between disaster severity and MNC entry. As we discussed in Chapter 4, natural disasters that show a pattern of the highest deadly consequences, year after year, become hard to ignore or dismiss as one-time historical anomalies or uncontrollable "acts of God." From 1995 to 2015, floods were the most frequent natural disasters, but they were second after storms in terms of loss of life, causing about 27 percent of all weather-related disaster fatalities (Wahlstrom & Guha-Sapir, 2016). Floods were also the second costliest natural disasters (after storms), generating around 25 percent (38 percent for storms) of the reported $1900 billion in economic loses generated by all natural disasters (including earthquakes and volcano eruptions) between 1995 and 2015 (Wahlstrom & Guha-Sapir, 2016).

A notable exception to the lack of significant moderating effects on the MNC entry models is the case of floods. Experience with high-impact floods does show a positive and significant moderating effect on the negative link between disaster severity and MNC entry. In 1995–2015, floods were the most frequent natural disasters, second after storms in terms of loss of life, causing about 27 percent of all weather-related disaster fatalities (Wahlstrom & Guha-Sapir, 2016).

This finding might be due to the fact that high-impact natural disasters show a pattern of the highest deadly consequences, year after year, and over time are difficult to ignore or to dismiss as one-time historical anomalies or uncontrollable "acts of God."

When we probed further into the type of natural disaster experience held by firms, we found that experience with low-impact terrorist attacks and technological disasters – *but not natural disasters* – is negatively and significantly related to expansion when these calamities occur in a host country. It is generally accepted in research on risk that individuals will rate natural disasters as relatively low risk, regardless of their probability or severity (Slovic, Fischhoff, & Lichtenstein, 2000). Natural disasters are seen as "acts of God" and largely outside the control of any individual or group. On the other hand, minor technological disasters such as industrial accidents that result in little damage or loss of life might evoke a surprisingly dramatic response if the event is seen as a signal of future technological disasters or if it raises questions about the integrity of relevant infrastructure or technology (Kasperson, et al., 1988). Likewise, terrorist events, no matter how small, are likely to be socially amplified by the media (Kasperson, Renn, Slovic et al., 1988). They create a sense of foreboding that might negatively influence new investment decisions when disasters occur.

Individuals tend to rate natural disasters as relatively low risk. Experience with low-impact terrorist attacks and technological disasters – *but not natural disasters* – is negatively and significantly related to expansion when these calamities occur in a host country.

In normal circumstances, where a host country experienced no disasters or only weak disasters, firms with experience in high-impact disasters did not appear to have particularly high investment rates. This suggests that a firm with catastrophic disaster experience is likely to be more conservative in making foreign entry and expansion decisions than firms without such experience. Nevertheless, when compared to firms with little to no disaster experience, these firms were more likely to invest – a finding we attribute to a greater relative understanding of such disasters. Firms need to recognize that the various types of disaster do not represent a single, homogeneous, exogenous shock. Different types of disasters appear to be associated with different patterns of impact on business.

Although our empirical analysis in this chapter was not designed to capture detailed firm-level decision-making processes around entry and expansion decisions – an analysis that would likely require extensive field work over a long period of time – we attempted to supplement our empirical findings with examples of the experiences of specific firms. In most cases, we found obtaining this type of firm-level data to be extremely difficult since firms generally do not publicly reveal their rationale for entering and leaving countries, particularly when the news is not positive. Moreover, this type of detail is often considered to be sensitive strategic information. Secondary sources, a possible alternative means of collecting data, often lack detailed information on the internal decision-making and rationale of firms.

For instance, we were able to determine from our data that before the tsunami hit Indonesia in 2004, the French cement firm Lafarge had three subsidiaries in Indonesia between 2001 and 2004. After the tsunami, Lafarge had only one subsidiary between 2005 and 2006. Through additional research, we discovered that at least one of these subsidiaries, P.T. Semen Andalas Indonesia (SAI), was completely destroyed in the disaster. We found reports from the press and from the Asian Development Bank that in the first two years after the disaster, despite the hefty cost of rebuilding (reportedly $45 million in 2007), Lafarge reinvested in the same location by reconstructing the subsidiary (Asian Development Bank, 2008). In a future study, we hope to gain access to managers at a number of companies who have experienced a disaster to gain insight into how and why they decided to reinvest in (or perhaps exit from) a country and what they learned in the process.[4]

---

[4] Another example is a French utility firm's (AREVA) safety management plan for industrial accidents such as fires, water pollution, and radiation. According to annual reports, since 2001 AREVA has inspected any minor deviations and anomalies in its domestic and foreign facilities. In order to respond to more stringent government requirements regarding industrial safety, the company has reinforced its use of lessons learned to ensure the highest level of safety in its

Expanding our examples to non-European firms, the experience of Procter & Gamble (P&G), in Louisiana, is illustrative and bears discussion. P&G accounts for 40 percent of all the coffee sold in the United States and has more than half its production based in New Orleans. Despite the fact that much of its operations were located in the areas hit hardest by Hurricane Katrina in 2005 (a Folgers plant, one of four P&G facilities in the area, experienced over $10 million in damages and for many days was only accessible by helicopter) P&G was one of the first businesses back in operation after it ended. In an article examining P&G's post-Katrina response, the company is credited with developing a detailed business continuity plan, one that was designed for each of their facilities and rehearsed annually. In the case of its operations in New Orleans, any hurricane entering the Gulf of Mexico automatically triggers a series of emergency measures including the transfer of inventory to distribution centers outside the New Orleans area, the sending of inventory backup tapes to corporate headquarters in Ohio, and the advent of shutdown procedures (Supply Chain Brain, 2006).

While outside the scope of our chapter analysis, the source of this experiential advantage presumably arises from a greater understanding of high-impact discontinuous natural disasters that enables firms to pursue investments in locations facing similar conditions. We interpret this finding to mean that experience with major discontinuous disasters provides firms with experience gains that can be leveraged in future investments. This experience enables firms to more accurately assess potential risk to the firm and perhaps manage it more effectively. Firms with little to no experience with high-impact disasters appear to be deterred from entering markets with high-risk environments because they perceive them to be high-threat contexts in which to operate. These findings lend support for resource-based notions of competitive advantage since we find possible evidence that firm capabilities built around experience and learning may lead firms to increase entry into foreign markets and further expansion.

facilities. It has also carried out a number of impact studies in foreign countries such as Canada, Niger, and Kazakhstan, as well as in its home country. Although the company has put in place strategies and procedures to control risks such as terrorism, natural disasters, airplane crashes, and equipment malfunctions, it admits that it is not always able to control the factors that influence the severity of potential accidents that may affect its facility or the transportation of materials (AREVA Annual Report, 2009).

Although it may not be uncommon for individuals to assume that investment is ill advised after a major disaster, there is a growing body of research suggesting that there are often positive economic effects post disaster, at least at the macro-level. Indeed, this possibility has been identified in a new and growing body of economics research that has focused primarily on natural disasters (Cuaresma et al., 2008; Skidmore & Toya, 2002). In one study, the authors found that natural disasters have the potential to create a literal Schumpeterian effect. After a disaster, it is argued, old capital stock, which is more likely to be destroyed by a high-risk disaster, is replaced by newer technology that generates a boost in total factor productivity. In an empirical study comparing developed and developing countries, researchers found that "only countries with relatively high levels of development benefit from capital upgrading through trade after a natural catastrophe" (Cuaresma et al., 2008). According to Arcelor Mittal's 2008 Annual Report, the company has commercialized a modular building designed to facilitate the rapid construction of emergency housing for victims of natural disasters. Therefore, disasters may generate new business opportunities for some firms and industries, but, at the firm level, our results suggest that not all firms can take part in the country's capital upgrading during recovery. Only firms with relevant and qualified experience will be eligible to take advantage of new business opportunities.

Limitations and Future Directions

Although we do not look at the process of learning *within* organizations, we want to recognize the emergent and closely related body of literature examining how firms learn from unusual events (e.g., Baum & Dahlin, 2007; Christianson, Farkas, Sutcliffe, & Weicke, 2009; Madsen, 2009; Rerup, 2009; Starbuck, 2009; Zollo, 2009). This literature may serve as a model for developing subsequent studies examining organizational learning from disasters.

Although we strengthened our empirical results with examples, as with all empirical research there are limitations associated with our study, which we must note. First, our sample consists of wholly owned subsidiaries from European MNCs. It is possible that results may differ when one considers subsidiaries of U.S., Japanese, Chinese, or MNCs in other countries. Second, joint ventures, alliances or other organizational types may exhibit behavior different than that of wholly owned subsidiaries. Third, we took the number of subsidiaries in a country as a measure of expansion from the literature. While we do not believe this count measure generates biased results, the inclusion of scale measures such as sales and assets would ease additional statistical concerns. Fourth, although we efficiently controlled for the problem of missing variables by using industry-, country-, and year-fixed effects, other factors – such as host country market opportunity, communication systems within organizations, and the characteristics of top management teams and boards of directors – might influence risk-taking behavior of MNC managers with respect to discontinuous risks. Fifth, in this chapter we analyzed MNCs' entry and expansion in 109 countries; a natural next step would be to delve into entry and expansion decisions at the subnational level with a longer observation period in order to investigate the micro behavior of MNCs. Subnational analyses of very large countries, such as the U.S., Canada, China, Russia, and India, may focus on noticeable subnational characteristics and observe how disasters influence only certain parts of a country. Although our robustness checks provided strong support for our results, only future work can establish our conclusions with certainty.

In terms of future directions, our findings indicate the need to probe more deeply into experience effects to better understand the specific knowledge obtained from managing in high-impact disasters and how such knowledge and learning is leveraged across markets and investments. Additionally, it is important to understand what the performance effects are for firms that enter into and expand within countries experiencing high-impact disasters.

In addition, our robustness check shows that a general disaster risk index does not properly represent realized disaster risks. Together with the main results, our findings indicate that experience effects vis-à-vis discontinuous risks are different from the same effects relative to continuous risks, such as ongoing political and economic instabilities. We presume that differences arise from the probability of risk occurrence as well as from the risk perception of managers. Our robustness check also shows that outdated disaster experience does not help MNCs overcome disaster risks. An alternative explanation for the short-lived nature of disaster experience is that experienced firms take advantage of opportunities during the recovery period – opportunities that affected and less experienced firms are unaware of or are too badly damaged by the disaster to pursue. An important avenue for future research is to design studies that will provide a better understanding of (1) the factors affecting the longevity of disaster experience and (2) the differences between disaster experience and disaster recovery experience. Thus, responses to experience with discontinuous risk is likely to be different from responses to continuous risks. Unfortunately, we could not explicitly test the difference between continuous and discontinuous risk and the differences between experience with entry and expansion decisions, or in business strategy decisions more broadly. Likewise, the relationship between discontinuous risks and MNC entry and expansion and the moderating effects of experience on the relationship differs across types of discontinuous risk. Future research should determine the reasons for these differences.

The scope of our study prohibits us from drawing definitive conclusions on those factors which might link the research on risk perception with our findings. We can, however, suggest ideas and research questions for the future. For instance, does the research on how disaster characteristics affect risk perception apply after managers have experience with realized disasters? For example, once a high-impact natural disaster (or a terrorist event or a technological disaster) is experienced, will responses tend to converge or will there still be key and perhaps subtle differences in responses across disaster types?

One well-established finding in studies of risk assessment and perception is that while "technologically sophisticated analysts employ risk assessment to evaluate hazards, the majority of citizens rely on intuitive judgments" (Slovic, 2000). In a future study, it would be interesting to analyze how firms go about assessing risk (for example, is the process technical in nature or instead based on media reports and other social influences); what the relationship is between the method of risk assessment and a firm's response to each of the disasters (Slovic, 2000); and what the link is between type of risk assessment approach and financial performance of current and future investment decisions.

Lessons drawn from particular disasters also need to be assessed. For example, why does BP continue to have oil spills and technological accidents despite the fact that it faced ample opportunities to learn from past spills? There may exist an internal mechanism or organizational culture that transforms experience (tacit knowledge) into implementable strategy and practice within an organization. It would be valuable to analyze how this internal mechanism is established, how it operates, and what the determinants of its effectiveness are. While much remains to be done, we believe this study has made a seminal contribution toward answering these questions.

Conclusion

Our aim in this chapter was to extend the research on the role of firm experience in managing risk by specifically analyzing MNC experience with major discontinuous risks, specifically natural disasters (compared to terrorist attacks and technological disasters). Firm experience with high-impact natural disasters was seen to be related to higher levels of expansion into other markets experiencing such risks. International experience alone and firm experience with low-impact disasters was seen not to have the same effect, however, on new foreign entry and expansion.

> **Only the experience that is gained from encounters with high-impact natural disasters – truly learning to carry the cat by the tail – provides what is needed for leveraging experience into other high-risk contexts.**

This indicates that experience related to specific types of disaster, and the quality of that experience, is necessary to overcome the deterrent effects of major discontinuities like natural disasters. Therefore, it appears that only the experience that is gained from encounters with high-impact natural disasters – truly learning to carry the cat by the tail – provides what is needed for leveraging experience in other high-risk contexts.

Appendix 8.1. *Top 25 countries affected by terrorism activities, natural disasters, and technological disasters during 2001–2007*[a]

Rank	Terrorism activities		Natural disasters		Technological disasters	
	Country	Number killed per year	Country	Number of killed per year	Country	Number killed per year
1	Iraq	155.4	Indonesia	25,158	China	9,850
2	Russia	93.4	Pakistan	10,813	Nigeria	5,922
3	Afghanistan	43.1	India	7,071	India	4,807
4	Israel	37.1	Iran, Islam Rep.	4,067	Bangladesh	3,424
5	United States	35.9	France	2,996	Indonesia	2,759
6	Indonesia	35.1	Italy	2,880	Egypt	2,618
7	Burundi	27.9	Spain	2,169	Iran, Islam Rep.	2,277
8	Spain	27.4	Germany	1,351	Russia	1,837
9	Pakistan	20.7	Thailand	1,309	Congo, Dem. Rep.	1,725
10	India	18.3	China	1,054	Senegal	1,459
11	Ethiopia	10.6	Philippines	904	Iraq	1,406
12	Egypt	10.3	Haiti	812	Pakistan	1,269
13	Philippines	10.0	Algeria	486	Peru	1,097
14	Saudi Arabia	10.0	United States	444	Brazil	1,059
15	Chad	8.9	Bangladesh	443	Saudi Arabia	1,010
16	Turkey	6.9	Portugal	396	Turkey	986
17	Colombia	6.3	Belgium	303	Tanzania	929
18	Congo, Rep.	5.9	Netherlands	281	United States	840

19	Sri Lanka	5.6	Viet Nam	249	Philippines	807
20	Algeria	4.9	Guatemala	248	South Africa	794
21	United Kingdom	4.4	Russia	229	Nepal	745
22	Somalia	4.0	Nepal	194	Korea, Rep.	646
23	Bangladesh	3.9	Ethiopia	188	Ukraine	635
24	Morocco	3.6	El Salvador	183	Kenya	620
25	Mauritania	3.4	Peru	179	Uganda	619

Note: [a] Number killed per year is an average of the number killed by each type of disaster during 2001–2007. Source of 'Terrorism activities' is International Terrorism Activity Database. Source of 'Natural disasters' and 'Technological disasters' is Emergency Events Database.

PART IV

Conclusions

9 | Business Adaptation to Climate Change

Conclusions, Limitations, and Future Research

During normal ecological conditions, humanity worships at the altar of technological progress. Science and ingenuity it is assumed can conquer the challenges posed by nature. For centuries, we have taken-for-granted ideal that humans will triumph over nature, an ideal that has been central to our worldview of progress and civilization (Montuschi, 2010). Alas, increasingly we are forced, one way or the other, to acknowledge our limits and muddle through to survive alongside nature's much messier, more complex, extreme, and often uncertain conditions. We are not free *from* nature, we are part of it, and our well-being is inseparable from the health of ecosystems. The COVID-19 pandemic (a natural disaster that has not been linked to climate change),[1] and its effect on people around the world, demonstrates how compounding risks can reverberate across geographies, particularly in those areas that are most vulnerable. Over the last few decades the world has repeatedly experienced record-breaking natural disasters (e.g. wildfires and hurricanes) combined with worsening

---

[1] It is important to emphasize that we are not suggesting the COVID-19 pandemic was caused by climate change. Yet, climate change trends are known to exacerbate the frequency and severity of not only weather-related disasters (such as floods, hurricanes, droughts) but also biological disasters such as epidemics and insect infestations (IPCC, 2014; McMichael et al., 2003). This is because climate change conditions, particularly temperature, precipitation, and humidity variations and extremes, can facilitate the transmission of tropical infectious diseases and plagues that get passed to humans from animals, insects, and other organisms (IPCC, 2014; McMichael et al., 2003). These zoonotic-pathogen spillovers from animals to humans, such as SARS, Ebola, Zika, Lyme, mad cow disease, COVID-19, etc., will only increase as adverse conditions linked to climate change push people closer to wildlife in newly deforested areas. Infectious viruses can then be spread very quickly through modern transportation systems that facilitate global travel. For instance, a person bit by a virus-infected bat from a cave near Cancún, Mexico (cave exploring is very popular among tourists visiting Cancún) can take a direct afternoon flight to Miami, New York, London, Frankfurt, etc., triggering, in a matter of hours, the spread of disease across continents.

chronic nature adversity conditions (e.g. warmer temperatures). These events give us a glimpse of what climate change may bring in the future: cascading and uncertain slow-onset nature adversity conditions and natural disasters that magnify loss of life and property damage to historic catastrophic proportions. Businesses have an important role to engage in mitigating and adapting to natural dynamics that can lead to disasters and human tragedy.

In this book we seek to advance our understanding of how businesses may adapt to climate change trends. Specifically, we focused on two general research questions: First, how do businesses adapt to chronic slow-onset nature adversity conditions linked to climate change? And second, how do firms adapt to weather-related natural disasters exacerbated by climate change? Despite, the strongly heated and long-lasting political debates surrounding responses to climate change, we know very little about these questions across business, government, and academia. Most businesses continue to pay little attention to measures that mitigate climate change or adapt to it. Moreover, multiple top business executives and national-level political leaders still argue that climate change might not be real and or caused by human activity. These skeptics also argue that even if climate change is happening, mitigation and adaptation have uncertain long-term benefits. The business community's tendency to disregard and ignore climate change threats is, in part, grounded on an ideological bias against global regulations, a myopic focus on short-term costs at the expense of long-term benefits, and a distrust of developing country governments willingness to avoid free-riding on global climate change efforts (see the detailed discussion of these factors in Chapter 1). At the same time, there are encouraging signs that some businesses are increasingly considering the risks and opportunities associated with climate change.

While the academic literature on climate change is quite large and growing, in both the natural and social sciences, business school academics and elite business journals show a strong tendency to ignore the challenges of climate change. **In top academic business journals, the proportion of articles focused on climate change adaptation and/or mitigation is close to zero.** As we highlight in the Introduction, only 0.15 percent of 22,903 articles published in the period between 1998 and mid-2015 in the 23 most elite business academic journals, mentioned "global warming," "climate change," "greenhouse," or "carbon" in the title, abstract, or list of key words (Diaz-Rainey et al., 2017). The dominant theories and frameworks of business management scholarship also ignore the fact that natural resources, and the positive externalities provided by ecosystems, allow humans to survive (e.g. clean air, a stable climate, and potable water). Instead, these theories give prominence to technology, capital, labor, and to a lesser degree the institutional environment as key contributors to business competitiveness and profitability.

A key premise of our book is that both mitigation and adaptation strategies and policies are mutually reinforcing and necessary for confronting the enormous challenges involved in reducing the negative effects of climate change (Haigh, 2019). Adaptation is not a panacea; it is a complement to climate change mitigation. This principle cannot be highlighted and reiterated enough. At the same time, our book's focus on business adaptation is motivated by the fact that adaptation is also fundamental to the long-term global prosperity and survival of humanity. The cumulative negative effects of climate change are going to continue for many centuries, even if (what seems like a miracle now) we could manage to completely stop emitting greenhouse gases today (IPCC, 2013).

Key Findings and Contributions

Our research examining business adaptation to slow-onset nature adversity conditions and to natural disasters exacerbated by climate change makes numerous theoretical and empirical contributions. We started this research in the early 2000s and have been publishing our findings in a series of academic journal articles, beginning in 2011 (see publication acknowledgments on page ix). The conclusions we outline in this final chapter are derived from these previous manuscripts and new empirical analyses included in this book. For instance, our conclusions about adaptation to slow-onset nature adversity conditions are derived from new empirical models examining how different business and economic context characteristics moderate the relationship between higher temperatures and adaptation by U.S. ski resorts. Given its high vulnerability to mild temperatures and snowfall variations, the ski industry is an illustrative harbinger of climate change challenges that may affect other industries in the future. United States ski resorts reportedly lost around $1 billion in revenue between 1999 and 2010, attributable to lower demand for skiing because of warmer temperatures and uncertain snowfall (Tashman & Rivera, 2016; Zeng, Broxton, & Dawson, 2018).

Regarding multinational corporations' adaptation to natural disasters, our conclusions extend beyond past research; we examine the combined effect of different categories of natural disasters on MNC investment by evaluating the severity of different categories of natural disasters. MNCs have high exposure to these disasters in multiple countries. Hence, their responses to natural disasters can be seen as a "canary in the coal mine" indication of what other businesses may need to do as climate change trends accelerate.

Adaptation to slow-onset nature adversity exacerbated by climate change

Multiple management literatures focus on a foundational topic of interest to business strategy scholars, namely, understanding how firms change their strategies to fit the external environment. Broadly, two general perspectives exist on this topic. The first perspective views organizational adaptation as likely to be constrained by inertial forces, attributing variation in organizations to their birth and death resulting from selection processes in the external environment (Hannan & Freeman, 1984; Staw, Sandelands, & Dutton, 1981). Alternatively, the second perspective tends to view firms as likely to be able to more deliberately adapt to changing external demands (Chakravarthy, 1982; March, 1991). In sum, these broad diverging views suggest that adverse external operating conditions tend to be either positively or negatively related to firm adaptation.

Scholars interested in this debate have long limited their attention to economic, competitive, political, and institutional factors, overlooking adverse conditions stemming from the natural environment. With our book, we contribute to this debate by examining the effect of slow-onset nature adversity intensity on firms' tendency to adopt protective adaptation measures that seek to preserve core organizational activities. To do this we analyzed the adaptation responses of ski resorts in the Western U.S. (2001–2013) to temperature and snowfall conditions (between 1995 and 2013) (see Chapter 6). The U.S. ski industry reportedly lost around $1 billion in revenue from 1999 to 2010, attributable to lower demand for skiing because of deteriorating snow conditions (Burakowski & Magnusson, 2012; Zeng, Broxton, & Dawson, 2018). **For instance, the Colorado's Rocky Mountains experienced a decline in snowfall of over 40 percent between 1982 and 2019** (O'Leary et al., 2019). Our findings indicate that firms tend to exhibit lower rates of protective adaptation at both lower and higher levels of nature adversity intensity. At the same time, firms also display greater levels of protective adaptation at medium levels of natural adversity intensity, yielding an inverted U-shaped relationship.

Building upon the ideas of resilience theory from socioecology, we posited (see Chapters 2 and 3) that mechanisms from both – traditionally diverging – organizational adaptation perspectives are necessary to explain the full extent and shape of the relationship between nature adversity intensity and firm protective adaptation (DesJardine, Bansal, & Yang, 2017; Gunderson & Holling, 2002). The first perspective views organizational adaptation as likely to be constrained by inertial forces, attributing the variation seen in organizations to their birth and death resulting from selection processes in the external environment (Hannan & Freeman, 1984; Staw et al., 1981). Alternatively, the second perspective tends to view firms as likely to be able to more deliberately adapt to changing external demands (Chakravarthy, 1982; March, 1991).

We believe that a counterbalancing combination of internal organizational inertial forces, organizational resilience resources and capabilities, and biophysical stressors explains our findings.

Our ski industry findings suggest a curvilinear variation in firms' adaptation responses (measured as acres of slope expansion) to nature adversity intensity (proxied as daily minimum temperatures). First, at lower than medium levels of nature adversity intensity, organizational inertial forces constrain organization willingness to adapt, despite the low and slowly growing costs of protective adaptation. Second, at medium levels of nature adversity intensity, the interplay between natural adversity signals and constraints, internal organizational inertial forces, and business resilience capabilities make firms more willing and able to implement greater protective adaptation. Third, at severe levels, growing natural forces eventually impose limits beyond which protective adaptation becomes unviable. Accordingly, we suggest an inverted U-shaped relationship between nature adversity intensity and protective adaptation such that firms facing lower or higher than medium levels of nature adversity intensity tend to adopt lower levels

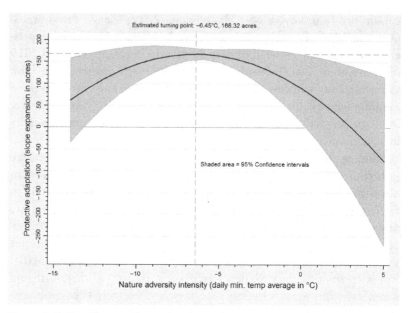

Figure 9.1 Curvilinear relationship between protective adaptation and nature adversity intensity.

of protective adaptation. This interplay of underlying mechanisms makes the initial positive link between nature adversity intensity and adaptation reach an apex point, after which it turns negative. This effect yields an inverted U-shaped relationship in which adaptation is highest at intermediate levels of nature adversity intensity (see Figure 9.1).

> Our findings indicate that firms tend to exhibit lower degrees of protective adaptation at both lower and upper range levels of nature adversity intensity while displaying greater levels of protective adaptation at medium levels, yielding an inverted U-shaped relationship.

> We believe that a counterbalancing combination of internal organizational inertial forces, organizational resilience resources and capabilities, and biophysical stressor barriers explains the curvilinear variation in firms' adaptation responses to nature adversity intensity.

These results contribute to the emerging literature examining firm adaptation to other slow-onset chronic dimensions of nature adversity in industries highly vulnerable to climate change such as the ski industry (Hoffmann et al., 2009; Linnenluecke & Griffiths, 2010; Pinkse &

Gasbarro, 2019; Tashman & Rivera, 2016; Winn et al., 2011). For instance, in examining how ski resorts response to uncertainty in the form of snowpack depth fluctuations, Tashman and Rivera (2016) find that greater snowpack variability from the long-term average has a significant and positive association with the adoption of snowmaking, and a marginally significant positive one with the adoption of slope expansion. This may be because snowpack variability alone does not impose strong physical constraints on firm adaptation. Snowpack variations might be detrimental or beneficial, respectively, for below or above average snowpack levels. To address this uncertainty, firms can thus focus on adaptive practices that confer more flexibility with regard to the availability of winter precipitation, such as snowmaking (Tashman & Rivera, 2016).

We advance this earlier research by showing that, controlling for snowpack uncertainty, the level of nature adversity intensity in the form of adverse temperature conditions may act as a key limiting factor in ski resort firms' ability to pursue protective adaptation. While rising temperatures may at first drive the uptake of protective adaptation practices like slope expansion, such practices may become increasingly unviable as warming temperatures exert stiffer adaptation constraints.

Factors that moderate the inverted U-shaped relationship between nature adversity intensity and protective adaptation. Our book also contributes to the research on how firms adapt to their external environment by identifying contingent factors that moderate the inverted U-shaped relationship between nature adversity intensity and protective adaptation. Our finding that **the slopes of this inverted U-shaped relationship are flatter for older ski resorts and in those operating in more stringent regulatory environments** suggests that these two factors (i.e. ski resort age and local regulatory stringency) seem to be inducing firms to face simultaneous challenges of nonadaptation and maladaptation. Because of stronger internal inertial forces, older firms may at first be reluctant to adapt, even as increasing nature adversity intensity levels require them to do so. Similarly, firms in more stringent regulatory environments may face initial barriers in their ability to implement preferred protective adaptation even as their need to do so increases with low to medium nature adversity intensity levels. However, because of the same inertial forces, older firms may be maladapting by persisting with protective adaptation that might no longer be effective once nature adversity intensity levels move from medium to high. Similarly, firms in more stringent regulatory environments may be locked into ineffective protective adaptation at these nature adversity intensity levels due to previously committed and high upfront investments.

We also found that that the slopes of the inverted U-shaped relationship between nature adversity intensity and protective adaptation are flatter for ski resorts with more slack resources. Here, such a flattening may indicate that firms with more slack resources do not tend to use protective adaptation as their primary adaptation strategy. Indeed, protective adaption may be part of a portfolio of adaptation practices that include diversification away from the core affected business. Because of the added buffer afforded by slack resources, these firms can more slowly ramp up and ramp down protective adaptation as needed according to the level of nature adversity intensity being experienced.

Additionally, our finding that the slopes of the inverted U-shaped relationship between nature adversity intensity and protective adaptation are steeper for firms that are publicly owned suggests that shareholder pressures lead firms to take a more short-term view of adaptation (Bansal & DesJardine, 2014). Firms may be induced to ramp up protective adaptation more rapidly and later ramp it down in a way that aligns more with short-run adaptive gains. Whether this is ultimately beneficial for longer-term resilience remains to be seen.

> The slopes of the inverted U-shaped relationship between nature adversity intensity and protective adaptation are flatter for older firms, in firms operating in more stringent regulatory environments, and/or in firms with more slack resources.

> Because of stronger internal inertial forces, older firms may at first be reluctant to adapt when facing moderate levels of nature adversity intensity and then persist with protective adaptation that might no longer be effective for dealing with severe nature adversity intensity.

> For firms with more slack resources, a flattened inverted U-shaped relationship may be indicative that these firms may not be using protective adaptation as their primary adaptation strategy.

> Conversely, our finding that the slopes of the inverted U-shaped relationship between nature adversity intensity and protective adaptation are steeper for publicly owned firms may be indicative of the fact that shareholders may pressure firms into taking a more short-term view of adaptation.

Multinational corporations and their foreign investment strategies in response to natural disasters. Natural disasters are not rare occurrences.

Among the 101 host countries examined in our book's cited studies between 2001 and 2006 (see Chapters 7 and 8), about 96 percent experienced natural disasters compared to 80 percent and 60 percent of countries experiencing technological disasters and terrorist attacks, respectively. Moreover, during this period, the average number of individuals killed in natural disasters – 757 deaths per year per country – was one or two orders of magnitude greater than for other types of disasters. The average number of individuals killed in terrorist activities, in contrast, was 4 per year per country, and for industrial accidents 73 per year per country. A key focus of our book was to examine how natural disasters, compared to technological disasters and terrorist attacks, shape MNCs' foreign subsidiary investments. Related to this general question, we also investigated: First, the effect of different subtypes of natural disasters on MNC foreign subsidiary investment. And second, we evaluated how host country governance characteristics moderate the relationship between disasters and subsidiary-level location and investment.

An important initial contribution of our research is the finding that MNC foreign subsidiary investment varies substantially depending upon the type of disaster involved. **More severe terrorist attacks and technological disasters decrease MNC foreign subsidiary investment. Alternatively, natural disaster severity does not appear to affect MNC foreign subsidiary investment.** These findings challenge the commonly accepted wisdom that managers employ a risk calculus where the firm's response would be in proportion to the loss of life and the duration and severity of the disaster. In Chapter 4, we argued that contrary to this "common wisdom," managers tend to ignore natural disasters and pay more attention to other types of disasters perceived to be more "controllable" and to some degree more preventable, such as terrorist attacks and technological disasters (Slovic et al., 2000). To be sure, as we mentioned earlier, between 2001 and 2006, the average number of individuals killed around the world by natural disasters, 757 deaths per year per country on average, was about 190 times greater than the number of fatalities for terrorist attacks and about 10 times greater than for technological disasters.

Managers may not respond in the same way to natural disasters as they do to other types of threats because such disasters are often considered uncontrollable events. Compared to natural disasters, terrorist attacks and industrial accidents often generate high levels of fear and anxiety and are socially amplified by the media. As such, this may exaggerate the perceived risk of terrorist attacks and industrial accidents. As a result, managers' decisions around market entry, expansion, and divestment in response to these events may not reflect the actual threat to a firm or its investments.

> Our findings challenge the commonly accepted wisdom that managers employ a risk calculus where the firm's response would be in proportion to the loss of life and the duration and severity of a disaster.

> Between 2001 and 2006, the average number of individuals killed around the world by natural disasters, 757 deaths per year per country on average, was about 190 times greater than the number of fatalities for terrorist attacks and about 10 times greater than for technological disasters Yet, we only found that more severe terrorist attacks and technological disasters significantly decrease MNC foreign subsidiary investment. Alternatively, natural disaster severity does not appear to affect MNC foreign subsidiary investment.

> Compared to natural disasters, the fear and anxiety associated with terrorist attacks and industrial accidents generates large biases that exaggerate their risks, leading firms to disinvest regardless of the actual threat. One exception to this finding concerns windstorms and storm surges, which do appear to increase the likelihood of divestment.

Additionally, our analysis of the differential effects of natural disaster subtypes indicates that windstorms and storm surges are the exception to this trend. The severity of windstorms and storm surges does appear to be linked to significantly higher MNC foreign subsidiary disinvestment. For all other subtypes of weather-related natural disasters – extreme temperatures, floods, droughts, wildfires, and landslides – there is no significant relationship between natural disasters and the number of MNC foreign subsidiaries in the host country. We argued in Chapter 4 that natural hazards that show a pattern of the highest deadly consequences, year after year, become hard to ignore or to dismiss as one-time historical anomalies or uncontrollable "acts of God." Compared to other natural disaster subtypes, windstorms and their related storm surges have been the deadliest weather-related disasters over the last few decades (Wahlstrom & Guha-Sapir, 2016). As we discussed in the introduction (Chapter 1), climate change trends are now known to have contributed toward exacerbating the severity of windstorms over the last few decades (IPCC, 2017).

> Despite the typical tendency to dismiss natural disasters as uncontrollable "acts of God," the most severe weather-related natural hazards, like

windstorms, become hard to ignore and underestimate as one-time historical anomalies.

Our findings also contribute to research and practice by assessing how country governance characteristics moderate disasters' direct effects on MNC foreign subsidiary investments. By focusing exclusively on the direct effects of disasters on subsidiary-level investment, managers might overestimate or underestimate the risk that major disasters pose. As a result, managers may mistakenly discontinue (or continue) their businesses and lose a competitive position in the market.

Another important contribution of our study is the finding that host country governance matters in different ways depending upon the type of risk involved. More specifically, we find that it is not wholly accurate to say that good governance is important to business investment in the aftermath of disasters. When considering our three generic disaster categories (i.e. natural, technological, and terrorist attacks), it appears that governance quality dimensions decrease the tendency of MNC disinvestment in the aftermath of terrorist attacks. Similarly, when considering natural disaster subtypes, **we found that the likelihood of MNC subsidiary disinvestment after weather-related disasters decreases as regulatory quality, political stability, and/or corruption control in a host country governance increase.**

An intriguing finding (contrary to what we proposed in Chapter 4) from our analysis indicates that in countries where voice and accountability are higher, MNC subsidiary disinvestment is significantly more likely after technological disasters. **Our analysis of individual natural disaster subtypes also indicates that higher voice and accountability (i.e. democratic freedoms) exacerbate the likelihood of MNC subsidiary disinvestment in the aftermath of specific natural disaster subtypes.** At first glance, this appears to be a puzzling finding: the more citizens enjoy democratic freedoms such as freedom of expression and are able to hold their governments accountable the more likely MNCs are to reduce investments after technological disasters and certain types of natural disasters. Public protest in the aftermath of technological disasters – although often vital for addressing systemic problems and alleviating a disaster – can be destabilizing to governments during an emergency. Public protest may spread concerns about a government's ability to address these types of disasters and raise the possibility that more technological accidents may be forthcoming. China's response to some technological and industrial crises may illustrate these concerns. After reports of lead in toys (2008), baby milk products tainted with melamine (2007), and an explosion at a state-owned chemical factory in Jilin City (2005), the Chinese government tried to suppress publicity surrounding the events in an effort to limit public protest (Oh & Oetzel, 2011).

Alternatively, we argued in Chapter 4 that higher disinvestment after technological disasters, and the most severe natural disaster subtypes, occurring in countries with higher levels of voice and accountability, may indicate that higher democratic freedoms allow civil society groups to more prominently highlight the negative consequences of technological and natural disasters. These enhanced freedoms and rights also allow civil society groups to pressure government to punish those responsible and to enact better disaster preparedness policies and regulations. This is because *free speech traditions* make it easier for populations to publicly and in a timely fashion convey concerns and demands to business managers, the media, and government officials about the consequences of problematic business practices that enhance the vulnerability to disasters (Rivera, Oetzel, DeLeon, & Starik, 2010).

Additionally, *freedom of association* facilitates the organization of advocacy groups and coalitions that are better able to debate, promote, and politically mobilize to maintain pressure on the government to respond to disasters and prevent similar events in the future (Rivera & Oh, 2013). *Freedom of political participation and the right to vote* also play a role in promoting adequate disaster prevention and recovery because groups advocating for regulations can support the election of like-minded politicians. Although these explanations are promising, clearly more empirical research is needed to determine exactly how freedom of expression and the ability of citizens to hold their governments accountable affects MNC response to natural disasters (and technological disasters), including when and whether such freedoms lead to greater subsidiary-level disinvestment.

> **Democratic freedoms may allow businesses and civil society groups to more prominently highlight the negative consequences of technological disasters, pressure governments to punish those responsible when appropriate, and enact better disaster preparedness policies.**

Additionally, *freedom of association* facilitates the organization of advocacy groups and coalitions that are better able to debate, promote, and politically mobilize to maintain pressure on the government to respond to disasters and prevent similar events in the future (Rivera & Oh, 2013).

Another finding that merits further discussion concerns the fact that regulatory quality was associated with a lower likelihood of subsidiary-level disinvestment after natural disasters. As we discussed in Chapter 4, regulatory quality is related to the degree of devastation ex post natural disaster. The ability of governments to formulate and enforce sound regulations was considered a key factor in the loss of many lives and a significant portion of the property damage after the earthquakes in Turkey in 1999 and China in 2008. In both cases, it was alleged that the Turkish and Chinese governments did not effectively impose regulatory controls on the construction of schools, offices, and other structures (Kinzer, 2001; Transparency International, 2008). On the other hand, in response to Hurricanes Katrina and Rita, the U.S. Department of Commerce supported and organized seminars and trade missions that promoted foreign investment and tightly monitored the recovery in the Gulf Coast (U.S. Department of Commerce, 2007). Companies may strategically transform natural catastrophic disasters from risks to opportunities in countries whose higher regulatory quality provides effective implementation of ex post disaster recovery, and in countries where preparedness plans lead to more favorable business investment environments. Depending upon the context in which disasters occur, entrepreneurial opportunities can be created if recovery plans are effective (Gopal, 2009).

Overall, our findings have relevant implications for global businesses. Given the increasing frequency and severity of weather-related disasters, MNCs that disregard these disasters do so at their own peril. Additionally, firms that overreact to disasters that are perceived to be more controllable, and to some degree preventable (such as terrorist attacks and technological accidents), and disinvest in response, may be forgoing valuable business opportunities. Effectively reacting to risk is a central concern in strategic management. If an MNC develops a competency around risk assessment and management, then it may evaluate the competitive benefits – rather than solely the costs – of foreign subsidiary investments or disinvestments in the aftermath of disasters (Li & Tong, 2007).

Understanding how country governance can mitigate or exacerbate the effect of major disasters on subsidiaries can help managers better calculate investment risk when formulating their location strategy. Prior research has shown that firms' experiences and capabilities around risk management can improve strategy formulation and firm performance (Delios & Henisz, 2003). Thus, a firm may be able to develop a competitive advantage through its location strategy and response to risk. For instance, managers will be better able to analyze a host country's ability to rebound from a natural disaster ex post and thus determine whether disinvestment is an appropriate strategic response.

For policy makers, these findings demonstrate that even though governments cannot always prevent disasters, they can minimize their impact and reduce the likelihood that foreign firms will disinvest by enhancing their capabilities for addressing them. While scholars have long noted that country-level disasters do not necessarily result in financial loss or firm failure, the literature in this area does not yet fully explain when, and under what conditions, these disasters are likely to threaten an MNC's subsidiary-level investment. For instance, if one were to examine only the direct effects of major disasters on subsidiary-level investment, one would conclude that terrorist attacks and technological disasters have a negative impact. This approach (only looking at direct effects) would lead managers to overestimate the risk and dissuade them from investing in countries that face greater risks. Similarly, those MNCs that have subsidiaries on the ground when a disaster occurs may unnecessarily disinvest rather than step back and analyze how the country will address the crisis and whether or not the government has the capabilities necessary to effectively do so.

The findings from our book may partially explain why scholars have found that similar disasters often produce widely differing casualty numbers, property losses, and economic disruptions in different countries (Davis & Seitz, 1982; Kasperson & Pijawka, 1985). For policy makers and government officials these findings suggest that host country governments can reduce the economic damage and loss of life associated with a disaster through effective governance, better regulatory quality, more effective rule of law, greater political stability, greater public voice, and more efficient control of corruption in the policy process. Through the same mechanisms, governments may also reduce the likelihood that MNCs will disinvest after a major disaster.

MNC disaster experience and foreign subsidiary investment. Is it possible for firms to gain experiential advantages from operating during seemingly unmanageable natural disasters and other catastrophes? That is, can firms gain experiential advantages associated with major natural disasters (compared to terrorist attack and technological disasters), and could these advantages enable firms to enter and expand into countries experiencing similar risks? The importance of these questions for firm survival has swelled dramatically given how climate change trends are increasingly exacerbating the frequency and severity of natural disasters. Additionally, if such experiential advantages are possible and valuable, then experience operating under natural disaster risk is a potential source of competitive advantage; an advantage that is difficult to acquire since it arises from learning by doing (Barkema, Bell, & Pennings, 1996). Moreover, for managers, understanding why some firms survive and even thrive after a major disaster while others go out of business may serve as a valuable source of knowledge, to be applied to major crisis management. After nearly every disaster there are many anecdotal stories about firms that survive and even expand after the crisis, suggesting that some firms may develop unique capabilities or response strategies for managing risk.

Our findings indicate that there do seem to be benefits from experience, specifically experience with high-impact natural disasters. **Firms that had experience with high-impact natural disasters were more likely to expand into a host country experiencing natural disasters.** Despite the fact that major natural disasters tend to occur irregularly and unexpectedly, and that they have traditionally been perceived to be outside the control or purview of managers, our study suggests that managers can gain experiential advantages from confronting major discontinuous natural disaster risks. We believe that the source of this experiential advantage arises from a greater understanding of high-impact discontinuous natural disasters. We interpret this finding to mean that experience with major discontinuous disasters provides firms with experience gains that can be leveraged in future investments in existing host countries. This experience enables firms to more accurately assess potential risk to the firm and perhaps manage it more effectively.

Noteworthy, however, is our finding that experience with high-impact natural disasters positively moderates the negative link between natural disaster severity and expansion into current host countries, but not new entry into new ones. These results are particularly interesting when considered against prior research on the value of experience managing political risk. Scholars have found that firms with more extensive international experience in countries with high political hazards, defined as those with greater policy uncertainty (Delios & Henisz, 2003), have higher entry rates into other high-risk countries

(Delios & Henisz, 2003; Holburn & Zelner, 2010). Our findings are closer to García-Canal and Guillén (2008), who found that greater experience operating in countries with a high degree of policy uncertainty discouraged managers from entering new markets with similar characteristics. We find that experience with high-impact natural disasters can be leveraged in an MNC's existing host country but not into other new countries experiencing similar high-impact disasters.

> Our findings suggest that managers can gain experiential advantages from operating during high-impact natural disaster risks. Experience with high-impact natural disasters can be leveraged to expand in an MNC's existing host country *but not to enter* into new countries experiencing similar high-impact disasters. Disaster experience needs to be accompanied by country-specific knowledge to be valuable. Contrary to experience with host country political risk, experience with natural disaster risk does not appear to be transferrable across borders.

One explanation for this finding may be that while firms show a lower tendency to enter new host countries experiencing major disasters, they are able to identify new business opportunities, ex post disaster, in countries where they currently operate. In the aftermath of major natural disasters, governments often spend large sums of money in the recovery process, which acts as a short-term stimulus (Vigdor, 2008). Additionally, it may also be that in the event of high-impact natural disasters, subsidiaries located close to the disaster experience lower output which, in turn, may spur expansion into other parts of the host country.

Since experience with natural disasters does not appear to lead to increased entry into new countries facing similar risks, a key contribution of our book is to indicate that disaster experience in the case of natural disasters needs to be accompanied by country-specific knowledge to be valuable. This is an important finding because it indicates that experience with political risks is more likely to be transferrable across borders, while experience with natural disasters risk needs to be context-specific to be valuable. Comparing our results with those of Delios and Henisz (2003), who found that experience in high-risk policy environments could be leveraged in new markets, we argue that it is the nature of the risk that explains, at least in part, the differences in our findings.

For instance, managers can study the decision-making process of the executive or legislative chambers (whether democratic or not) in a country prior to any investment. Knowledge of decision-making systems can then be applied to many country contexts, so although one cannot necessarily know, a priori, what specific policy changes might occur, one can understand how a particular government may react (or at least identify the likely range of responses) based on their typical processes and on precedent. García-Canal and Guillén (2008), for example, found that although firms in regulated industries were initially attracted to operating in countries whose governments were characterized by a high degree of policy discretion (and therefore policy uncertainty), greater experience operating in such environments actually diminished the likelihood that firms would enter similar markets in the future. Alternatively, a country's ability to respond to a disaster may only be known once the event occurs. If the event is infrequent or rare it will be more difficult to glean relevant information. Managers can gain knowledge about the general capacity of a country's government, but the manner in which local/regional governments, police, firefighters, and bureaucrats will respond when faced with a crisis may be knowledge that is only obtained from operating in that country.

A notable exception to this finding is the lack of a significant moderating effect of experience managing floods. Experience with high-impact floods does show a positive and significant moderating effect on the negative link between disaster severity and MNC entry into new host countries. As we argued in Chapter 4, natural hazards that result in high-impact disasters year after year become hard to ignore or to dismiss as one-time historical anomalies or uncontrollable "acts of God." Between 1995 and 2015, floods made up the most frequent of natural disasters, but they were second after storms in terms of loss of life, causing about 27 percent of all fatalities related to weather-related disasters (Wahlstrom & Guha-Sapir, 2016). Floods were also the second costliest natural disasters (after storms), generating around 25 percent (38 percent for storms) of the reported $1,900 billion in economic losses generated by all natural disasters (including earthquakes and volcano eruptions) from 1995 to 2015 (Wahlstrom & Guha-Sapir, 2016).

A notable exception to the lack of significant moderating effects of experience on MNC entry models is the case of floods. Experience with high-impact floods does show a positive and significant moderating effect on the negative link between disaster severity and MNC entry. Between 1995 and 2015, floods were the most frequent of natural

disasters. However, in terms of loss of life, they were second to storms, which caused about 27 percent of all fatalities related to weather related disasters (Wahlstrom & Guha-Sapir, 2016).

This may be due to the fact that high-impact natural disasters that occur year after year become hard to ignore or to dismiss as one time historical anomalies or uncontrollable "acts of God."

Main limitations of our empirical studies. We discuss in detail the limitations and future research implications of our empirical studies in Chapter 6 (for the ski industry) and in Chapters 7 and 8 (for MNCs' foreign investment studies). However, it is important to highlight the key limitations of these studies. First, we analyze only the adaptation strategies of large firms. Small firms are likely to have different strategic decision-making approaches for confronting slow-onset nature adversity and natural disasters. This is due to differences in, among others, their organizational resources, risk-taking behaviors, and regulatory constraints. Future research could explore those particular climate challenges that smaller business face. Second, our samples include only Western U.S. resorts or wholly owned subsidiaries from European MNCs. Future research needs to examine how adaptation to climate change-related adversity varies for firms operating in other industries and for MNCs from other countries such as the United States and China. And third, our empirical studies focus on examining adaptation to slow-onset nature adversity intensity or natural disaster severity. Future research could further theorize on and empirically test for a fuller range of nature adversity dimensions and how these may differentially shape firm adaptation strategies.

Additional Avenues for Future Research on Business Adaptation to Climate Change

By building on socioecology's resilience theory (see Chapters 2, 3, and 6) that explicitly considers firms and the natural ecosystems in which they operate as mutually dependent, our book suggests that future research can also explore how building resilience pathways can be aligned with broader sustainable development goals in a more holistic manner. Such an approach can enable us to widen our research scope from one focusing on how organizations can protect what they have or recover what they lost (Folke et al., 2010) to another that envisions what organizations can become. Thus, we propose that future research be organized around the following broad lines of inquiry.

How do firms adapt to nature adversity dimensions? One future research stream could focus on identifying the dimensions of nature adversity that have the potential to affect a firm's core business. Conceptually, this may mean teasing out the nature, timing, and intensity or magnitude of slow-onset nature adversity conditions and sudden natural disasters (U.S. Environmental Protection Agency, 1998). Other aspects of adversity may also be salient, such as its unpredictability and frequency (Wholey & Brittain, 1989). Empirically, this may mean establishing indicators of nature adversity that are both context-specific and locally specific as well as traceable over time in industries that are or might become vulnerable. Comparative studies could also be undertaken across sectors and geographic regions with different biophysical and socioeconomic conditions. Current frontline industries that heavily depend on natural systems, either directly or indirectly through their supply chains, include agriculture, forestry, tourism, coastal industries, energy, or food and beverage industries, among others (Risky Business Project, 2014). Salient nature adversity indicators in these contexts can include changes in temperature, rainfall, or snowfall patterns, as well as changes in sea level. Future research could also track the incidence and severity of sudden extreme events such as heat waves, floods, storms, and wildfires among others to consider how the combination of gradual and sudden changes in firms' natural environment may affect adaptation.

Once relevant dimensions of nature adversity have been outlined, the adaptations that are selected and implemented by firms during the exploitation and conservation phases of their adaptive cycles could be identified. Well-developed typologies of adaptation already exist in organizational research, particularly in the stream of literature addressing firm adaptation to climate change. Classifications vary according to the timing of actions relative to impacts (Smit, Burton, Klein, & Wandel, 2000), the stages these represent in decision-making processes (Berkhout, Hertin, & Gann, 2006; Weinhofer & Busch, 2013), as well as the nature of these actions (commercial, technological, financial, etc.) (Berkhout et al., 2006; Yohe & Tol, 2002).

Particularly useful for our discussion is the consideration of strategic objectives that adaptations aim to fulfill (Hoffmann et al., 2009). In particular, what adaptations do firms undertake as they attempt to protect their core business? In previous research that one of us implemented with Peter Tashman, we found that firms may prioritize securing access to critical core business resources (Tashman & Rivera, 2016). Firms may increase inventories of these resources, ensure that viable substitutes are at hand, or diversify their sources (Tashman & Rivera, 2016). From an empirical standpoint, future research could identify actions that match up with different adaptation objectives to understand the portfolio of adaptations that firms may use.

Future research could then model how this adaptation portfolio might evolve in response to changing nature adversity. In particular, scholars could examine whether engagement in adaptation is undertaken commensurately at low to moderate levels of nature adversity but then abandoned at higher levels of adversity. Scholars could identify potential turning points in specific industry and regional studies, that is, the nature adversity threshold after which adaptation becomes constrained. Such thresholds could have practical implications, as these would be indicative of existing or approaching adaptation limits in different study contexts.

How do firms undertake transformative change? In our theorizing (see Chapter 2), we outlined three potential trajectories for firms emerging from a reorganization phase. Along one trajectory, a firm may be unable to recover and cease operations completely or be acquired by another firm. Future research could track this trajectory by identifying firms in different study contexts that fail altogether or that register significant and persistent declines in performance upon reaching an adaptation limit.

Along another trajectory, a firm may recover and resume business as usual following its standard operating practices regime. Now, aware of the heightened risks posed by nature adversity, however, the firm may select different adaptive actions. Such actions should be better suited to the firm's new awareness of its altered operating environment. Future research could therefore track the extent to which a firm continues to be dependent on its original core affected business and whether its adaptation portfolio changes after reaching an adaptation limit. For instance, one could still expect to see the firm engage with protective adaptation, but through actions that have now built in a certain degree of resilience to nature adversity. In other words, new adaptation may still seek to secure critical resources but may now to do so in a way that is less vulnerable to adversity. One could also expect to see an emergence of complementary actions aimed at further reinforcing resilience. These may include spreading risk, namely financial risk

(Hoffmann et al., 2009), developing partnerships and collaborations (Berkhout et al., 2006; Hertin, Berkhout, Gann, & Barlow, 2003), or enhancing knowledge (Berrang-Ford et al., 2011).

The final trajectory focuses on transformation, during which a firm may shift to an entirely new operational regime. The first potential question for future research that emerges here is: what would organizational transformation consist of? While well-defined typologies have been developed for organizational adaptation, this is not yet the case for transformation. Transformation may involve a reassessment of organizational goals or a strategic reorientation; the development of entirely new resources, processes, capabilities, and products; the emergence of new networks and patterns of interaction; geographic relocation; or a transition toward more radical changes in organizational structure, size, and operations; among other possibilities (Berkhout, 2011; Folke et al., 2010; IPCC, 2014b; Kates, Travis, & Willbanks, 2012; Linnenluecke & Griffiths, 2010; Newman, 2000; Yang, Bansal, & DesJardine, 2014). As a starting point, future research could consider how transformative change may be categorized along a spectrum.

A second emerging question pertains to the relationship between adaptation and transformation. Specifically, is transformation mainly reactive *after* an adaptation limit is reached, or can it also be undertaken in an anticipatory manner *before* an approaching limit? Future research could examine which of the two may be more likely. If the former is more likely, from an empirical standpoint, one would expect to see an increased engagement in transformative actions only after a firm has started to forgo protective adaptation under high levels of nature adversity. If the latter is more likely, one would expect to see increased engagement in transformative actions simultaneously with protective adaptation at low to moderate levels of adversity. Future research could also consider the extent to which the type, level, and timing of previous investments in adaptation reduce or enhance potential transformation options down the line.

A third emerging question pertains to the *conditions* under which firms may undertake transformation as opposed to returning to business as usual or alternatively collapsing. This would mean identifying potential enablers of transformation, particularly those that would allow a firm to be ambidextrous. How does a firm strike the balance between building capacity for a potentially complete reorganization while simultaneously protecting its core business by leveraging existing competencies? The literatures on loose coupling (Weick, 1976) and organizations managing at the edge of chaos (Brown & Eisenhardt, 1998) offer extensive resources on which to draw for describing these enablers of transformation. In particular, extant research suggests that the ability to transform may be centered on a capacity for continued novelty and diversity in organizational capital and functions (Kemp, Loorbach, & Rotmans, 2007; Nyström & Folke, 2011). Attributes of such a capacity might include active and continual learning and experimentation (Loorbach, 2010; Vogus & Sutcliffe, 2007), future search and monitoring (Linnenluecke & Griffiths, 2010; Loorbach, 2010), strong leadership (Kates et al., 2012), and flexibility in organizational form (Loorbach, 2010). Future research could seek to operationalize these attributes, identify potential others, and relate them to different typologies of transformation. Finally, future research could also ask whether transformation actually results in a more favorable operational regime. For instance, do firms that undertake transformation perform better in the long run compared to firms that return to business as usual? Are they more resilient to subsequent nature adversity?

How can the interdependence between organizational and ecosystem resilience be better understood? In conceptualizing firms and ecosystems as components of broader socioecological systems, we reiterate that resilience should be examined not just at the firm level, but also in relation to the broader ecosystem in which a firm operates. This is especially the case if the firm is heavily dependent on ecosystem services for its core business or for adaptation. Such an avenue of inquiry would make resilience research a truly interdisciplinary field. Business strategy scholars have a real opportunity to build bridges with the environmental, ecological, geographic, and climate sciences to develop a better understanding of resilience-building processes within socioecological systems.

Future research could model the relationship between the level of protective adaptation undertaken by firms and its effects on local ecosystems. From an empirical standpoint, direct observation of shifts in ecosystem function is inherently difficult due to the larger spatial and longer time scales at which ecosystems operate. Carpenter, Westley, and Turner (2005) thus suggest the use of "surrogates," through which changes in key variables are tracked as signals of such ecosystem shifts.

Ecosystem service-provisioning variables, in terms of quantity and quality, and derived measures, such as rate of change, could be used as surrogates. Examples of ecosystem services include water resources, soil composition, biodiversity, and vegetative cover, among others (MEA, 2005). Future research could also model potential feedback relationships, for example the extent to which changes in the level of ecosystem provisioning constrains or enables firm adaptation or, alternatively, firm transformation. Finally, future research could also consider how the effects in both of these relationships may be compounded by other factors, including other indicators of nature adversity or the presence of other potentially competing users.

Rather than asking how adaptation can lead to vicious cycles of resilience deterioration in both firms and ecosystems, future research could also ask the opposite question: How can adaptation and transformation strategies at the firm level actually contribute to enhancing ecosystem service provisioning? In a case study of two different urban woodland parks that had undergone both climate and human-related disturbances, Carreiro and Zipperer (2011) examined how policy-making processes at the municipal and national levels enhanced or inhibited adaptation and induced transformations within these park systems. This type of study could be undertaken in the organizational context, paying particular attention to the extent to which firms are able to make sense of and account for the dynamics of adaptive cycles at the ecosystem level.

Future research could also ask whether a firm may enable virtuous feedback cycles that eventually strengthen and sustain resilience in the firms' socioecological system. If it does enable virtuous feedback cycles, what does this have to do with the type of adaptation or transformation undertaken by the firm? Prior work on transformation, notably in the area of policy and governance, suggests that this may be the case. Kemp et al. (2007) argue that achieving sustainable development goals may require a proactive transformation of entire socioeconomic systems. They suggest that such a transition should be *managed* so as to emphasize a reflexive and iterative approach combining short-term actions and flexible long-term perspectives (Loorbach, 2010). In the organizational context, future research could consider whether ambidextrous firms may be able to manage their interdependencies more holistically over the long term within the broader systems of resources where they operate.

What other cross-level factors may influence organizational resilience? While we have emphasized firm-ecosystem linkages in our theorizing in

Chapter 2, future research could also consider how firms' embeddedness within communities of institutions, competitors, collaborators, civil society actors, and other stakeholders could complement the socioecological system view outlined in this chapter. The extant organizational literature suggests that networks of various types of actors and their differentiated roles may help foster or alternatively restrict firms in their ability to undertake processes of change (Adger, 2009; Folke, Hahn, Olsson, & Norberg, 2005; Kemp et al., 2007; Kraatz, 1998; Linnenluecke & Griffiths, 2013).

For instance, Alexandrescu, Martinát, Klusácek, and Bartke (2014) examine the role of government actors in encouraging or delaying change in the context of firm environmental management initiatives. In another example, Hahn and Pinske (2014) emphasize how the dynamics of competition between firm and nongovernmental organization actors involved in cross-sector partnerships affect the effectiveness of these partnerships in dealing with environmental issues. This recent work highlights the need for further research to unpack specific firm relationships within different types of networks and their potential effects on firm adaptation and transformation.

To this end, future research could operationalize different types of networks, comprised of different actors, particularly in terms of structure (e.g. cohesive, sparse, or hybrid networks) and content (e.g. range, node diversity, or types of actors), and examine how these may affect firm resilience. Are firms in certain types of networks better able to anticipate potential adaptation limits? Are they more likely to undertake transformation? Does this translate to better firm performance even under conditions of nature adversity? It would also be interesting to examine if certain types of networks lead to firm adaptation and transformation that sustain local ecosystems.

How does experience affect multinational corporation response to natural disasters? Finally, future research also needs to probe more deeply into experiential learning to better understand what specific knowledge is obtained from managing in high-impact natural disasters and how this knowledge and learning is leveraged across countries. We find that (see Chapter 8) outdated disaster experience does not help MNCs to overcome disaster risk. Thus, an important avenue for future research is to gain a better understanding of (1) factors affecting the longevity of disaster experience and (2) differences between disaster experience and disaster recovery experience.

Bibliography

Abadie, A. (2006). Poverty, political freedom, and the roots of terrorism. *American Economic Review*, 96(2), 50–56.

Abadie, A., and Gardeazabal, J. (2003). The economic costs of conflict: a case study of the Basque country. *American Economic Review*, 93(1), 113–132.

Adger, N. (2006). Vulnerability. *Global Environmental Change*, 16(3), 268–281.

Adger, W. W. N. (2009). Are there social limits to adaptation to climate change? *Climatic Change*, 93, 335–354.

Adger, W. N., and Barnett, J. (2009). Four reasons for concern about adaptation to climate change. *Environment and Planning A*, 41(12), 2800–2805.

Akaike, H. (1974). A new look at the statistical model identification. *IEEE Transactions on Automatic Control*, 19(6), 716–723.

Alexander, D. E. (2000). *Confronting Catastrophe: New Perspectives on Natural Disasters*. Terra Publishing: Harpenden, UK.

(2006). Globalization of disaster: trends, problems and dilemmas. *Journal of International Affairs*, 59(2), 1–22.

Alexandrescu, F., Martinát, S., Klusácek, P., and Bartke, S. (2014). The path from passivity toward entrepreneurship: public sector actors in brownfield regeneration processes in Central and Eastern Europe. *Organization and Environment*, 27(2), 181–201.

Allen, C. R., Angeler, D. G., Garmestani, A. S., Gunderson, L. H., and Holling, C. S. (2014). Panarchy: theory and application. *Ecosystems*, 17, 578–589.

Almeida, P., and Phene, A. (2004). Subsidiaries and knowledge creation: the influence of the MNC and host country on innovation. *Strategic Management Journal, August–September Special Issue*, 25, 847–864.

Amburgey, T. L., Kelly, D., and Barnett, W. P. (1993). Resetting the clock: the dynamics of organizational change and failure. *Administrative Science Quarterly*, 38(1), 51–73.

Aragon-Correa, J. A., and Sharma, S. (2003). A contingent resource-based view of proactive corporate environmental strategy. *Academy of Management Review*, 28(1), 71–88.

AREVA (2009). AREVA Annual Report, 2009.

Armenakis, A. A., and Bedeian, A. G. (1999). Organizational change: a review of theory and research in the 1990s. *Journal of Management*, 25(3), 293–315.

Arregle, J.-L., Beamish, P. W., and Hébert, L. (2009). The regional dimension of MNEs' foreign subsidiary localization. *Journal of International Business Studies*, 40(1), 86–107.

Asian Development Bank (2008). Towards the cliff. Quezon City, Philippines. NGO Forum on ADB.

Astley, W. G., and Van de Ven, A. H. (1983). Central perspectives and debates in organization theory. *Administrative Science Quarterly*, 28(2), 245–273.

Baird, I. S., and Thomas, H. (1985). Toward a contingency model of strategic risk taking. *Academy of Management Review*, 10(2), 230–243.

Baker, K., and Coulter, A. (2007). Terrorism and tourism: the vulnerability of beach vendors' livelihoods in Bali. *Journal of Sustainable Tourism*, 15(3), 249–266.

Banerjee, S., Oetzel J., and Ranganathan, R. (2006). Private provision of infrastructure in emerging markets: do institutions matter? *Development Policy Review*, 24(2), 175–202.

Bansal, P., and DesJardine, M. R. (2014). Business sustainability: it is about time. *Strategic Organization*, 12(1), 70–78.

Bansal, P., Kim, A. K., and Wood, M. O. (2018). Hidden in plain sight: The importance of scale on organizational attention to issues. *Academy of Management Review*, 43(2), 217–241.

Bansal, P., and Knox-Hayes, J. (2013). The time and space of materiality in organizations and the natural environment. *Organization and Environment*, 26(1), 61–82.

Barkema, H. G., Bell, J. H., and Pennings, J. M. (1996). Foreign entry, cultural barriers and learning. *Strategic Management Journal*, 17(2), 151–166.

Barkema, H. G., and Schijven, M. (2008). Toward unlocking the full potential of acquisitions: the role of organizational restructuring. *Academy of Management Journal*, 51(4), 696–722.

Barnett, J. (2003). Security and climate change. *Global Environmental Change*, 13, 7–17.

Barnett, J., and O'Neill, S. (2010). Maladaptation. *Global Environmental Change*, 20, 211–213.

Barney, J. (1991). Firm resources and sustained competitive advantage. *Journal of Management*, 17(1), 99–120.

(1996). The resource-based theory of the firm. *Organization Science*, 1, 469.

Baum, J., Calabrese, T., and Silverman, B. (2000). Don't go it alone: alliance network composition and startups' performance in Canadian biotechnology. *Strategic Management Journal, March Special Issue*, **21**, 267–294.

Baum, J. A. C., and Dahlin, B. (2007). Aspiration performance and railroads' rates of learning from train wrecks and crashes. *Organization Science*, **18**(3), 368–385.

Beermann, M. (2010). Linking corporate climate change adaptation strategies with resilience thinking. *Journal of Cleaner Production*, **19**, 836–842.

Beisner, B. E., Haydon, D. T., and Cuddington, K. (2003). Alternative stable states in ecology. *Frontiers in Ecology and the Environment*, **1**(7), 376–382.

Benson, C., and Clay, E. (2004). *Understanding the economic and financial impacts of natural disasters*. World Bank: Washington, DC.

Berkhout, F. (2011). Adaptation to climate change by organizations. *WIREs Climate Change*, **3**(1), 91–106.

Berkhout, F., Hertin, J., and Gann, D. (2006). Learning to adapt: organizational adaptation to climate change impacts. *Climatic Change*, **78**(1), 135–156.

Berrang-Ford, L., Ford, J. D., and Paterson, J. (2011). Are we adapting to climate change? *Global Environmental Change*, **21**(1), 25–33.

Bloom, M., and Milkovich, G. T. (1998). Relationships among risk, incentive pay, and organizational performance. *Academy of Management Journal*, **41**(3), 283–297.

Blunt, K., and Gold, R. (2019). PG&E knew for years its lines could spark wildfires, and didn't fix them. *The Wall Street Journal*, July 10, 2019. www.wsj.com/articles/pg-e-knew-for-years-its-lines-could-spark-wild fires-and-didnt-fix-them-11562768885.

Branch, J. (2014). As snow fades, California ski resorts are left high and very dry. *The New York Times*, November 23, 2014. www.nytimes.com/2014/11/24/sports/skiing/as-snow-fades-california-ski-resorts-face-a-brown-future.html?_r=0.

Brown, S. L., and Eisenhardt, K. M. (1998). *Competing on the Edge: Strategy as Structured Chaos*. Harvard Business School Press: Boston, MA.

Brozovic, N., and Schlenker, W. (2010). Optimal management of an ecosystem with an unknown threshold. *Ecological Economics*, **70**(4), 627–640.

Bruneau, M., Chang, S. E., Eguchi, R. T., et al. (2003). A framework to quantitatively assess and enhance the seismic resilience of communities. *Earthquake Spectra*, **19**(4), 733–752.

Buckley, P. J., and Casson, M. C. (1998). Analyzing foreign market entry strategies: extending the internalization approach. *Journal of International Business Studies*, **29**(3), 539–562.

Burakowski, E., and Magnusson, M. (2012). *Climate Impacts on the Winter Tourism Economy in the U.S.* Natural Resources Defense Council: New York.

Burton, I., Kates, R. W., and White, G. F. (1978). *The Environment as Hazard.* Oxford University Press: New York.

Busch, T. (2011). Organizational adaptation to disruptions in the natural environment: the case of climate change. *Scandinavian Journal of Management,* 27, 389–404.

Business Roundtable (2008). Business Roundtable releases strategic CEO-level guidance to combat terrorism and protect the nation's assets. Sep 23rd.

Capelle-Blancard, G., and Laguna, M.-A. (2010). How does the stock market respond to chemical disasters? *Journal of Environmental Economics and Management,* 59(2), 192–205.

Carpenter, S. R., Westley, F., and Turner, M. G. (2005). Surrogates for resilience of social ecological systems. *Ecosystems,* 8(8), 941–944.

Carreiro, M. M., and Zipperer, W. C. (2011). Co-adapting societal and ecological interactions following large disturbances in urban park woodlands. *Austral Ecology,* 36, 904–915.

Cave, D. (2019). Australia burns again, and now its biggest city is choking. *The New York Times,* December 6, 2019. www.nytimes.com/2019/12/06/world/australia/sydney-fires.html?searchResultPosition=1.

Central Intelligence Agency (2008). *World Factbook 2008.* www.cia.gov/library/publications/the-world-factbook.

Chakravarthy, B. S. (1982). Adaptation: a promising metaphor for strategic management. *Academy of Management Review,* 7(1), 35–44.

Chang, S. J. (1995). International expansion strategy of Japanese firms: capability building through sequential entry. *Academy of Management Journal,* 38(2), 383–407.

Chattopadhyay, P., Glick, W. H., and Huber, G. P. (2001). Organizational actions in response to threats and opportunities. *Academy of Management Journal,* 44(5), 937–955.

Christensen, J., and Olthoff, A. (2019). *Lessons from a Decade of Emissions Gap Assessments.* United Nations Environment Programme: Nairobi.

Christianson, M. K., Farkas, M. T., Sutcliffe, K. M., and Weick, K. E. (2009). Learning through rare events: significant interruptions at the Baltimore & Ohio Railroad Museum. *Organization Science,* 20(5), 846–860.

Chung, C., and Beamish, P. W. (2005). The impact of institutional reforms on characteristics and survival of foreign subsidiaries in emerging economies. *Journal of Management Studies,* 42(1), 35–62.

Clement, V., and Rivera, J. (2017). From adaptation to transformation: an extended research agenda for organizational resilience to adversity in the natural environment. *Organization & Environment,* 30(4), 346–365.

Compustat Global (2008). Standard & Poor's. wrds.wharton.upenn.edu.

Continental Magazine (2008). In control: the biggest storm in Houston's history proved no match for a well-rehearsed response – and a resilient business community. magazine.continental.com/200812-houston-recovery.

Cuaresma, J. C., Hlouskova, J., and Obersteiner, M. (2008). Natural disasters as creative destruction? Evidence from developing countries. *Economic Inquiry*, 46(2), 214–226.

Cuervo-Cazurra, A., and Genc, M. (2008). Transforming disadvantages into advantages: developing country MNEs in the least developed countries. *Journal of International Business Studies*, 39(6), 957–979.

Cumming, D. H. M. (1999). Living off 'biodiversity': whose land, whose resources and where? *Environment and Development Economics*, 4(02), 203–236.

Cyert, R. M., and March, J. G. (1963). *A Behavioral Theory of the Firm*. Prentice-Hall: Englewood Cliffs, NJ.

Dahlhamer, J. M., and D'Souza M. J. (1997). Determinants of business-disaster preparedness in two U.S. metropolitan areas. *International Journal of Mass Emergencies and Disasters*, 15(2), 265–281.

DANONE (2011). Governance. phx.corporate-ir.net/phoenix.zhtml?c= 95168&p=irol-riskManagement.

Daude, C., and Stein, E. (2007). The quality of institutions and foreign direct investment. *Economic & Politics*, 19(3), 317–344.

Davis, M., and Seitz, S. (1982). Disasters and governments. *Journal of Conflict Resolution*, 26, 547–568.

Delacroix, J., and Swaminathan, A. (1991). Cosmetic, speculative, and adaptive organizational change in the wine industry: a longitudinal study. *Administrative Science Quarterly*, 36(4), 631–661.

Delios, A., and Beamish, P. W. (2001). Survival and profitability: the roles of experience and intangible assets in foreign subsidiary performance. *Academy of Management Journal*, 44(5), 1028–1038.

Delios, A., and Henisz, W. J. (2000). Japanese firms' investment strategies in emerging markets. *Academy of Management Journal*, 43(3), 305–323.
   (2003). Political hazards, experience, and sequential entry strategies: the international expansion of Japanese firms, 1980–1998. *Strategic Management Journal*, 24(11), 1153–1164.

DesJardine, M., Bansal, P., and Yang, Y. (2017). Bouncing back: building resilience through social and environmental practices in the context of the 2008 global financial crisis. *Journal of Management*, doi.org/10 .1177/0149206317708854.

Dess, G. G., and Beard, D. W. (1984). Dimensions of organizational task environments. *Administrative Science Quarterly*, 29(1), 52–73.

Diaz-Rainey, I., Robertson, B., and Wilson, C. (2017). Stranded research? Leading finance journals are silent on climate change. *Climatic Change* 143, 243. doi.org/10.1007/s10584–017-1985-1

Doh, J., Rodriguez, P., Uhlenbruck, K., Collins, J., and Eden, L. (2003). Coping with corruption in foreign markets. *Academy of Management Executive*, **17**(3), 114–127.

Dolsak, N., and Prakash, A. (2018). The politics of climate change adaptation. *Annual Review of Environment and Resources*, **43**(1), 1–25.

Dow, K., Berkhout, F., Preston, B. L., et al. (2013). Limits to adaptation. *Nature Climate Change*, **3**, 305–307.

Doz, Y. (1986). *Strategic Management in Multinational Companies*. Pergamon Press, New York.

Drakos, K., and Kutan, A. M. (2003). Regional effects of terrorism on tourism in three Mediterranean countries. *Journal of Conflict Resolution*, **47**(5), 621–641.

Dunning, J. H. (1998). Location and the multinational enterprise: a neglected factor? *Journal of International Business Studies*, **29**(1), 45–66.

Eden, L., and Miller, S. R. (2004). Distance matters: liability of foreignness, institutional distance and ownership strategy. *Advances in International Management*, **16**, 187–221.

Eisenhardt, K. M., and Martin, J. A. (2000). Dynamic capabilities: what are they? *Strategic Management Journal*, **21**(10), 1105–1121.

Eisensee, T., and Strömberg, D. (2007). News droughts, news floods, and U.S. disaster relief. *Quarterly Journal of Economics*, **122**(2), 693–728.

EM-DAT (2008). Emergency Events Database, Center for Research on the Epidemiology of Disaster at Université Catholique de Louvain.

(2009). The OFDA/CRED international disaster database. www.emdat .net. Université Catholique de Louvain: Brussels, Belgium.

England, R. W. (1988). Disaster-prone technologies, environmental risks, and profit maximization. *Kyklos*, **41**(3), 379–395.

Errunza, V. R., and Senbet, L.W. (1984). International corporate diversification, market valuation, and size-adjusted evidence. *Journal of Finance*, **39**(3), 727–743.

Escaleras, M., and Register, C. A. (2011). Natural disasters and foreign direct investment. *Land Economics*, **87**(2), 346–363.

Evan, W. M., and Manion M. (2002). *Minding the Machines: Preventing Technological Disasters*. Prentice Hall: Englewood Cliffs, NJ.

Fatehi-Sedeh, K., and Safizadeh, M. H. (1989). The association between political instability and flow of foreign direct investment. *Management International Review*, **29**(4), 4–13.

Fiksel, J. (2003). Designing resilient, sustainable systems. *Environmental Science and Technology*, **37**(23), 5330–5339.

Finz, S. (2013). Farmers cultivate alternative revenue. *The San Francisco Chronicle*. www.sfgate.com/business/article/Farmers-cultivate-alternative-revenue-4500755.php.

Fishman, C. (2015). How California is winning the drought. *The New York Times*, August 19, 2015. www.nytimes.com/2015/08/16/opinion/sunday/how-california-is-winning-the-drought.html.

Fitzpatrick, M. K. (1983). The definition and assessment of political risk in international business: a review of the literature. *Academy of Management Review*, 8(2), 249–254.

Folke, C., Carpenter, S. R., Walker, B., et al. (2010). Resilience thinking: integrating resilience, adaptability, and transformability. *Ecology and Society*, 15(4), 20. http://www.ecologyandsociety.org/vol15/iss4/art20/

Folke, C., Hahn, T., Olsson, P., and Norberg, J. (2005). Adaptive governance of socio-ecological systems. *Annual Review of Environment and Resources*, 30, 441–473.

Fratianni, M., and Oh, C. H. (2009). Expanding RTA, trade flows, and the multinational enterprise. *Journal of International Business Studies*, 40(7), 1206–1227.

Frederick, W. C. (1998). Creatures, corporations, communities, chaos, complexity: a naturological view of the corporate social role. *Business and Society*, 37(4), 358–388.

Fremeth, A., and Shaver, M. (2014). Strategic rationale for responding to extra-jurisdictional regulation: evidence from firm adoption of renewable power in the U.S. *Strategic Management Journal*, 35(5), 629–651.

Fuller, C., and Flavelle, T. (2020). A climate reckoning in fire-stricken California. *The New York Times*, October 27, 2020. www.nytimes.com/2020/09/10/us/climate-change-california-wildfires.html?smid=em-share

Fuller, T. (2019). PG&E outage darkens Northern California amid wildfire threat. *The New York Times*, October 10, 2019. www.nytimes.com/2019/10/09/us/california-power-outage-PGE.html.

García-Canal, E., and Guillén, M. F (2008). Risk and the strategy of foreign location choice in regulated industries. *Strategic Management Journal*, 29, 1097–1115.

Garvey, J., and Mullins, M. (2008). Contemporary terrorism: risk perception in the London options market. *Risk Analysis*, 28(1), 151–160.

Gasbarro, F., Rizzi, F., and Frey, M. (2016). Adaptation measures of energy and utility companies to cope with water scarcity induced by climate change. *Business Strategy and the Environment*, 25, 54–72.

Gassebner, M., Keck, A., and Teh, R. (2006). *The Impact of Disasters on International Trade*. WTO Staff Working Paper ERSD-2006-04. World Trade Organization: Geneva, Switzerland.

Gavetti, G. (2012). Toward a behavioral theory of strategy. *Organization Science*, 23(1), 267–285.

Gavetti, G., Greve, H. R., Levinthal, D. A., and Ocasio, W. (2012). The behavioral theory of the firm: assessment and prospects. *Academy of Management Annals*, 6(1), 1–40.

Ghemawat, P. (2007). *Redefining Global Strategy*. Harvard Business School Press: Boston, MA.

Globerman, S., and Shapiro, D. (2003). Governance infrastructure and U.S. foreign direct investment. *Journal of International Business Studies*, **34**(1), 19–39.

Godschalk, D. R., Beatley, T., Berke, P., Brower, D. T., and Kaiser, E. J. (1998). *Natural Hazard Mitigation*. Island Press: Washington, DC.

Golden, B. R. (1992). The past is the past – or is it? The use of retrospective accounts as indicators of past strategy. *Academy of Management Journal*, **35**(4), 848–860.

Goodall, A. H. (2008). Why have the leading journals in management (and other social sciences) failed to respond to climate change? *Journal of Management Inquiry*, **17**(4), 408–420. journals.sagepub.com/doi/10 .1177/1056492607311930.

Gopal, P. (2009). The natural disaster stimulus plan. *Business Week*, April 2, 2009. www.businessweek.com/lifestyle/content/apr2009/bw2009042_ 829447.htm.

Greene, W. H. (2001). FIML estimation of sample selection models for count data. In T. Negishi, R. V. Ramachandran, and K. Mino (eds.), *Economic Theory, Dynamics, and Markets: Essays in Honor of Ryuzo Sato*. Kluwer: Norwell, MA, pp. 73–91.

(2010). Testing hypotheses about interaction terms in nonlinear models. *Economics Letters*, **107**(2), 291–296.

Greening, D. W. and Johnson, R.A. (1996). Do managers and strategies matter? A study in crisis. *Journal of Management Studies* **33**(1), 25–51.

Gunderson, L. H. (2000). Ecological resilience: in theory and application. *Annual Review of Ecology and Systematics*, **31**, 425–439.

Gunderson, L. H., and Holling, C. S. (2002). *Panarchy: Understanding Transformations in Human and Natural Systems*. Island Press: Washington, DC.

Gupta, A. K., Govindarajan, V., and Roche, P. (2001). Converting global presence into global competitive advantage. *Academy of Management Executive*, **15**(2), 45–58.

Haans, R. F. J., Pieters, C., and He, Z. (2016). Thinking about U: Theorizing and testing U- and inverted U-shaped relationships in strategy research. *Strategic Management Journal*, **37**(7), 1177–1195.

Hahn, T., and Pinkse, J. (2014). Private environmental governance through cross-sector partnerships: tensions between competition and effectiveness. *Organization and Environment*, **27**(2), 140–160.

Haigh, N. L. (2019). *Scenario Planning for Climate Change: A Guide for Strategists*. New York: Routledge.

Haigh, N., and Griffiths, A. (2012). Surprise as a catalyst for including climatic change in the strategic environment. *Business & Society*, **51**(1), 89–120.

Halkos, G., Skouloudis, A., Malesios, C., and Evangelinos, K. (2018). Bouncing back from extreme weather events: some preliminary findings on resilience barriers facing small and medium-sized enterprises. *Business Strategy and the Environment*, 27, 547–559.

Hannah, L., Roehrdanz, P. R., Ikegami, M., et al. (2013). Climate change, wine, and conservation. *Proceedings of the National Academy of Sciences of the United States of America*, 110(17), 6907–6912.

Hannan, M. T., and Freeman, J. (1984). Structural inertia and organizational change. *American Sociological Review*, 49(2), 149–164.

Hardin, G. (1968). The tragedy of the commons. *Science*, 162, 1243–1248.

Hatem, F. (1997). *International Investment: Towards the Year 2001*. United Nations: Geneva, Switzerland.

Haveman, H. A. (1992). Between a rock and a hard place: organizational change and performance under conditions of fundamental environmental transformation. *Administrative Science Quarterly*, 37(1), 48–75.

Hayes, T. C. (1992). Business technology: how the offshore rigs rode out gulf's storm. *The New York Times*, October 21, 1992.

Heckman, J. J. (1976). The common structure of statistical models of truncation, sample selection and limited dependent variables and a simple estimator for such models. *Annals of Economic and Social Measurement*, 5(4), 475–491.

(1979). Sample selection bias as a specification error. *Econometrica*, 47(1), 153–161.

Helpman, E., Melitz, M., and Rubinstein, Y. (2008). Estimating trade flows: trading partners and trading volumes. *Quarterly Journal of Economics*, 123(2), 441–457.

Henisz, W. J. (2000). The institutional environment for multinational investment. *Journal of Law, Economics, and Organization* 16(2), 334–364.

(2002). The institutional environment for infrastructure investment. *Industrial and Corporate Change*, 11(2), 355–389.

Henisz, W. J., and Delios, A. (2001). Uncertainty, imitation, and plant location: Japanese multinational corporations, 1990–1996. *Administrative Science Quarterly*, 46(3), 443–475.

Henisz, W. J., and Macher, J. T. (2004). Firm- and country-level tradeoffs and contingencies in the evaluation of foreign investment: the semiconductor industry, 1994–2002. *Organization Science*, 15(6), 537–554.

Henisz, W. J., and Williamson, O. E. (1999). Comparative economic organization within and between countries. *Business and Politics*, 1(3), 261–276.

Hertin, J., Berkhout, F., Gann, D., and Barlow, J. (2003). Climate change and the UK house building sector: perceptions, impacts and adaptive capacity. *Building Research and Information*, 31(3), 278.

Hitt, M. A., Hoskisson, R. E., and Kim, H. (1997). International diversification: effects on innovation and firm performance in product-diversified firms. *Academy of Management Journal*, **40**(4), 767–798.

Hoffman, A. (2011). Talking past each other? Cultural framing of skeptical and convinced logics in the climate change debate. *Organization & Environment*, **24**(1), 3–33.

Hoffmann, V. H., Sprengel, D. C., Ziegler, A., Kolb, M., and Abegg, B. (2009). Determinants of corporate adaptation to climate change in winter tourism: an econometric analysis. *Global Environmental Change*, **19**(2), 256–264.

Holburn, G., and Zelner, B. A. (2010). Political capabilities, policy risk, and international investment strategy: evidence from the global electric power industry. *Strategic Management Journal*, **31**, 1290–1315.

Holling, C. S. (2001). Understanding the complexity of economic, ecological, and social systems. *Ecosystems*, **4**, 390–405.

Hollnagel, E. (2006). Resilience: the challenge of the unstable. In E. Hollnagel, D. D. Woods, and N. C. Leveson (eds.), *Resilience Engineering: Concepts and Precepts*. Ashgate: Aldershot, UK, pp. 9–18.

Hoskisson, R. E., Eden, L., Lau, C. M., and Wright, M. (2000). Strategy in emerging economies. *Academy of Management Journal*, **43**(3), 249–267.

IPCC (2012). Summary for policy makers. In C. B. Field, V. Barros, T. F. Stocker et al. (eds.), *Managing the Risks of Extreme Events and Disasters to Advanced Climate Change Adaptation*. Cambridge University Press: Cambridge, UK, pp. 1–19.

(2013). Summary for policymakers. In T. F. Stocker, D. Qin, G.-K. Plattner et al. (eds.), *Climate Change 2013: The Physical Science Basis*. Working Group I contribution to the Fifth Assessment Report of the Intergovernmental Panel on Climate Change. Cambridge University Press: Cambridge, UK, and New York.

(2014a). Summary for policymakers. In C. B. Field, V. R. Barros, D. J. Dokken et al. (eds.), *Climate Change 2014: Impacts, Adaptation, and Vulnerability. Part A: Global and Sectoral Aspects*. Working Group II contribution to the Fifth Assessment Report of the Intergovernmental Panel on Climate Change. Cambridge University Press, Cambridge, UK, and New York, pp. 1–32.

(2014b). *Climate Change 2014: Synthesis Report*. Working Groups I, II, and III contribution to the Fifth Assessment Report of the Intergovernmental Panel on Climate Change. Core Writing Team, R. K. Pachauri and L. A. Meyer (eds.), IPCC: Geneva, Switzerland, 151 pp.

(2014c). Summary for policymakers. In C. B. Field, V. R. Barros, D. J. Dokken et al. (eds.), *Climate Change 2014: Impacts, Adaptation, and Vulnerability. Part A: Global and Sectoral Aspects*. Working Group II contribution to the Fifth Assessment Report of the Intergovernmental

Panel on Climate Change. Cambridge University Press: Cambridge, UK, and New York.

(2014d). *Climate Change 2014: Mitigation of Climate Change*. Working Group III contribution to the Fifth Assessment Report of the Intergovernmental Panel on Climate Change, O. Edenhofer, R. Pichs-Madruga, Y. Sokona et al. (eds.), Cambridge University Press: Cambridge, UK, and New York.

(2018). Summary for policymakers. In V. Masson-Delmotte, P. Zhai, H.-O. Pörtner et al. (eds.), *Global Warming of 1.5°C*. An IPCC special report on the impacts of global warming of 1.5°C above pre-industrial levels and related global greenhouse gas emission pathways, in the context of strengthening the global response to the threat of climate change, sustainable development, and efforts to eradicate poverty. In press.

Johanson, J., and Vahlne, J. E. (1977). The internationalisation process of the firm: a model of knowledge development and increasing market commitments. *Journal of International Business Studies*, 8(1), 23–32.

Kapoor, R., and Klueter, T. (2013). Decoding the adaptability-rigidity puzzle: evidence from pharmaceutical incumbents' pursuit of gene therapy and monoclonal antibodies. *Academy of Management Journal*, 58(4), 1180–1207.

Kasperson, R. E. (1992). The social amplification of risk: progress in developing an integrative framework. In S. Krimsky and D. Golding (eds.), *Social Theories of Risk*. Praeger: Westport, CT, pp. 153–178.

Kasperson, R. E., and Pijawka K. D. (1985). Societal response to hazards and major hazard events: comparing natural and technological hazards. *Public Administration Review*, 45, 7–18.

Kasperson, R. E., Renn, O., Slovic, P., et al. (1988). The social amplification of risk: a conceptual framework, *Risk Analysis*, 8(2),177–187.

Kates, R. W., Travis, W. R., and Wilbanks, T. J. (2012). Transformational adaptation when incremental adaptations to climate change are insufficient. *Proceedings of the National Academy of Sciences*, 109(19), 7156–7161.

Kaufmann, D., Kraay, A., and Mastruzzi, M. (2008). Governance matters VII: aggregate and individual governance indicators, 1996–2007. World Bank Policy Research. Working Paper No. 4654. World Bank: Washington, DC.

Kaufmann, D., Kraay, A., and Zoido-Lobatón, P. (1999). Aggregating Governance Indicators. World Bank Policy Research. Working Paper No. 2195. World Bank: Washington, DC.

Kelly, D., and Amburgey, T. L. (1991). Organizational inertia and momentum: a dynamic model of strategic change, *Academy of Management Journal*, 34(3), 591–612.

Kemp, R., Loorbach, D., and Rotmans, J. (2007). Transition management as a model for managing processes of co-evolution towards sustainable development. *International Journal of Sustainable Development and World Ecology*, 14, 78–91.

Kennedy, D. (2002). Science, terrorism, and natural disasters. *Science*, 295 (5554), 405.

King, A. (1995). Avoiding ecological surprise: lessons from long standing communities. *Academy of Management Review*, 20(4), 961–985.

King, G., Tomz, M., and Wittenberg, J. (2000). Making the most of statistical analyses: improving interpretation and presentation. *American Journal of Political Science*, 44(2), 341–355.

Kinzer, S. (2001). Turkey's political earthquake. *Middle East Quarterly*, 8(4), 41–48.

Kobrin, S. J. (1978). When does political instability result in increased investment risk? *Columbia Journal of World Business*, 13(3), 113–122.

Kobrin, S. J., Basek, J., Blank, S., and La Palombara, J. (1980). The assessment and evaluation of noneconomic environments by American firms: a preliminary report. *Journal of International Business Studies*, 11(1), 32–47.

Kogut, B., and Zander, U. H. (1993). Knowledge of the firm and the evolutionary perspective of the multinational corporation. *Journal of International Business Studies*, 24, 625–645.

Kordos, M., and Vojtovic, S. (2016). Transnational corporations in the global world economic environment. *Procedia–Social and Behavioral Sciences*, 230, 150–158.

Kraatz, M. S. (1998). Learning by association? Interorganizational networks and adaptation to environmental change. *Academy of Management Journal*, 41(6), 621–643.

Kraatz, M. S., and Zajac, E. J. (2001). How resources affect strategic change and performance in turbulent environments: theory and evidence. *Organization Science*, 12(5), 632–657.

La Porta, R., Lopez-de-Silanes, F., Shleifer A., and Vishny, R. W. (1998). Law and finance. *Journal of Political Economy*, 106(6), 1113–1155.

Lampel, J., Shamsie, J., and Shapira, Z. (2009). Experiencing the improbable: rare events and organizational learning. *Organization Science*, 20(5), 835–845.

Lansing, J. S. (2003). Complex adaptive systems. *Annual Review of Anthropology*, 32, 183–204.

Le Mens, G., Hannan, M. T., and Pólos, L. (2011). Founding conditions, learning, and organizational life chances: age dependence revisited. *Administrative Science Quarterly*, 56(1), 95–126.

Lengnick-Hall, C. A., and Beck, T. E. (2005). Adaptive fit versus robust transformation: how organizations respond to environmental change. *Journal of Management*, 31(5), 738–757.

Levin, S. A., Barrett, S., Aniyar, S., et al. (1998). Resilience in natural and socioeconomic systems. *Environment and Development Economics*, 3(2), 221–262.

Levinthal, D. A. (1991). Organizational adaptation and environmental selection: interrelated processes of change. *Organization Science*, 2(1), 140–145.

Levinthal, D., and Rerup, C. (1994). Surviving Schumpeterian environments: an evolutionary perspective. In J. A. C. Baum and J. V. Singh (eds.), *Evolutionary Dynamics of Organizations*. Oxford University Press: New York, pp. 167–178.

(2006). Crossing an apparent chasm: bridging mindful and less-mindful perspectives on organizational learning. *Organization Science*, 17(4), 502–513.

Lewin, A. Y., Weigelt, C. B., and Emery, J. D. (2004). Adaptation and selection in strategy and change. In M. S. Poole and A. H. Van de Ven (eds.), *Handbook of Organizational Change and Innovation*, Oxford University Press: Oxford, UK, pp. 108–160.

Lewis, J. (2005). Earthquake destruction: corruption on the fault line? datum .gn.apc.org/PDFs/Transparency%20Int%20Corruption%20&%20%20Earthquakes.pdf.

Li, J., Tong, T. W. (2007). Real options theory and international strategic management. In S. Tallman (ed.), *A New Generation in International Strategic Management*, Edward Elgar: Northampton, MA, pp. 100–117.

Lin, I.-I., Chen, C.-H., Pun, I.-F., Liu T., and Wu, C.-C. (2009). Warm ocean anomaly, air sea fluxes, and the rapid intensification of tropical cyclone Nargis (2008). *Geophysical Research Letters*, 36(3), LO3817.

Lind, J. T., and Mehlum, H. (2010). With or without U? The appropriate test for a U-shaped relationship. *Oxford Bulletin of Economics and Statistics*, 72(1), 109–118.

Linnenluecke, M. K., and Griffiths, A. (2010). Beyond adaptation: resilience for business in light of climate change and weather extremes. *Business & Society*, 49(3), 477–511.

(2012). Assessing organizational resilience to climate and weather extremes: complexities and methodological pathways. *Climatic Change*, 113(3), 933–947.

(2013). The 2009 Victorian bushfires: a multilevel perspective on organizational risk and resilience. *Organization and Environment*, 26(4), 386–411.

Linnenluecke, M. K., Griffiths, A. and Winn, M. (2012). Extreme weather events and the critical importance of anticipatory adaptation and organizational resilience in responding to impacts. *Business Strategy and the Environment*, 21, 17–32.

Linnenluecke, M. K., Griffiths, A., and Winn, M. I. (2013). Firm and industry adaptation to climate change: a review of climate adaptation studies in the business and management field. *Climate Change*, 4(5), 397–416.

Liou, D.-Y., and Lin C.-H. (2008). Human resources planning on terrorism and crises in the Asia Pacific region: cross-national challenge reconsideration, and proposition from western experiences. *Human Resource Management,* 47(1), 49–72.

Llorca-Vivero, R. (2008). Terrorism and international tourism: new evidence. *Defence and Peace Economics,* 19(2), 169–188.

Loorbach, D. (2010). Transition management for sustainable development: a prescriptive, complexity-based governance framework. *Governance,* 23(1), 161–183.

Lumpkin, G. T., and Dess G. G. (1996). Clarifying the entrepreneurial orientation construct and linking it to performance. *Academy of Management Review* 21(1), 135–172.

Luthar, S. S., Cicchetti, D., and Becker, B. (2000). The construct of resilience: a critical evaluation and guidelines for future work. *Child Development,* 71(3), 543–562.

Madsen, P. M. (2009). These lives will not be lost in vain: organizational learning from disaster in U.S. coal mining. *Organization Science,* 20(5), 861–875.

Maguire, S., McKelvey, B., Mirabeau, L., and Öztas, N. (2006). Complexity science and organization studies. In S. R. Clegg, C. Hardy, T. B. Lawrence, and W. R. Nord (eds.), *The SAGE Handbook of Organization Studies.* SAGE Publications: London, pp. 165–214.

March, J. G. (1991). Exploration and exploitation in organizational learning. *Organization Science,* 2(1), 71–87.

March, J. G., Shapira, Z. (1987). Managerial perspectives on risk and risk taking. *Management Science,* 33(11), 1404–1418.

Mata, J., Portugal, P. (2002). The survival of new domestic and foreign-owned firms. *Strategic Management Journal,* 23(4), 323–343.

McCarthy, B, and Casey, T. (2008). Love, sex, and crime: adolescent romantic relationships and offending. *American Sociological Review,* 73, 944–969.

McFayden, M. A., and Cannella, A. A (2004). Social capital and knowledge creation: diminishing returns of the number and strength of exchange relationships. *Academy of Management Journal,* 47(5), 735–746.

McKendrick, D. G., Wade, J. B., and Jaffee, J. (2009). A good riddance? Spin-offs and the technological performance of parent firms. *Organization Science,* 20(6), 979–992.

McNamara, G., and Bromiley, P. (1999). Risk and return in organizational decision making. *Academy of Management Journal,* 42(3), 330–340.

Meyer, K. E., Estrin, S., Bhaumik, S. K., and Peng, M. W. (2009). Institutions, resources, and entry strategies in emerging economies. *Strategic Management Journal,* 30(1), 61–80.

Mickolus, E. F., Sandler, T., Murdock, J. M., and Fleming, P. (2008). *International Terrorism: Attributes of Terrorist Events, 1968–2007 (ITERATE)*. Vinyard Software: Dunn Loring, VA.

Millennium Ecosystem Assessment (2005). Ecosystems and human well-being: opportunities and challenges for business and industry. www.millenniumassessment.org/en/index.html.

Miller, K. D. (1992). A framework for integrated risk management in international business. *Journal of International Business Studies*, 23(2), 311–331.

(1993). Industry and country effects on managers' perceptions of environmental uncertainties. *Journal of International Business Studies*, 24(4), 693–714.

(1998). Economic exposure and integrated risk management. *Strategic Management Journal*, 19(5), 497–514.

Miller, P. A. (1999). Exxon Valdez Oil Spill: Ten Years Later. Technical Background Paper for Alaska Wilderness League.

Miller, S. T., and A. Parkhe. (1998). Patterns in the expansion of U.S. banks' foreign operations. *Journal of International Business Studies*, 29(2), 359–390.

Mitchell, J. K. (1996). *The Long Road to Recovery: Community Responses to Industrial Disasters*. United Nations University Press: New York.

Mitroff, I., Srivastava, P., and Udwadia, F. E. (1987). Effective crisis management. *Academy Management Executive*, 1(4), 282–292.

Montuschi, E. (2010). Order of Man, Order of Nature: Francis Bacon's Idea of a 'Dominion' over Nature. Discussion Paper. Centre for Philosophy of Natural and Social Science, London School of Economics and Political Science: London.

Morel, B., and Ramanujam, R. (1999). Through the looking glass of complexity: The dynamics of organizations as adaptive and evolving systems. *Organization Science*, 10(3), 278–292.

Morrow, J. D., Siverson, R. H., and Tabares, T. E. (1998). The political determinants of international trade: the major powers, 1907–1990. *American Political Science Review* 92(3), 649–661.

Mulcahy, S. (2021). Many Texans have died because of the winter storm. Just how many won't be known for weeks or months. *The Texas Tribune*, February 19, 2021. www.texastribune.org/2021/02/19/texas-power-outage-winter-storm-deaths.

Mullahy, J. (1986). Specification and testing of some modified count data models. *Journal of Econometrics*, 33(3), 341–365.

Nanto, D. K. (2004). *9/11 Terrorism: Global Economic Costs*. Congressional Research Service, Washington, DC.

National Academies of Sciences, Engineering, and Medicine (NAS) (2016). *Attribution of Extreme Weather Events in the Context of Climate Change.*The National Academies Press: Washington, DC.

National Consortium for the Study of Terrorism and Responses to Terrorism (2008). *Global Terrorism Database, a Center for Excellence of DHS.* University of Maryland. www.start.umd.edu/start.

National Hurricane Center (2010). Hurricane History, February 24, 2010.

National Ski Areas Association (NSAA) (2016). Industry Stats. www.nsaa .org/press/industry-stats.

National Snow and Ice Data Center (NSIDC) (2015). All About Snow. nsidc .org/cryosphere/snow/science/formation.html.

Nearly, J. P. (2007). Cross-border mergers as instruments of comparative advantage. *Review of Economic Studies*, 74(4), 1229–1257.

Nelson, D. R., Adger, W. N., and Brown, K. (2007). Adaptation to environmental change: contributions of a resilience framework. *Annual Review of Environmental Resources*, 32, 395-419.

Newman, K. L. (2000). Organizational transformation during institutional upheaval. *Academy of Management Review*, 25(3), 602-619.

Nickell, S. (1981). Biases in dynamic models with fixed effects. *Econometrica* 49(6) 1417–1426.

Nijhuis, J. (2014). When the snow fails. *National Geographic.*

Nitsch, V, and Schumacher, D. (2004). Terrorism and international trade: an empirical investigation. *European Journal of Political Economy*, 20(2), 423–433.

Nolte, C. (2019). PG&E power Shut-off: Diablo winds to blame for extreme wildfire concerns. *San Francisco Chronicle*, October 8, 2019. www .sfchronicle.com/california-wildfires/article/PG-E-power-shut-off-Diablo-winds-to-blame-for-14501564.php.

North, D. C. (1990). *Institutions, Institutional Change, and Economic Performance.* Cambridge University Press: New York.

Nyström, M., and Folke, C. (2001). Spatial resilience of coral reefs. *Ecosystems*, 4, 406–417.

O'Brien, K., Sygna, L., and Haugen, J. E. (2004). Vulnerable or resilient? A multi-scale assessment of climate impacts and vulnerability in Norway. *Climatic Change*, 63(1–2), 193–225.

Oetzel, J. (2005). Smaller may be beautiful but is it more risky? Assessing and managing political and economic risk post FDI in Costa Rica. *International Business Review*, 14(6), 765–790.

Oetzel, J., and Oh, C. H. (2014). Learning to carry the cat by the tail: Firm experience, disasters, and multinational subsidiary entry and expansion. *Organization Science*, 25(3), 732–756.

Oh, C. H., and Oetzel, J. (2011). Multinationals' response to major disasters: How does subsidiary investment vary in response to the type of disaster and the quality of host country governance? *Strategic Management Journal*, 32(6), 658–681.

Oh, C. H., Oetzel, J., Rivera, J., and Lien, D. (2020). Natural disasters and MNC sub-national investments in China. *Multinational Business Review*, 28(2), 245–274.

Oh, C. H., and Reuveny, R. (2010) Climatic natural disasters, political risk, and international trade. *Global Environmental Change*, 20, 243–254.

Okuyama, Y., and Chang, S. E. (2004). *Modeling Spatial and Economic Impacts of Disasters*. Springer-Verlag: Berlin.

O'Leary III, D., Hall, D. K., Medler, M., et al. (2019). Snowmelt timing maps derived from MODIS for North America, version 2, 2001-2018. ORNL DAAC: Oak Ridge, Tennessee, USA, doi.org/10.3334/ORNLDAAC/1712.

Ortiz-de-Mandojana, N., and Bansal, P. (2016). The long-term benefits of organizational resilience through sustainable business practices, *Strategic Management Journal*, 37(8), 1615–1631.

Ostrom, E. (2010). Beyond markets and states: polycentric governance of complex economic systems. *American Economic Association*, 100(3), 641–672.

Perrow, C. (2007). *The Next Catastrophe: Reducing Our Vulnerabilities to Natural, Industrial, and Terrorist Disasters*. Princeton University Press: Princeton, NJ.

Pickering, C. (2011). Changes in demand for tourism with climate change: a case study of visitation patterns to six ski resorts in Australia. *Journal of Sustainable Tourism*, 19(6), 767–281.

Pierce, J. R., and Aguinis, H. (2013). The too-much-of-a-good-thing effect in management. *Journal of Management*, 39(2), 313–338.

Pinkse, J., and Gasbarro, F. (2019). Managing physical impacts of climate change: an attentional perspective on corporate adaptation. *Business & Society*, 58(2), 333–368.

Political Risk Services (2008). International Country Risk Guide. www .icrgonline.com.

PRISM Climate Group, Oregon State University (2004). www.prism .oregonstate.edu.

(2016). prism.oregonstate.edu/explorer.

Ramanujam, R. (2003). The effects of discontinuous change on latent errors in organizations: the moderating role of risk. *Academy of Management Journal*, 46(5), 608–617.

Repenning, N. P., and Sterman, J. D. (2002). Capability traps and self-confirming attribution errors in the dynamics of process improvement. *Administrative Science Quarterly*, 47(2), 265–295.

Rerup, C. (2009). Attentional triangulation: learning from unexpected rare crises. *Organization Science*, 20, 876–893.

Restuccia, A. (2021). U.S. officially rejoins Paris Climate Agreement. *The Wall Street Journal*, February 19, 2021. www.wsj.com/articles/u-s-offi ciall-rejoins-paris-climate-agreement-11613747961.

Reuer, J. J., and Tong, T. W. (2005). Real options in international joint ventures. *Journal of Management*, 31, 403–423.

Rickards, L. (2013). Transformation is adaptation. *Nature Climate Change*, 3, 690.

Rindova, V. P., and Kotha, S. (2001). Continuous 'morphing': competing through dynamic capabilities, form, and function. *Academy of Management Journal*, 44(6), 1263–1280.

Risky Business Project (2014). Risky business: the economic risks of climate change in the United States. riskybusiness.org/report/overview/executive-summary.

Rivera, J. (2010). *Business and Public Policy: Responses to Environmental and Social Protection Processes*. Cambridge University Press: Cambridge, UK.

Rivera, J., and Clement, V. (2019). Business adaptation to climate change-American ski resorts and warmer temperatures. *Business Strategy and the Environment*, 28, 1285–1301.

Rivera, J., and de Leon, P. (2004). Is greener whiter? Voluntary environmental performance of western ski areas. *Policy Studies Journal*, 32(3), 417–437.

Rivera, J., de Leon, P., and Koerber, C. (2006). Is greener whiter yet? The sustainable slopes program after five years. *Policy Studies Journal*, 34(2), 195–221.

Rivera, J., Oetzel J., de Leon, P., and Starik, M. (2009). The policy process and business political environmental management strategies in developing countries. *Policy Sciences*, 42(1), 3–32.

Rivera, J., and Oh, C. (2013). Environmental regulations and MNC foreign market entry. *Policy Studies Journal*, 41(2), 243–272.

Rockström, J., Steffen, W., Noone, K., et al. (2009). A safe operating space for humanity. *Nature*, 461, 472–475.

Romanelli, E., and Tushman, M. L. (1994). Organizational transformation as punctuated equilibrium: an empirical test. *Academy of Management Journal*, 37(5), 1141–1166.

Root, F. R. (1972). Analyzing political risks in international business. In A. Kappor and P. A. Grub (eds.), *The Multinational Enterprise in Transition*. Darwin Press: Princeton, NJ, pp. 354–365.

Rose, A., and Liao, S. (2005). Modeling regional economic resilience to disasters: a computable general equilibrium analysis of water service disruptions. *Journal of Regional Science*, 45(1), 75–112.

Sahagun, L. (2015). Drought devastates cherry crops, puts some growers out of business. *The Los Angeles Times*. www.latimes.com/local/california/la-me-cherries-drought-20150618-story.html.

Sarangi, S. (1995). Bhopal disaster: judiciary's failure. *Economic and Political Weekly*, 30(46), 2907–2909.

Scheffer, M., Carpenter, S., Foley, J., Folke, C., and Walker, B. (2001). Catastrophic shifts in ecosystems. *Nature*, 413, 591–596.

Scott, D., and McBoyle, G. (2007). Climate change adaptation in the ski industry. *Mitigation and Adaptation Strategies for Global Change*, 12(8), 1411–1431.

Scott, D., McBoyle, G., Minogue, A., and Mills, B. (2006). Climate change and the sustainability of ski-based tourism in eastern North America: a reassessment. *Journal of Sustainable Tourism*, 14(4), 376–398.

Scott, W. R. (2001). *Institutions and Organizations*. Sage: Thousand Oaks, CA.

Serrano, A., Rubenstein, S., and Morris, J. (2019). PG&E blacks out parts of 17 counties, looks ahead to bigger outage that could start Saturday. *San Francisco Chronicle*, October 25, 2019. www.sfchronicle.com/california-wildfires/article/PG-E-blacks-out-parts-of-15-counties-and-14558470.php.

Shapira, Z. (1995). *Risk Taking: A Managerial Perspective*. Russell Sage Foundation: New York.

(2017). Entering new markets: the effect of performance feedback near aspiration and well below and above it. *Strategic Management Journal*, 38(7), 1416–1434.

Shimizu, K. (2007). Prospect theory, behavioral theory, and the threat-rigidity thesis: combinative effects on organizational decisions to divest formerly acquired units. *Academy of Management Journal*, 50(6), 1495–1514.

Singh, J. A. (1986). Performance, slack, and risk taking in organizational decision making. *Academy of Management Journal*, 29(3), 562–585.

Ski Area Citizens Coalition (SACC) (2014). www.skiareacitizens.org.

Skidmore, M., and Toya, H. (2002). Do natural disasters promote long-run economic growth? *Economic Inquiry*, 40(4), 664–687.

Slawinski, N., and Bansal, P. (2015). Short on time: intertemporal tensions in business sustainability, *Organization Science*, 26(2), 531–549.

Slovic, P. (1992). Perception of risk: reflections on the psychometric paradigm. In S. Krimsky and D. Golding (eds.), *Social Theories of Risk*. Praeger: Westport, CT, pp. 117–152.

(2000). Perception of risk. In P. Slovic (ed.), *The Perception of Risk*. Earthscan Publications Ltd.: London, pp. 220–231.

Slovic, P, Fischhoff, B., and Lichtenstein, S. (2000). Rating the risks. In P. Slovic (ed.), *The Perception of Risk*. Earthscan Publications Ltd: London, pp. 104–120.

Slovic, P., Fischhoff, B., and Lichtenstein, S. (2000). Rating the risks. In P. Slovic, (ed.). *The Perception of Risk.* Earthscan Publications Ltd.: London, pp. 104–120.

Smit, B., Burton, I., Klein, R. J. T., and Wandel, J. (2000). An anatomy of adaptation to climate change and variability, *Climatic Change*, 45, 223–251.

Sönmez, S. F., and Graefe, A. R. (1998). Influence of terrorism risk on foreign tourism decisions. *Annals of Tourism Research*, 25(1), 112–144.

Starbuck, W. H. (2009). Cognitive reactions to rare events: perceptions, uncertainty, and learning. *Organization Science*, 20(5), 925–937.

Starik, M., and Kanashiro, P. (2013). Toward a theory of sustainability management: uncovering and integrating the nearly obvious, *Organization & Environment*, 27, 107–112.

Starik, M., and Rands, G. P. (1995). Weaving an integrated web: multilevel and multisystem perspectives of ecologically sustainable organizations. *Academy of Management Review*, 20(4), 908–935.

Staw, B. M., Sandelands, L. E., and Dutton, J. E. (1981). Threat rigidity effects in organizational behavior: a multilevel analysis. *Administrative Science Quarterly*, 26(4), 501–524.

Stockholm Resilience Center (2014). What is resilience? An introduction to social-ecological research. www.stockholmresilience.org/21/research/what-is-resilience.html.

   (2015). Regime shifts and their implications in social-ecological systems. www.stockholmresilience.org/21/research/research-themes/regime-shifts.html.

Stone, R. (2006). Facing a tsunami with no place to run. *Science*, 314(5798), 408–409.

Strömberg, D. (2007). Natural disasters, economic development, and humanitarian aid. *Journal of Economic Perspective*, 21(3), 199–222.

Suder, G. S. (2004). *Terrorism and the International Business Environment: The Security-Business Nexus.* Edward Elgar: Cheltenham, UK.

Supply Chain Brain (2006). P&G, after devastation of Hurricane Katrina, shows the value of best-laid plans. www.supplychainbrain.com/content/research-analysis/supply-chain-innovation-awards/single-article-page/article/pg-after-devastation-of-hurricane-katrina-shows-the-value-of-best-laid-plans-1.

Sutcliffe, K. M., and Vogus, T. J. (2003). Organizing for resilience. In K. Cameron, J. E. Dutton, and R. E. Quinn (eds.), *Positive Organizational Scholarship–.* Berrett-Koehler: San Francisco, CA, pp. 94–110.

Tallman, S. B. (1988). Home country political risk and foreign direct investment in the United States. *Journal of International Business Studies*, 19(2), 219–234.

Tashman, P., and Rivera, J. (2016). Ecological uncertainty and organizational adaptation and mitigation in the U.S. ski resort industry. *Strategic Management Journal*, 37(7), 1507–1525.

Teece, D., Pisano, G., and Shuen, A. (1997). Dynamic capabilities and strategic management. *Strategic Management Journal*, 18(7), 509–533.

Tisch, D., and Galbreath, J. (2018). Building organizational resilience through sensemaking: the case of climate change and extreme weather events. *Business Strategy and the Environment*, 27, 1197–1208.

Transparency International (2008). Transparency Watch July. www.transparency.org/publications/newsletter/2008/july_2008/in_the_news/chinese_earthquake_reveals_weak_construction.

Tushman, M. L., and O'Reilly, C. A. (1996). The ambidextrous organization: managing evolutionary and revolutionary change. *California Management Review*, 38, 1–23.

UNDP (2004). *Reducing Disaster Risk: A Challenge for Development*. United Nations Development Programme: New York.

UNEP (2019). *Emissions Gap Report 2019. Executive Summary*. United Nations Environment Programme: Nairobi, Kenya.

U.S. Census Bureau (2012). Population Estimates. www.census.gov/popest/data/historical/index.html.

U.S. Department of Agriculture, Natural Resources Conservation Service (USDA NRCS) (2016). www.wcc.nrcs.usda.gov/webmap/index.html.

U.S. Department of Commerce (2007). The Gulf Coast: economic recovery two years after the hurricanes. www.eda.gov/PDF/GulfCoast2yr20808.pdf.

U.S. Environmental Protection Agency (1998). Guidelines for Ecological Risk Assessment. www2.epa.gov/sites/production/files/2014-11/documents/eco_risk_assessment1998.pdf.

Vaaler, P. (2008). How do MNCs vote in developing country elections? *Academy of Management Journal*, 51(1), 21–43.

Vaaler, P., and McNamara, G. (2004). Crisis and competition in expert organizational decision making: credit-rating agencies and their response to turbulence in emerging markets. *Organization Science*, 15(6), 687–703.

Vachani, S. (1991). Distinguishing between related and unrelated international geographic diversification: a comprehensive measure of global diversification. *Journal of International Business Studies*, 22(2), 307–322.

Valente, M. (2010). Demystifying the struggles of private sector paradigmatic change: business as an agent in a complex adaptive system. *Business and Society*, 49(3), 439–476.

Van der Vink, G., DiFiore, P., Brett, A., et al. (2007). Democracy, GDP and natural disasters. *Geotimes*, 52(10), 36–39.

Vernon, R. (1983). Organizational and institutional responses to international risk. In R. J. Herring (ed.), *Managing International Risk*, Cambridge University Press: Cambridge, UK, pp. 191–216.

Vigdor, J. (2008). The economic aftermath of Hurricane Katrina. *Journal of Economic Perspective*, **22**(4), 135–154.

Vogus, T. J., and Sutcliffe, K. M. (2007). Organizational Resilience: Towards a Theory and Research Agenda. Paper presented at the International Institute of Electrical and Electronics Engineers (IEEE) Conference on Systems, Man and Cybernetics, Montreal, QC.

Wadhwa, A., and Kotha, S. (2006). Knowledge creation through external venturing: Evidence from the telecommunications equipment manufacturing industry. *Academy of Management Journal*, **49**(4), 819–835.

Wahlstrom, M., and Guha-Sapir, D. (2016). *The Human Cost of Weather-Related Disasters 1995–2015*. Centre for Research on the Epidemiology of Disasters: Brussels, Belgium.

Walker, B., Abel, N., and Anderies, J. M. (2009). Resilience, adaptability, and transformability in the Goulburn–Broken catchment, Australia. *Ecology and Society*, **14**(1), 12.

Walker, B., Holling, C. S., Carpenter, S., and Kinzig, A. (2004). Resilience, adaptability and transformability in social–ecological systems. *Ecology and Society*, **9**(2), 5. http://www.ecologyandsociety.org/vol9/iss2/art5/.

Walker, B. H., and Abel, N. (2002). Resilient rangelands: adaptation in complex systems. In L. H., Gunderson and C. S. Holling (eds.), *Panarchy: Understanding Transformations in Human and Natural Systems*. Island Press: Washington, DC, pp. 9–18.

Wan, W. P., and Hoskisson, R. E. (2003). Home country environments, corporate diversification strategies, and firm performance. *Academy of Management Journal*, **46**(1), 27–45.

Webb, G. R., Tierney, K. J., and Dahlhamer, J. M. (2002). Predicting long-term business recovery from disaster: a comparison of the Loma Prieta earthquake and Hurricane Andrew. *Global Environmental Change*, **4**(2/3), 45–58.

Weick, K. E. (1976). Educational organizations as loosely coupled systems. *Administrative Science Quarterly*, **21**(1), 1–19.

(1995). *Sensemaking in Organizations*. Sage: London.

Weick, K. E., and Sutcliffe, K. M. (2001). *Managing the Unexpected: Resilient Performance in an Age of Uncertainty*, 1st edition. Jossey-Bass: San Francisco, CA.

(2006). Mindfulness and the quality of organizational attention. *Organization Science*, **17**(4), 514–524.

Weinhofer, G., and Busch, T. (2013). Corporate strategies for managing climate risks. *Business Strategy and Environment*, **22**, 121–144.

Wernerfelt, B. (1984). A resource-based view of the firm. *Strategic Management Journal*, **5**(2), 171–180.

Wernick, D. A. (2006). Terror incognito: international business in an era of heightened geopolitical risk. In G. S. Suder (ed.), *Corporate Strategies under International Terrorism and Adversity*. Edward Elgar: Cheltenham, UK, pp. 59–82.

White, H. (1980). A heteroskedasticity-consistent covariance matrix estimator and a direct test for heteroskedasticity. *Econometrica*, **48**(4), 817–838.

Whiteman, G., and Cooper, W. H. (2011). Ecological sensemaking. *Academy of Management Journal*, **54**(5), 889–911.

Wholey, D. R., and Brittain, J. (1989). Characterizing environmental variation. *Academy of Management Journal*, **32**(4), 867–882.

Williams, A. P., Abatzoglou, J. T., Gershunov, A., et al. (2019). Observed impacts of anthropogenic climate change on wildfire in California. *Earth's Future*, **7**, 892–910. agupubs.onlinelibrary.wiley.com/doi/pdf/10.1029/2019EF001210.nbv.

Williamson, O. E. (1996). *The Mechanisms of Governance*. Oxford University Press: New York.

Winn, M. I., Kirchgeorg, M., Griffiths, A., Linnenluecke, M. K., and Gunther, E. (2011). Impacts from climate change on organizations: a conceptual foundation. *Business Strategy and Environment*, **20**, 157–173.

Winn, M. I., and Pogutz, S. (2013). Business, ecosystems, and biodiversity: new horizons for management research. *Organization and Environment*, **26**(2), 203–229.

Woodward, D. P., and Rolfe, R. (1993). The location of export-oriented foreign direct investment in the Caribbean basin. *Journal of International Business Studies*, **21**(1), 121–144.

Wooldridge, J. (2002). *Econometric Analysis of Cross Section and Panel Data*. MIT Press: Cambridge, MA.

World Atlas of Global Issues (2018). Multinational Corporations. espace-mondial-atlas.sciencespo.fr/en/topic-strategies-of-transnational-actors/article-3A11-EN-multinational-corporations.html.

World Bank (2004). Natural Disasters: Counting the Cost.

(2008a). World Development Indicators 2008. publications.worldbank.org/subscriptions/WDI.

(2008b). World Governance Indicators 2008. publications.worldbank.org/subscriptions/WDI.

World Resources Institute (2019). Estimating the Economic Benefits of Climate Adaptation Investments, Technical Paper. World Resources Institute: Washington, DC.

Worthington, W. J., Collins, J. D., and Hitt, M. A. (2009). Beyond risk mitigation: enhancing corporate innovation with scenario planning. *Business Horizons*, **52**(5), 441–450.

Yang, Y., Bansal, P., and DesJardine, M. R. (2014). What doesn't kill you makes you stronger: a multi-level process theory of organizational resilience. *Academy of Management Proceedings*, **2014**(1), 13934.

Yohe, G., and Tol, R. S. (2002). Indicators for social and economic coping capacity: moving toward a working definition of adaptive capacity. *Global Environmental Change*, **12**(1), 25–40.

Zajac, E. J., and Westphal J. D. (1996). Who shall succeed? How CEO/board preferences and power affect the choice of new CEOs. *Academy of Management Journal*, **39**(1), 64–90.

Zanini, M. (2009). 'Power curves': what natural and economic disasters have in common. *McKinsey Quarterly, June*, 10–15.

Zelner, B. A. (2009). Using simulation to interpret results from logit, probit, and other nonlinear models. *Strategic Management Journal*, **30**(12), 1335–1348.

Zeng, X., Broxton, P., and Dawson, N. (2018). Snowpack change from 1982 to 2016 over conterminous United States. *Geophysical Research Letters*. doi.org/10.1029/2018GL079621.

Zimmerman, R. (1985). The relationship of emergency management to governmental policies on man-made technological disasters. *Public Administration Review*, **45**, 29–39.

Zollo, M. (2009). Superstitious learning with rare strategic decisions: theory and evidence from corporate acquisitions. *Organization Science*, **20**(5), 894–908.

Zollo, M., and Reuer, J. J. (2010). Experience spillovers across corporate development activities. *Organization Science*, **21**(6), 1195–1212.

Zollo, M., Winter, S. G. (2002). Deliberate learning and the evolution of dynamic capabilities. *Organization Science*, **13**(3), 339–351.

Index

Printed in the United States
by Baker & Taylor Publisher Services